THINKING STRAIGHT

fourth edition

THINKING STRAIGHT

Principles of Reasoning

for Readers and Writers

MONROE C. BEARDSLEY
Temple University

PRENTICE-HALL, INC., ENGLEWOOD CLIFFS, NEW JERSEY

Library of Congress Cataloging in Publication Data

BEARDSLEY, MONROE C
Thinking straight.

1. Logic. I. Title.
BC71.B32 1975 160 74-16349
ISBN 0-13-918235-7
ISBN 0-13-918227-6 (pbk.)

10 9 8 7 6 5 4 3 2 1

Printed in the United States of America

PRENTICE-HALL INTERNATIONAL, INC., *London*
PRENTICE-HALL OF AUSTRALIA, PTY. LTD., *Sydney*
PRENTICE-HALL OF CANADA, LTD., *Toronto*
PRENTICE-HALL OF INDIA PRIVATE LIMITED, *New Delhi*
PRENTICE-HALL OF JAPAN, INC., *Tokyo*

PREFACE

In rewriting this book for the fourth edition, I have preserved the basic structure, the logical principles, and nearly all the technical terminology, of the previous edition. But I have provided new examples throughout the text, and have replaced all the quizzes and exercises with new ones; I have tried to make the book a little more concise; and here and there I have added new distinctions or principles or further clarifications that seemed to be called for either by my own reflections or by the comments of students and teachers who have used the book.

Thanks are due, and gladly given, to those whose advice helped so much with the revision; to students and teachers who have written to me from time to time with their questions or suggestions; to Professor Parks C. Hunter, Jr., of Texas A and M University, Ms. Sandra M. Berwind, of Bryn Mawr College, and Professor Alfred L. Crabb, Jr., of the University of Kentucky, whose reviews of the manuscript were very useful to me; to Mrs. Grace Stuart, for her typing and many helpful suggestions; to Professor Göran Hermerén for some valuable critical comments on the third edition; to Professor William Wisdom, for other acute criticisms; and especially to Lars Aagaard-Mogensen, for his deeply and keenly reflective reading of the manuscript, which led to many improvements, though not all the changes he would wish to see.

I hope that this edition, like its predecessors, will be found useful in various ways as a textbook: in introductory courses in practical logic, rather than logical theory; in English composition courses (combined with a standard rhetoric or essay–reader), in courses in speech and argument (combined with a text on oral communication). I believe it can also be profitably used in private study. But anyone who wishes to take it up will find, I think, that much more can be learned if two or three people work on it together, exchanging their answers to the exercises and their interpretations of the examples. The book is elementary, but I hope that it can be studied with profit—and not without pleasure—by persons at various stages of experience and education.

M. C. B.

CONTENTS

THINKING STRAIGHT

PREVIEW

It seems to be a basic feature, if not of the human condition then at least of Western civilization, that while practically everyone is in favor of progress, problems are our most important product. This fact—if it is a fact—is ironic, but it is also understandable, given the interlockings of natural processes and the interconnections of human knowledge. For each step of progress, as most people see it, consists in solving a problem, as, for example, the invention of detergents solved the problem of getting large quantities of dirty clothes sparkling clean at relatively low cost. But the knowledge, both theoretical and technological, that must be obtained to solve one problem often combines with previous knowledge to suggest other things that might be done, if we decide to do them. And the application of new knowledge to practical situations, as we have seen so clearly in the case of detergents, brings along with it consequences that are seldom adequately foreseen, and even if they were foreseen would still confront us with new choices: Are all these sparkling and cheaply clean clothes worth the death of Lake Erie, say? When we didn't have detergents, we didn't have the problem of deciding whether or not to use them; but now we do have the problem, and it is a shiny new one we ourselves created. This process by which solutions often generate more and bigger problems than those they solve goes on constantly, and, as years go by, at an apparently accelerating rate. We see it all about us in the so-called "crises" that elbow each other off the front pages of the daily newspaper—energy crises, power blackouts, transportation deterioration, gasoline shortages, oil spills, nuclear plant hazards, nerve-gas leakages, and the rest of the familiar litany of our modern woes—nor must we lose sight of those many nagging older problems that still plague and sometimes terrify us, such as how to cope with crime and mental illness, and how to achieve a closer approximation to genuinely equal opportunity.

There are, of course, many divergent, and even passionately divergent, views of what is to be done about these problems. It is no part of the purpose of this book to offer solutions. Its fundamental advice—so general as perhaps to seem trivial, even frivolous in view of the seriousness of our many predicaments—is that, whatever else we do about the problems, we must *think*.

In a popular sense, the word "thinking" is applied charitably to almost anything that passes through the mind—idle daydreams, free associations, random recollections, half-hearted resolutions about the morrow. I use it more narrowly. Thinking is a series of ideas that is directed toward the solution of a problem. The problem may be an urgent practical one, like those mentioned earlier; or it may be a highly theoretical one, which has no time-limit attached: How large is the universe? How did human speech originate? But if what goes through our minds is initiated by a question that we want to answer, and aims at attaining the answer, and is guided by the conditions set by the question itself, then that mental process is thinking.

What thinking is after is simply the truth. It is successful when it eventuates in a true and warranted belief, that is, when the thinker acquires new knowledge.

If thinking often seems to lead to more problems than it solves, it is not to be wondered at that there are backlashes against it from time to time. Nowadays, thinking, in the sense adopted here, is sometimes called "objective thinking"—because it responds to articulated questions, it uses words and other symbols as a medium, and it submits itself to standards of judgment (such as we shall be discussing in this book). "Objective thinking" is said to be cold, narrow, inhuman, and unimportant—after all, where does it get you? And something called "subjective thinking" is raised in its place as more natural and suitable to human beings, more worthy of being cultivated and practiced. The philosophical issues are complicated, and they deserve a great deal of reflection. One difficulty is that, as often described, "subjective thinking" seems to amount to feeling strongly that it would be nice if something were true, and then believing it; any protest that there is no evidence or no logical basis for the belief, or that it is incoherent or confused, is dismissed as just what you would expect to hear from an "objective thinker." There is more to the matter, of course. My chief concern here is to confess at the start the general commitment of this book: Whatever problems thinking may lead us to, there is no genuine alternative to it; even if we choose not to think on a particular occasion (for example, if we decide to toss a coin), we ought to make *that* choice on the basis of good thinking.

It is useful to distinguish two fundamentally different aspects of thinking: its *creative* aspect and its *critical* aspect. Good thinking is to a marked degree both creative and critical.

Creative thinking is thinking that generates new ideas, unsuspected solutions to problems that we have been wrestling with. By way of contrast, I recall a recent case in Dallas. A man had been sentenced to seven concurrent life sentences for robbery and burglary, and was paroled after nine years. Shortly thereafter, he stole two credit cards, and was once again caught. This time the jury sentenced him to 1,000 years in prison. That's the kind of thinking-in-a-rut that keeps doggedly plugging away trying to make the same old ideas work, despite all the evidence—from the criminal or economic or military or diplomatic front—of their futility. So one person, whose dog refuses to sit still to be weighed on a scale, keeps putting the restless creature back on the scale until he gives up in disgust; while another, pausing to think and to cast about for alternatives, hits upon the idea of holding the dog in his arms for weighing, and subtracting his own weight from the combined total. Here, in a small way, is creative thinking, which uses imagination to restructure the situation so that its elements appear in quite different relationships; which sees frustrating obstacles as potential means and instruments; which re-examines tacit assumptions and wonders what would follow if some of the most cherished ones were given up.

Creative thinking has been much studied by psychologists and others, and something is known about the conditions that seem to foster it: for example, experiences that exercise our imagination and encourage us to break down familiar conceptual systems and rearrange them in new, even in random, ways. But there is still much mystery about this aspect of thinking. There is undoubtedly an art, at which some are much more skilled than others. Whether, and to what extent, it can be taught, I do not know. The reports are mixed. Some rather general bits of advice have been found helpful when people are stuck on a problem: Consider the assumptions you are tacitly making, and try rejecting them; reverse the direction of your thinking (if you cannot move X to Y, try moving Y to X); let your mind range freely over other things the situation reminds you of, however farfetched the comparison; get away from the situation and seek out a variety of stimuli, which may suggest new approaches and methods.

In this book we shall be concerned with critical thinking, which comes into play when you have an idea to try out, a theory to test, a proposition that someone is defending or objecting to. Is the so-called

"Sinn Fein Oath" a hoax? Can the "energy crisis" be solved without firm measures to conserve all forms of fuel? Is there really a "generation gap," and if there is, would it be largely bridged if we abandoned our system of higher education, in which young people are segregated by age for several years, while so many older people take it for granted that their education is over? When we want answers to such questions as these—questions which implicitly propose an idea that is open to study or investigation—we have to do some critical thinking.

There are, of course, many varities of critical thinking; it varies in important ways with the subject to be thought about. Lawyers, literary critics, composers, stockbrokers, grocers, have their own ways of thinking, and their own standards for distinguishing between good thinking and poor thinking. For unless there are such standards, generally accepted (on reasonable grounds) among those who engage together in a particular form of activity, there can be no way of determining when thinking is going straight, and when it is going astray. There are also general standards that apply to thinking whatever its subject-matter may be, and these are the concern of *logic*. The business of logic is to discover those conditions that must be satisfied by any critical thinking if it is to be good, and therefore have the best chance to be successful.

Good critical thinking—that is, critical thinking that conforms to the general principles of logic—is what I am calling *straight thinking*. In the course of this book we shall have to look at numerous examples of crooked thinking, in order to get clear about the ways in which it differs from straight thinking. But our chief aim will be to understand the nature of thinking that is cogent and effective because its steps have a logical order.

Like most subjects, logic can be studied in itself as a systematic body of knowledge—that is pure logic, or logical theory—and it can be studied in its application to concrete problems, as applied, or practical, logic. The difference is that between physics and engineering, or biochemistry and medicine. In the first half of this book we shall be concerned with applied logic, and, more specifically, with the application of logic to the problems we meet with in the ordinary affairs of life, as responsible persons and as citizens of a modern democratic society, when we try to deal sensibly and intelligently with our relationships to other people and to our physical environment. How shall I vote? (Or is it worthwhile to vote at all?) What kind of life (what career, what goals) shall I choose? Should I be working for, or against, abortion laws? Does the United States need to spend so much money on armaments? What lessons, if any, can we learn from the last election? These are the kinds of questions we have to think about, if we are to realize our potentialities, and perhaps even survive. Of course, it takes more than skill in logical reasoning to handle them—indeed, it takes imagination, sensitivity, persistence, concentration, the ability to obtain and connect much relevant information. But without some skill in logic, the task is hopeless.

Most of the problems we face as persons and as citizens come to us in the medium of words, spoken or written. Most of the information we must bring to bear upon these problems comes to us in words, mainly through the mass media. And most of our thinking is done in words. Until we articulate an idea in a sentence, we cannot be sure what it is, we cannot connect it with other ideas that may affect its truth, and we cannot be confident that we see what is right and what is wrong with it. Critical thinking is impossible without skill in handling language: analyzing and distinguishing meanings, grasping the significance of grammatical constructions, comprehending the basic structure of thought in a paragraph or series of paragraphs. So in the second half of this book we shall be concerned with certain fundamental features of language, considered as a vehicle of critical thinking—and especially with ways of making language, in our own writing or speaking, work to help, rather than hinder, our thinking.

Any extended piece of writing or speech (that is, one containing more than a paragraph) can be looked at in many ways, from many points of view. The literary critic may be most interested in its style; the psychoanalyst may be most interested in the light it may throw upon the subconscious processes of its author. In this book, we shall adopt the logical point of view: that is, we shall be interested in writing or speech as an exemplification of thinking—asking how far the *quality* of its thinking enables it to further knowledge and understanding. Describing, reporting, predicting, arguing, refuting, questioning, inquiring, explaining, clarifying—all these, and many other, activities involving language are of special interest from the logical point of view. So some writings and speeches—newspaper or radio editorials, insertions in the Congressional Record, political orations, advertisements—are most naturally, or most appropriately, approached from this point of view. Still, anything in words (and not only such things) *can* be so approached—even a poem or a joke.

Since most of this book will be developing and explaining the logical point of view, there is no need to say a great deal at this preliminary stage. But it may be clarifying to note the difference between this point of view and a quite different one that is sometimes confused with it. To regard a piece of language from the *rhetorical* point of view is (in one good sense of this term) to take an interest in its *persuasiveness*. Will it in fact get the voters to pull the top lever? Will it sell quantities of

Chocolate Malted Soy Bubble breakfast cereal? Will it win the debate, or the trial? These are questions for the rhetorician: He is concerned to discover general principles governing the use of words for getting people to believe or feel or act. The logician is not concerned with what actually persuades, but with what *ought* to persuade; he inquires not whether the advertisement gets people to buy the cereal, but whether it gives them a *good reason* to buy the cereal; not whether in the "making of a president," a successful "image" is projected to the electorate, but whether a plausible case has been made out for voting one way rather than another. We might say: Rhetoric studies persuasiveness; logic studies *convincingness*—but remember that the logical question is never "Will it actually convince?" but "Is it convincing?" (that is, "*Should* it convince?").

Since this book is designed to be practical, to help you learn to think better, it contains a good many quizzes and exercises. By doing the exercises, you will become familiar with the principles set forth in the text. It is even better to make your own collection of examples as you go along. If you keep your eyes open, you will find odd or dubious thinking turning up from time to time in your favorite periodicals or broadcast programs. Copy them and label them. There is no better way to make sure that you are mastering the subject than to take logic, so to speak, outside the laboratory and into the field.

You may be interested to obtain a preliminary rough sense of the kinds of crooked thinking that will be discussed and analyzed later—and you may like to see how far you have already developed your logical skill. If you wish, turn to the final exercise in this book (Exercise 31) and examine the passages assembled there. Can you see where they go wrong, and explain clearly in your own words just how they go wrong? You might jot down your notes now, and take a look at them again after you have studied this book.

chapter one

ANALYZING AN ARGUMENT

Among the things we encounter from time to time are strings of words, spoken or written: newspaper articles, answers to questions by television interviewers, billboards, novels, advertisements for films, idle chatter, and so on, in practically endless variety. It will be convenient to have a single term to cover them all, so any series of words that are organized into sentences by the grammatical rules of some language I shall call a **discourse**. The term is not meant to imply a formal character, as it does, say, in the title of Descartes's *Discourse on Method* or the *Discourses* of Epictetus; it is, in this book, simply a catch-all term for coherent pieces of language.

A discourse may interest us in many ways, and for many reasons—because it is funny, or beautiful, or promises financial profit, or stirs our moral indignation at public officials who have betrayed the public trust. But when we approach it from the logical point of view, we must temporarily set aside these other considerations and concentrate our attention on its rational convincingness. We must analyze; that is, we must take it apart to see how its parts work and examine their relations with one another. From the logical point of view, the working parts of a discourse are the statements of which it is composed.

The term "statement" can be used in many ways; we can even tell someone in a parliamentary situation to "state his question." But I propose to use it here to mark an extremely fundamental distinction. A **statement** is a sentence, or a part of a sentence, that can be true or false.

§ 1. Statements and Arguments

To tell whether a sentence, or sentence-part, is a statement, we see whether it makes sense to speak of it as true or false, to agree or disagree with it in the usual way. Simple exclamations are certainly excluded: to say "Dammit!" is to show that one is cross about something, but it is not to say what is or is not the case. Simple interrogative sentences are excluded: for example, the question "Will it rain tomorrow?" —though the reply, "The probability of precipitation is 60%" is a statement, even if it doesn't exactly answer the question. Simple imperative sentences are excluded: The command "Get lost!" can be complied with by the rejected hearer, but when he makes himself scarce, the command doesn't become true. All these forms of speech play important roles in many discourses, of course; nor can we utterly ignore them, even from the logical point of view. But for the present we may set them aside.

Sentences that are about nonexistent persons, places, and things also fall short of being statements. In the first chapter of Joseph Heller's *Catch-22* we learn that "Yossarian was in the hospital with a pain in his liver that fell just short of being jaundice." Is this true or false? It's not really either, since it refers to a fictional character. We can make it true by transforming it from a statement about Yossarian to a statement about the novel: "*Catch-22* opens with its protagonist in the medical hospital with an alleged pain in his liver." If you have no briefcase, it makes no sense to ask whether your briefcase is brown or black. Works of prose fiction can, of course, include sentences about real objects and events, which can be true or false: as, for example, *Catch-22* truly says that there was bombing in Italy in World War II.

Parts of sentences can also be statements. This is plainly true of compound sentences, and of complex sentences with nonrestrictive clauses: "The candidate fired his campaign-aides, who had accepted illegal campaign contributions" can be quite satisfactorily recast in two sentences: "The candidate fired his campaign-aides. The campaign-aides had accepted illegal campaign contributions." But of course if the comma had been omitted, making the subordinate clause restrictive, the sentence would consist of only one statement: In "The candidate fired his campaign-aides who had accepted illegal campaign contributions," the subordinate clause simply tells us which of the aides were fired.

Things can get more complicated. You might read in a newspaper that

> The Supreme Court let stand today a ruling that the National Labor Relations Board may not penalize a "runaway" shop by requiring its

owners to recognize the same union in Florida that prompted them to move out of New York. [*The New York Times*, June 6, 1967.]

If you have difficulty grasping this sentence, you can sort out its parts, beginning at the end. What it says is that

(1) Union practices in New York City led the owners of a shop to move their business to Florida.

(2) The National Labor Relations Board required the owners to recognize the Florida branch of the same union they fled from in New York.

(3) On appeal, a Federal District Court ruled that the NLRB could not legally require this.

(4) On appeal, the U. S. Supreme Court let the District Court's ruling stand.

Complex exclamations include statements: "Oh what a tangled web we weave / When first we practice to deceive" includes the statement that deceiving weaves a tangled web. So do complex questions: "When did Copernicus, the great astronomer, live?" says that Copernicus was a great astronomer. So do negative questions: "Didn't Copernicus live in the fifteenth century?" is a perhaps somewhat hesitant and tentative way of saying that Copernicus did live in the fifteenth century. And so do complex imperative sentences: "Write your Congressman today to protest the proposal to give away national timberlands to private lumbering interests!" includes the statement that there *is* such a proposal, or that such a proposal has been made.

Except for the kinds of sentence I have specifically excluded—simple nondeclarative sentences and those sentences that refer to nonexistent things—I shall regard all sentences as being wholly or partly true or false, and hence as statements. This decision deliberately sets aside some difficult and fundamental philosophical questions that must be raised on appropriate occasions but do not, I think, require our attention in this book. It is sometimes thought, for example, that judgments of value, more particularly judgments of right and wrong and (most particularly) judgments of artistic goodness, are to be classed with simple exclamations and not counted as straightforward statements. But I do not exclude them here, though I shall not give my reasons. It is sometimes thought that some declarative sentences express "matters of opinion," and consequently fall short of full statement-status. I take matters of opinion to be matters that it is difficult to make confident judgments about, and that should therefore not be judged dogmatically; but a sentence that is hard to verify, or even one that might be in practice impossible for us to verify, may still be true or false, and is a statement: for example, "If the United States had refrained from certain actions with regard to Russia in 1945, when World War II was ending, the Cold War would never have come about."

To utter a statement is to produce it in some public, or at least potentially public, fashion—to speak the words, or write them down, or cause them to be inscribed, emblazoned, carved, printed, or whatever. To **assert** a statement is to utter it in such a manner as to evince belief in it and invite belief in it. Normally uttering amounts to asserting: When you tell a bewildered pedestrian how to get to the nearest Post Office, or when you fill out an application for a job, your tone of voice, your air of seriousness and sincerity, convert utterance into assertion. Of course you can lie—that is, pretend to believe the statement without believing it, and intend to deceive others—but lying is asserting. And even when you are sincere, you may fail to get others to believe what you say—but you are asserting, nevertheless. The context of utterance is often decisive: Statements pronounced from the bench or pulpit are reasonably taken as assertions; statements in the mouths of television situation-comedy heroines or stand-up nightclub comics are presumed not to be asserted. Of course we can make mistakes about this—as when we think someone is telling a joke, but in fact he is giving a report of what happened to him on the way to the testimonial dinner.

A case in point is provided by an issue of *Environmental Action* (May 12, 1973):

> TO THE EDITOR:
>
> I have read with interest your article, "Sewage treatment: Where do we go from here?" . . . The thing that prompts me to write is your sentence, "Of course, when Thomas Crapper invented the commode in 1884, he didn't know that it was an ecological mistake." . . .
>
> I hate to distract you from the more serious business of trying to straighten out our environment, but on the other hand your article has distracted me from the important business of conserving people's hearing. [The writer is a professor of Audiology.] Therefore, were you kidding when you wrote this sentence? . . .
>
> *The author replies:* . . . No, I was not kidding. However, it turns out that I was wrong. . . . Thomas Crapper was invented in 1969 by the British humorist Wallace Reyburn who wrote about him in a book called *Flushed with Pride.* According to Reyburn, Crapper lived from 1837 to 1910 in England. . . . The book, I might add, is not very funny. In fact, it is so dry and boring that the Library of Congress fell for the same hoax that I did. Instead of listing the book under "Fiction–Humor," the library placed it under "Technical–Building and Construction."

Generally we do not confuse asserted with unasserted utterances, yet a few reminders are in order. (1) When you quote someone else's assertion, you are not making the assertion yourself ("Shakespeare says, 'All the world's a stage' ") unless you endorse the statement ("*As* Shakespeare says, . . ."). (2) When you say, "If it rains tomorrow, I'll stay home," you are, of course, asserting the whole statement, but *not* that it will rain or that you will stay home. (3) When you say, "I believe it will be sunny," or "I don't doubt that it will be sunny," you are asserting, among other things, that it will be sunny—but not if you say "I hope . . . ."

A discourse that consists of, or contains, asserted statements may be called **assertive discourse**. This is the sort of discourse that we are to be concerned with in this book; for these are the discourses that invite us to approach them from the logical point of view—and that seem likely to reward us when we approach them from the logical point of view. So, from this point on, when I refer to discourses, let it be understood that I mean assertive discourses.

The next distinction I propose to make divides the class of assertive discourses into two subclasses. This distinction is not perfectly sharp, but it can be made sufficiently clear, and it is logically fundamental. In some assertive discourses, statements are not merely presented for our information (or misinformation, as the case may be); they are connected in a specific logical way: some of them are offered as *reasons* for others.

Suppose you are reading a book on the growth of the United States interstate highway system, and the vast complex of economic interests and powers that has nurtured it.

> At the end of World War II the American Association of State Highway Officials estimated that necessary improvements on all state highway systems required $11 billion. Then, in 1955, just prior to enactment of the $101 billion highway program (inaugurating the interstate highways), a report to Congress estimated the highway needs for thirty years after 1955 at $297 billion dollars. However, in 1968 the state highway officials testified before Congress that highway needs during the ten years from 1975 to 1985 were $285 billion. . . .

This passage, as you see, consists of a series of assertions, with a common topic. The facts are presented for our consideration, but we are not, at this point, being invited to go beyond them in our thinking. Now consider another passage from the same book:

> The subway-gray reputation of transit has its reasons, of course. For over a half-century it has remained undeveloped, underfed, and shackled. The fact that it returned to carry an unprecedented burden in World War II, despite severe handicaps, only contributes to its bad memories. And the bad memories reinforce equally bad logic.
>
> Capacities illustrate the addictive unreality. An ordinary street lane can serve about 300 cars per hour, but auto passengers are never likely

> to exceed 600. A freeway lane may serve 1,500 cars in a peak hour, but commuters there are not likely to rise above 2,500. Even a humble streetcar track could carry five times as many. Express subway trains are rated at 60,000 persons per hour per track—twenty-four times the freeway lane. . . .

Here the statements are not merely presented and related; some are given as reasons for others. This logical connection is not very explicitly marked, but it is there in the sentence "Capacities illustrate the addictive unreality." We can make the connection explicit with the help of the word "therefore":

> Cars transport so many persons. . . . Transit systems transport so many persons, . . . *Therefore,* it is a serious mistake ("unreal") to let transit systems fall into disuse.

The logical connection is wholly implicit in a passage like this:

> The power of auto conquest is on every side. While the federal government spent seventy-three cents of its transportation dollar on highways in 1967, only three cents served public transit.

It is not a distortion, I think, to read this as saying, roughly, that (1) far more federal money goes into supporting highway construction than into expanding and improving public transit; *therefore* (2) the political power of the "auto complex" (producers of cars, gasoline, cement, asphalt, steel, glass, rubber; as well as truckers and union officials) is very considerable. For here we are not invited by the author merely to note the comparative expenditures, but to draw an inference from them: to see what they show about "the power of auto conquest."[1]

An **argument** is a discourse that not only makes assertions but also asserts that some of those assertions are reasons for others. In ordinary speech the term "argument" often means a dispute, or a situation in which persons holding opposed views on some arguable or debatable matter try to change each other's minds. But in logic, an argument is a special kind of discourse, embodying the claim that one or more specific statements ought to be accepted as true, or probably true, just because certain other statements are true. To believe one statement because you think it is well supported by another is to make an *inference.* Making inferences is reasoning. An argument is reasoning's verbal record.

[1]The three quotations above are from Kenneth R. Schneider, *Autokind vs. Mankind* (New York: Norton, 1971), as reprinted in Philip L. Beardsley, ed., *Whose Country America? An Introductory Reader on American Politics* (Encino and Belmont, California: Dickenson, 1973). Of course the passages quoted are only fragments of a long and complex argument, and do not reveal their full force when taken out of context.

An **exposition** is an assertive discourse that is not an argument. This term is often used more narrowly, and perhaps less usefully, in books on rhetoric that classify discourses as "exposition," "argument," "description," and "narration." Some description, as in poems and stories, is not assertive discourse at all; but within the category of assertive discourse, description is exposition that deals, on the whole, with fairly concrete things: We describe a missing cat, a cottage, a bank robber, a bank robbery. Narration is description of a series of events: a bank robbery, a European tour, the rise and fall of a commune.

The minimal ingredients of an argument are (1) at least one statement that is reasoned *for* (this is the *conclusion* of the argument), (2) at least one statement that is alleged to support it, and (3) some signal or suggestion that an argument is under way (where this is a word or phrase, we shall call it the *logical indicator*). A great variety of English expressions, some rather roundabout, can serve as logical indicators, so you have to be on the lookout for them. Perhaps it will be useful to list the commonest ones. Each of the following words or phrases usually shows that the statement that follows is a conclusion:

therefore . . .
hence . . .
thus . . .
so . . .
implies that . . .
entails that . . .
which shows that . . .
proves that . . .
indicates that . . .
consequently . . .
allows us to conclude that . . .
we may deduce that . . .
points to the conclusion that . . .
suggests very strongly that . . .
leads me to believe that . . .
bears out my point that . . .
from which it follows that . . .

And each of the following words or phrases usually shows that the statement that follows is a reason:

for . . .
since . . .
because . . .
for the reason that . . .
in view of the fact that . . .
on the correct supposition that . . .

assuming, as we may, that . . .
may be inferred from the fact that . . .
may be deduced from . . .
as shown by . . .
as indicated by . . .
as is substantiated by . . .

It is convenient to take "therefore . . ." as a standard logical indicator; when we wish to make logical relationships very clear, the other indicators can be translated into it. If someone writes, "Since current government policies are encouraging a high rate of inflation, price controls should be instituted immediately," his argument can be restated (no doubt somewhat artificially) as:

> Current government policies are encouraging a high rate of inflation.
> *Therefore:*
> Price controls should be instituted immediately.

The term "therefore" must not be taken too strongly: it does not commit the writer to the claim that his reason is utterly conclusive, or that it is the only reason that can or need be given, or that its connection with the conclusion is obvious—but it does make the claim that what precedes it gives what follows it some logical support, some weight of credibility, some justification for acceptance. Nor do I mean to suggest that all the logical indicators are exactly synonymous; each has its subtle individual sense, and its special uses. But they do share an important logical sense, and that is what we are concerned with at the moment.

It is not always easy to tell whether a discourse is an argument; indeed, sometimes its status—unless the circumstances are very helpful—remains forever in doubt. The presence of a logical indicator is quite decisive—but even here it is important to be sure that the logical indicator is being used in a logical sense, rather than in some other sense. Many of these terms have such other senses. "Since," in many contexts, is purely temporal: "The position has remained vacant since the Deputy Undersecretary resigned" is not an argument, and has no logical indicator. Sometimes the logical indicator is suppressed, and the relationship between the statements is supposed to stamp the discourse as an argument: It is pretty obvious, for example, that in "The Undersecretary is incompetent. He should resign," the second statement is supposed to be supported by the first. It would no doubt be a little tedious to insert "therefore" here. Yet, on the whole, where there is a serious risk of misunderstanding, a little extra logical explicitness is worth the effort.

Another borderline case is the discourse that hovers on the verge of coming to a conclusion without quite coming out with it. If we list a number of obvious objections to a proposed new superhighway that would cut through a valued old part of the city, anyone can see that we are against it, and understand our conclusion to be something like "The highway should not be built there." But things are not always so plain. You have to exercise care and sensitivity to the nuances of language, and draw on what you know, if anything, about the writer and his situation, then make the best judgment you can. If the matter is important (if, for example, you are strongly in favor of building that highway, despite the objections), you can always reply to the objections anyway, on the ground that someone *might* draw the negative conclusion.

In this book we shall be concerned primarily with arguments, with their logical soundness or unsoundness—that is, we shall be asking whether reasons are good reasons, or how good they are. When a reason is very good, an argument amounts to a proof. But many arguments that fall short of this high standard are nevertheless of great moment to us; we may have to reply on them in many practical situations. To estimate the soundness of an argument requires a special skill; to help you develop this skill is the main purpose of this book.

A check-up quiz

Some of the following passages are arguments. What is the conclusion, and what is the logical indicator, in each?

1. Since Congress passed the Civil Rights Act of 1964, the number of black voters and office-holders in Southern states has increased considerably.
2. The wiretapper is not to blame for what he did. He believed he was acting under White House instructions.
3. If it is true that the election was won by trickery and deceit, then it should be voided by the court.
4. Why do I insist that New York City is still the best place in the country to live? Look at the unequalled variety of drama, music, art, educational opportunity available there.
5. The union has called a strike because the company is refusing to meet its terms.
6. The company must be refusing to meet the union's terms, because the union has called a strike.
7. The government is distrusted by many citizens, the reason being that it has misled them too often.
8. I do not regard the government as trustworthy, my reason being that it has misled us too often.

9. Beef will soon be scarce. The price freeze on beef has been continued.
10. Beef will soon be scarce. Lobsters will be scarce, too.

§ 2. Getting the Point

To recognize a discourse as an argument—if it is an argument—is one of the first things we must do in approaching it from a logical point of view. The next step is to get a clear map, so to speak, of its logical anatomy. What is it arguing *for*? What is it arguing from? Where is it going, and from what basis does it start? In an argument of any complexity, some statements will be used to support other statements, and will themselves be supported by still other statements. There may be a chain of inferences—or, better, a network, since a given statement may support more than one statement, and may be supported by more than one statement.

When the structure of an argument either is too complex to be immediately apparent, or is obscured by carelessness in style and organization, it can be clarified by a diagram. Consider, to begin with, a fairly simple argument:

> Should it be legal for newspaper and television reporters to refuse to reveal their confidential sources? Indeed it should. For the reporter-informant relationship, is, after all, similar to those of priest and penitent, lawyer and client, physician and patient—all of which have a degree of privacy under the law; moreover, if it were not protected, the sources of information needed by the public would dry up. It follows that Congress should pass appropriate legislation at once.

You may find yourself wanting to take issue with this argument, to point out flaws, to bring in considerations that have been overlooked, to advance a counter-argument of your own. But let us take one step at a time; before we can criticize it effectively, we must be sure we know exactly what the argument is.

First, we want to know what is the *point of the argument.* Unless the argument goes in a circle—a possibility we shall consider in Chapter 2—there will be at least one assertion (perhaps more) that is supported by reasons but is not itself used as a reason to support other assertions. It could be so used in other arguments; but in this one it is the end of the line. This assertion is the argument's final conclusion, and it is the point of the argument. If there are several such assertions then the argument has several points. On the other hand, there will be at least one assertion that is presented as a reason, but is not itself a conclusion from any other assertions. Such assertions are the *basic reasons* in the argument. They might be supported in other arguments, at another time, but in this argument they are the foundations on which it rests.

It is the logical indicators we must look to first for clues to the logical structure. In our example, they are "For," at the beginning of the third sentence, and "It follows that" at the beginning of the fourth sentence. But we must also identify the constituents of the arguments, the various assertions it consists of. For example, the first two sentences seem to go together as a simple assertion. In preparing to diagram an argument it may be useful to rewrite it, separating the assertions by brackets and numbering them, and underlining or italicizing the logical indicators:

> ① [Should it be legal for newspaper and television reporters to refuse to reveal their confidential sources? Indeed it should.] *For* ② [the reporter-informant relationship is, after all, similar to that of priest and penitent, lawyer and client, physician and patient—all of which have a degree of privacy under the law;] moreover, ③ [if it (the reporter-informant relationship) were not protected, the sources of information needed by the public would dry up.] *It follows that* ④ [Congress should pass appropriate legislation at once.]

The relationship between Assertion 1 and Assertions 2 and 3 is clearly marked by "For": evidently Assertions 2 and 3 are both reasons for Assertion 1. But how is Assertion 4 connected with the others? Here we must rely to some extent—as we often do—on our understanding of the statements and of how it might be at least plausible to relate them. It seems fairly plain that this writer is advancing Assertion 1 as a reason for Assertion 4, which is then the final conclusion. Thus the diagram of the argument (in which the assertions are referred to by their numbers, and the arrow stands for "therefore") would look like this:

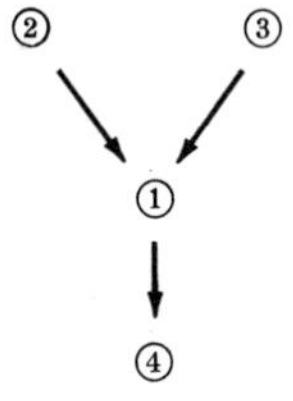

You need not, of course, be prepared to diagram every argument you run across; but the method is sometimes useful when it takes effort to see how an argument hangs together. Some practice with the method should sharpen your ability to grasp the structure of an argument quickly and clearly. It should also help you give your own arguments a firmer structure, and make that structure more evident, when you write them out.

Consider the following passage, which has something to commend it, but also some difficulties:

> The present system of financing political campaigns is far too costly because it makes it almost impossible for anyone who is not a millionaire or a friend (or employee) of millionaires to achieve high public office. This is why the alternative system, under which elections are publicly financed, ought to be adopted; but there is also the point that the public-financing system would help to democratize the process of choosing public officials by automatically involving every citizen in that process. It would certainly be desirable to free legislators as far as possible from dependence on particular economic interests, as well as to equalize the opportunities of candidates, for their merits ought to count more than their money in winning.

There is something confused and confusing about the way the argument is presented. Can we rewrite it, to make its structure, and therefore its logical cogency (or lack of cogency), more clear?

Let us begin by sorting out its constituent assertions and the logical indicators:

> ① [The present system of financing political campaigns is far too costly,] *because* ② [(under the present system it is) almost impossible for anyone who is not a millionaire or a friend (or employee) of millionaires to achieve high public office.] *This is why* ③ [the alternative system, under which, elections are publicly financed, ought to be adopted;] but there is also the point that ④ [the public-financing system would help to democratize the process of choosing public officials by automatically involving every citizen in the process.] ⑤ [It would certainly be desirable to free legislators as far as possible from dependence on particular economic interests,] as well as ⑥ [(it would be desirable) to equalize the opportunities of candidates,] *for* ⑦ [their merits ought to count more than their money in elections.]

Assertion 5 is introduced a bit abruptly, without any indication of its relationship to what went before, but we can discern the most likely one. So the structure can be represented thus:

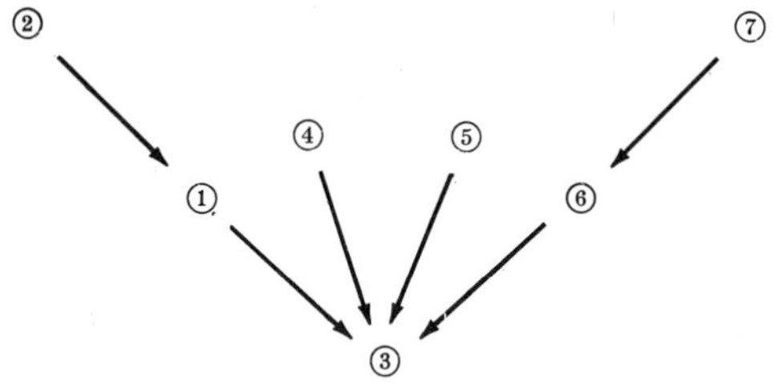

This diagram can give us guidance in recasting the argument to present it in a more orderly way.

The writer's main problem, in formulating an argument, is to make the elements of verbal texture—the syntax, the order of words and topics, the connectives—bring into the open the logical relationships of the argument. Here there are two fundamental rules to keep in mind. The *Rule of Grouping* is, briefly, that as far as possible, reasons for the same conclusion should be kept together, and their similar logical status called to the reader's attention. This can sometimes be done by parallel grammatical construction; in complex contexts, the reasons may have to be numbered and the system of numbering explicitly introduced. In our example, the writer has a problem, because Assertions 1, 4, 5, and 6 are all (as I read the passage) reasons for Assertion 3, yet two of them are in turn supported by other reasons. His solution (or non-solution) is a rather haphazard scattering about of these assertions, leaving it to the reader to pick up the pieces and assemble the puzzle. The *Rule of Direction* is that when there is a series of assertions, each being a reason for the next one, the argument should move in a single direction, so the order of the words helps to remind us of the order of the thought. Logically, it does not matter whether you go from reason to conclusion to conclusion from that conclusion, or from final conclusion to its reason, to the reason for that reason; though other important considerations (such as rhetorical considerations) may decide which procedure is preferable in a particular case. But notice that in our example, the Rule of Direction is violated by the first three assertions, where the logical order is 2, 1, 3, rather than 1, 2, 3, or 3, 2, 1.

The two rules I have suggested—and of course they are not absolute—are not rules of logic, but rules of rhetoric—but they are rules of rhetoric that have to do with making logical order clear. There are other rules of rhetoric (again, in the nature of rules of thumb, or general guiding principles, not without exceptions) that bear upon logic, though not so directly. For example, Assertions 2 and 5 are rather closely related, since they both concern the adverse effects on officeholders of being beholden to individuals or groups who have practically paid for their election; it would help the reader to place these two arguments together, so their relationship is easy to see, rather than separating them by Assertion 4, which involves quite different considerations.

When we rewrite the passage with these rules in mind, it will undoubtedly be improved. There are several ways of doing this, and I am anxious not to suggest that one way is necessarily the best. I shall rewrite the passage so that it seems reasonably clear, but it is quite possible that there are better ways of rewriting it, and that you will find one of them. Here, then, is a possible version:

It is time for us to adopt a system under which all elections are financed wholly by public funds. There are at least four compelling reasons for this. First, the present system of unlimited private contributions is just too costly, for the system makes it almost impossible for anyone who is not a millionaire or a friend (or employee) of millionaires to achieve high public office. Second, it is highly desirable to free legislators as far as possible from all dependence on particular economic interests. Third, it is highly desirable to equalize the opportunities of candidates, since their merits ought to count more than their money in elections. And fourth, the public-financing system would help to democratize the process of choosing public officials by automatically involving every citizen in the process.

If you renumber the statements in the order in which they now appear, the diagram of the rewritten argument will look like this (and note that it is a good deal easier to construct):

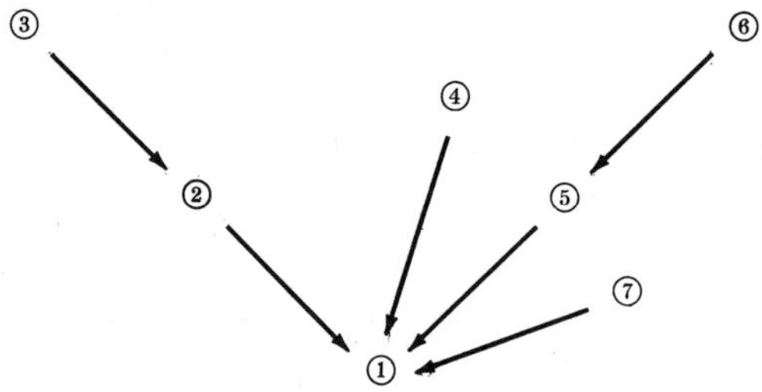

To bring out the nature of logical structure and the usefulness of the diagrammatic method, I have given artificially simplified examples—arguments in which the reasons consist mostly of single sentences or clauses. In an extended argument, of course, a reason may be developed in a paragraph, or even in an entire chapter, with numerous illustrations, embellishments, and digressions. Such arguments must be summarized in key sentences before their basic structure can be diagrammed. And of course many ideas that turn up in the course of the argument will be set aside—but only temporarily—to get at that main structure. Statements made in the course of an argument may play various important logical roles besides serving as reasons or conclusions or providing logical indicators: A writer may state a view that he disagrees with and is about to rebut; he may cite reasons given by others, though only to reject them as unworthy of serious attention; he may tell us something of the past history of the issue he is dealing with, so we can see how it came to be an issue, and thus may understand it better—even though this history is not strictly a part of the argument itself. In later chapters we shall note some of these complications.

A check-up quiz

What is the point of each of the following arguments? If the point is not explicitly stated, put it in your own words.

1. Granted that the druggist made a mistake in substituting the tranquilizer Nardil for the contraceptive drug Norinyl in filling Mrs. Troppi's prescription. But how can he be legally liable for damages to her, when any damages she sustained are far outweighed by the birth of a fine, healthy eighth child?

2. People are always complaining about air pollution and demanding clean air. They do not realize the prohibitive costs involved. We would need exhaust controls for every car (not just new ones), smoke-free factories and municipal incinerators, municipal collection of leaves, thousands of inspectors to police factories and homes. The price of everything would go up, to cover the expense of eliminating smoke.

3. Motorcycles, when properly muffled, do not make more noise than diesel trucks; they produce far less carbon monoxide than large sedans; they can get through city traffic, without violating traffic regulations, several times as fast as a car; they get 150 miles per gallon of gas, instead of twelve or thirteen; they take up only a tenth of the parking-space of a car; and they carry as many passengers (namely, one) as most commuter cars. Even if they have disadvantages, these facts ought to answer those people who are prejudiced against motorcycles and want to ban them.

4. In the long run our greatest medical danger lies in our most admired medical successes. Saving and prolonging the lives of the least fit among us, including constitutionally defective infants, enables individuals to multiply hereditary weaknesses to future generations.

5. One cannot but agree with those drama critics who hold that, because of its broad humanity, insight into human nature, inexorable dramatic development, and capacity to move us, Arthur Miller's *Death of a Salesman* is his best play; and it is interesting to see this judgment confirmed by its lasting popularity among theater and television audiences.

§ 3. Induction and Deduction

To cope successfully with an argument, you have to recognize what kind of argument it is, or at least purports to be, for only then are you in a position to apply the appropriate standards and decide how well it meets them. In the following chapters we shall distinguish the main varieties of argument, and consider the ways they can go wrong or go right. Underlying all these distinctions is a most fundamental one: All arguments fall into one or the other of two jointly exhaustive and mutually exclusive categories.

In making this distinction for our practical purposes, we shall have to overlook important refinements and qualifications that must be attended to in a more advanced and systematic study of logic. Nor can the concepts we require be made as precise in this context as they can be made in a more technical treatise. But what can be said here is substantially correct, and will be found indispensable as we proceed.

The essential feature of an argument, as we have seen, is that it aims (or is aimed) to get us to accept a certain assertion as true, by appealing to a reason—that is, another assertion that we are already disposed to accept and that we can recognize as lending logical support to the proposed conclusion. The argument embodies a claim that the conclusion is made worthy of belief, at least to some degree, by the reason set forth.

Now there are two possibilities here. The argument may actually give a conclusive reason for its conclusion, a reason so strong and compelling that any reasonable person who understands and accepts the reason is bound to accept the conclusion. Or the argument may fall short of conclusiveness, though lending some degree of support to the conclusion: perhaps very heavy support, so that it seems safe to accept the conclusion unreservedly, or perhaps very meager support, so that all we can say is that, in view of the reason given, it would be a little more sensible to accept the conclusion than to reject it—if we have to make the choice.

It is easy to cite simple examples of utterly conclusive arguments—of arguments, in other words, where the reason is amply sufficient, and no further reasons could be demanded.

> Today is Saturday,
> *Therefore:* Tomorrow is Sunday.
>
> Dr. Clark is Gerald's grandfather.
> *Therefore:* Gerald is Dr. Clark's grandchild.

Of course it's possible that tomorrow will never come; the sun may not rise. But if it does come, and if today is Saturday (and assuming that we are referring throughout the argument to the same part of the earth), then it is impossible for tomorrow to be anything but Sunday. And if Dr. Clark is Gerald's grandfather, Gerald has got to be Dr. Clark's grandchild. No way around it.

These little arguments illustrate *logical implication* (or, as it is sometimes called, logical entailment). "Dr. Clark is Gerald's grandfather" logically implies "Gerald is Dr. Clark's grandchild"—meaning that if the first statement is true, the second must be true; it follows necessarily from the first. You can't have the one without the other. In the first example, the implication goes both ways, but not in the second. For suppose "Dr. Clark" is the name of a woman: then Gerald could be a grandchild, without Dr. Clark's being a grandfather at all. We can argue:

> Gerald is Dr. Clark's grandchild.
> *Therefore:* Dr. Clark is Gerald's grandparent.

And we can argue:

> Gerald is Dr. Clark's grandchild, and Dr. Clark is male.
> *Therefore:* Dr. Clark is Gerald's grandfather (i.e., male grandparent).

When we want to draw a logical implication, we have to make sure that the reason contains all that is needed for the conclusion.

When an argument moves from reason to conclusion with logical necessity, it is said to be **valid**. And it is a deductive argument. But even if an argument is not valid, it may still *claim* to be valid; it may have the (deceptive) look of a valid argument, or be offered as such. A **deductive argument** is an argument that either is or claims to be valid. All other arguments are **inductive**. When the validity claim is not put forward very firmly, we cannot be very sure that an argument is deductive. Certain words, such as "necessarily," "it follows that," "consequently," "implies," generally (though they do not always) signal that a claim to validity is being made. An argument that moves from general statements to more limited ones, or from universal statements to statements about particular things, can be recognized as deductive by its logical form, whether or not it is valid. When you become more familiar, in the following chapter, with some basic forms of deductive argument, you will find it easier to classify arguments that you come across. And, in any case, you can tentatively treat any argument as deductive, if there is some plausibility in doing so. You can determine whether it is in fact valid; if it is not, you know at least that it wouldn't be a very good deductive argument if it were offered as one, and you can move on to the next question, which is: How good an inductive argument would it make?

In a deductive argument, the statements that make up the reason are called the **premises** of the argument. Two premises that work together and depend on one another for help in supporting the conclusion are considered to constitute a single reason. In the example just above,

"Gerald is Dr. Clark's grandchild" and "Dr. Clark is male" are two statements, but they combine to yield the conclusion validly, and so count as a single reason. On the other hand, an argument may be deductive, and recognizably so, even if a premise is missing. If we are given some assurance that a valid deduction is being offered, and can supply the statement that is tacitly assumed, we may legitimately treat the argument as deductive though incomplete. "All mathematicians love music, so Jones must love music"—here it is plainly assumed that Jones is a mathematician, and when that premise is added to the other, the argument becomes valid. Erasmus Darwin wrote, in his *Botanic Garden,*

> That the moon possesses little or no atmosphere is deduced from the undiminished luster of the stars, at the instant when they emerge from behind her disk.

Here it may not be quite so easy to see exactly what is required to complete the argument ("If the moon has an atmosphere, the luster of the stars will be diminished when they emerge from behind her disk")—but you will get more help with this sort of problem in the following chapter.

In an inductive argument, the reasons are called the **evidence** for the conclusion. They are facts, or alleged facts, from which the conclusion is induced. An inductive argument marshalls its evidence so as to bring it to bear on the conclusion in the strongest possible way:

> Eleven minutes after Flight 629 took off from Denver at 6:52 p.m., November 1, 1955, it crashed on farmland north of Denver. Wreckage was strewn over an area five miles long and two miles wide. The tail section and nose section were found virtually intact, far apart, but the engines, wings, and main cabin section were destroyed. Many bits of metal looked like shell fragments. Some remnants of the plane had the acrid smell of gunpowder. A thorough investigation turned up no indication of malfunction of the plane or of the crew. Farmers in the area told of hearing loud reports just before the crash. Officials of the Civil Aeronautics Board and the F.B.I. properly concluded that a bomb had been placed in the luggage compartment and that its explosion had caused the crash.

There is more to this story, but what I have given is enough to show the pattern. Even granted all the facts gathered and listed, it does not follow necessarily that there was an explosion, but the evidence is very strong, and the argument carries weight.

Inductive arguments are not always clearly marked by logical indicators, though expressions like "probably," "likely," "suggests," "it seems," "apparently," "evidently," are often used for induction. Indicators may also give a rough estimate of the degree of convincingness claimed for the argument—"it seems" is a weaker claim than "very probably." An argument that moves from statements about particular things to general statements can be recognized as inductive by its form, though many inductive arguments do not have this form (see Chapter 3).

The division of arguments into deductive and inductive may at first seem to leave out a good many arguments that do not readily fit either pattern. Indeed, some philosophers would defend the view that the division is not really exhaustive, that there are arguments which are neither. The issues are too complex to deal with here, but something more ought to be said by way of clarification, at least. There are many arguments, of which we have already seen a few examples and will see many more, in which the conclusion plays another role besides simple assertion. It may be used to make a moral or aesthetic judgment, to recommend a course of action or dissuade us from that course, to commend or disparage a person's character or style of life. There is no doubt such arguments—often grouped together as being *normative*—have an especially complex structure. Moreover, there are features of these structures that are still not fully understood or generally agreed upon. Still, I shall assume here that even such arguments have conclusions which are statements, and that these conclusions are asserted. Such arguments are, then, either deductive or inductive, like any other. If there is a claim, legitimate or illegitimate, that the conclusion is conclusively established, the argument is deductive:

> It is a cardinal principle with me that no painting can be a good painting unless, directly or indirectly, it makes a clear reference to our experience of the world or of life. This painting makes no such reference, and therefore simply cannot be good art.

This argument is even valid.

Another art-critic's discussion might shape up in this fashion:

> I am not in the habit of applying any absolute rules to paintings, and I acknowledge that there are many—very many—ways in which paintings can be good. But consider this canvas, with its single hard-edged slanting red line across a field of plain yellow. It is somewhat striking, at first glance, no doubt, and it illustrates a simple sort of angular tension. But it generates no visual complexities for the eye to explore at length. It develops no new shapes or color-harmonies. It speaks to us not at all of anything in our human condition. It simply doesn't have much to offer, and I would judge that it is a poor painting.

Here the judgment, "This is a poor painting," is backed by various reasons, carefully deployed; the claim is not that the judgment is proved, but that a case has been made out for rating the painting aesthetically low. This is a form of argument of particular significance in many fields; it consists in applying certain *criteria* (in this case, criteria of what constitutes a good painting), as when a jeweller appraises a diamond, or an appraiser tells you how much a house is worth, or *Consumer Reports* rates various refrigerators after making appropriate tests. Such arguments have interesting peculiarities, but what concerns us at present is just that they fall under the broad characterization of inductive arguments.

Whichever sort of argument we are dealing with, its success or failure as an argument depends on the relationship between the reason and the conclusion. In order to lend support to the conclusion, the reason must be connected with it in a logical way. The logician's business is to study such logical connections, and to reduce them as far as possible to rules. These are *rules of inference;* they license certain inferences, so to speak, and prohibit others. An argument is a good one only if it proceeds in accordance with some rule of inference and thus can be justified by appeal to that rule. If it purports to conform to a rule of inference, and thus acquires some plausibility, though in fact it violates that rule, then it is said to be fallacious, or to contain a **fallacy**.

In the course of this book we shall encounter a number of fallacies. They are important to understand if we want to elude many common traps of reasoning. But of course we shall not be interested only in poor reasoning. Our main purpose in the end is to learn how to recognize good reasons when we meet them, and (above all) how to tell whether the reasons we give in our own arguments are good ones.

A check-up quiz

Which of the following arguments are deductive, and which inductive?

1. I read about a girl who got divorced at the age of twelve; she must have married quite young.
2. The chair was priced at $79.95, and I paid $21.35 down; according to my calculations I still own $58.50.
3. The Presidential aide looked grim as he emerged from the Grand Jury room; it looks as if they gave him a hard time.
4. Probably he will live to a ripe old age; certainly he is in excellent physical condition.
5. There is alcohol in his urine; evidently he has been drinking.

6. A house is a dwelling, so a house's chimney is a dwelling's chimney.
7. There are more people in the world than there are hairs on any one person's head; it follows that there must be at least two people with the same number of hairs on their heads.
8. Mammals are warm-blooded; so whales must be warm-blooded.
9. This stone is quartz, has been chipped and flaked, is shaped like an arrowhead; it must be an Indian artifact.
10. The police say he committed the crime; so he committed the crime.

OUTLINE-SUMMARY: chapter one

A sentence, or part of a sentence, that is either true or false is a *statement*. A statement is an *assertion* when it is uttered (that is, spoken, written, etc.) in such a way as to manifest and solicit belief that it is true.

A *discourse* is a sentence, or a series of sentences. If it consists of, or contains, assertions it is an *assertive discourse*. An *argument* is an assertive discourse that contains reasons; all others are *exposition*.

An argument contains (1) one or more assertions set forth as *conclusions*, (2) one or more assertions set forth as *reasons* in support of the conclusions, and (3) a claim that the reasons support the conclusions. This claim is generally made by means of a *logical indicator*, but it may be merely suggested, as may the conclusion itself.

An argument is *deductive* if it claims that its conclusion follows necessarily from its *premises;* if this claim is made good the argument is *valid*. It is *inductive* if it claims only that the *evidence* it provides renders the conclusion more or less worthy of belief.

In a good argument the conclusion is drawn according to a logical *rule of inference,* which prescribes that reasons of such-and-such a sort yield conclusions of such-and-such a sort. If an argument has the appearance of conforming to a rule of inference but actually violates it, the argument commits a *fallacy*.

Exercise 1

Which of the following sentences either are or include statements? If part of a sentence is a statement, rewrite that part as a sentence.

1. Vote Republican! Pull the third lever!
2. Under what circumstances, if any, is a person justified in committing an act of civil disobedience like making "classified" government documents public?

3. I do not wish to see the United States of America become a pitiful helpless giant.

4. The diameter of Jupiter is approximately 11.5 times that of earth.

5. The residents of the apartment, who did not have leases, were evicted by court-order.

6. Don't forget that we have an appointment for Friday.

7. How generous of Henry to lend them his car in the emergency!

8. Why did you neglect to tell the grand jury that you were present at the meeting on May 16th?

9. The only United States president to serve five terms was a Republican.

10. What is truth?

11. In all probability, inflation will continue.

12. Small world, isn't it?

13. Shakespeare's best sonnets are better poems than Shelley's best sonnets.

14. The wages of sin is death.

15. The sky-jackers took along the passengers who were on the plane at the time of the sky-jacking.

16. Thomas Gray was right: "The paths of glory lead but to the grave."

17. Hopefully, next week will be less hectic than this one.

18. If your own relatives won't help you, who will?

19. Support your local police!

20. Some say the world will end in fire / Some say in ice.

Exercise 2

Read each of the following paragraphs carefully, and decide whether it is exposition or argument. If it is argument, pick out the conclusion, or, if the conclusion is only implicit, supply it in your own words.

1. How can one read about 23,736 fans paying four to eight dollars to see the "world's richest demolition derby"—in which brand new 1973 model cars, including a Rolls Silver Shadow and a Lincoln Mark IV were deliberately crashed into each other and wrecked—without finding in this event another indication of the madness of our affluent society, and an

explanation of the atmosphere that has made vandalism and destruction such a constant feature of our urban life?

2. The push for birth control and, indeed, the entire idea of the "population explosion," is only another attempt at deceiving the masses. The idea is to make the people think that the problems we are facing are due to overpopulation and the gross misuse of the natural resources, so that we will turn away from our fight against capitalism and imperialism and deal with ecology. The problem is not that there are too many people on this planet but that an elite few control the resources and have allowed capitalistic exploitation to cause the resources to dissipate.

3. I'll be glad to tell you my opinion of sex-education courses in the public schools. They stir up interest in sex where it didn't exist before; they encourage immorality by making sex seem natural and nothing to be "uptight" about; they give the schools a job that is the responsibility of the parents; they are a filthy Communist plot.

4. At least $600 billion of real estate in the United States goes untaxed each year, although if it were taxed it would yield nearly $15 billion annually in desperately-needed revenue for local governments. Well over $100 billion of this consists of church-owned real estate. All of this property is policed, protected from fire, and in many ways serviced by the cities and townships and boroughs in which it exists. No wonder that a city like Newark, New Jersey, which has almost 50 percent of its assessed valuation in property exempt from taxation, is going broke. (Though it certainly helps to have had a succession of corrupt administrations before the present one.)

5. One of the insistent slogans of the day is that U. S. institutions are not "responsive" to people's wishes. Thus the Electoral College is an easy target. In designing a new nation, nothing perplexed the drafters of the Constitution quite so much as the question of how the President should be elected. As it turned out, the Electoral College devised by them has three times denied the country's highest office to the candidate receiving the greatest number of popular votes. Twice it has resulted in, and several times—most recently in 1968—it has threatened, the chaos of a disputed election's being thrown to Congress for resolution. Last year, in the wake of that recent near fiasco, a proposed constitutional amendment for direct election of the President was passed by the House of Representatives. [*Time,* May 4, 1970]

6. Opponents of the [constitutional] amendment are raising a more serious and thoughtful argument against the plan, focusing on three main considerations: 1) what effect change would have on the two-party system, 2) whether it would favor geographical or popular representation, and 3) whether it would give the edge to a liberal or a conservative candidate. [*ibid.*]

7. "Progress" is what everyone wants, and who can be against it? Yet let us stop from time to time to consider what it means, and what it involves. I suppose it would be widely agreed that the introduction of electricity, and its application to household and industrial tasks, saving countless hours of labor, is one of the most significant examples of progress in the past century and a half since electricity was first discovered. Yet as the industrial designer Victor Papanek recently pointed out, there are more people without electricity in the world today than there were 150 years ago!

8. Preventive detention reverses the traditional presumption that a person is innocent until proved guilty; one can be jailed just for being accused of a crime. It takes away the constitutional right to bail and the right to due process of law. It deprives people of the right to a fair trial by making it harder for them to defend themselves. It is totally illogical in punishing people for what they *might* do, or what someone thinks they will do, instead of what they *have* done.

Exercise 3

Show the structure of each of the following arguments by means of a diagram.

1. Requiring a worker to contribute financially to the labor union that is the recognized collective bargaining agent in his shop does not violate the worker's civil liberties. Because the union has both the authority and the responsibility to represent all employees in that unit, and because the agreement negotiated by the union regulates terms and conditions of employment, the union can properly be said to be an instrument of the worker's industrial government, and therefore the workers who benefit from it can be required to share its cost.

2. Only when there is a compelling need should the government have the right to classify information and withhold it from the citizens—as when it concerns necessarily secret technical and tactical aspects of military planning and activity, or covert intelligence operations abroad, or confidential diplomacy. For the public has a fundamental right, under the Constitution, to know what its government is up to. It follows that the government had no right to conceal from the American people the fact that it was bombing Cambodia, with no legislative or constitutional justification at all—since this was not news to the Cambodians or their allies. It is a further consequence of the public's fundamental right that all classification should be for a short and fixed period of time, and, moreover, that it should be done by a quasi-judicial commission, independent of the government—especially since, as we know, it is the habit of administrations, when they are highly secretive, to protect themselves by keeping the public ignorant of their mistakes and their unwarranted acts.

3. That American parents are under an increasing strain in bringing up children is shown by the rapid and horrible rise in the incidence of child abuse. Obviously the government must provide substantial help to the family, which means there should be a broad system of day-care centers for children of working parents. The number of working mothers is constantly increasing, so that small children are bound to be even more neglected unless there are day-care centers. Moreover, we now know how important it is for children to be stimulated and given the chance to learn at the earliest ages, and this need can best be filled by such centers.

4. It is all very well to complain that in recent years the power of the executive branch of the United States government has grown at the expense of the legislative branch. Unfortunately it does not look as though Congress is in a position to reassert its constitutional equality with the President. It does not enforce its own regulaions providing that campaign contributions of over $100 must be reported; which shows that Congress is no purer than the President's campaign seems to have been in 1972. The regulations of lobbying are a farce: special-interest representatives swarm all over Capitol Hill, carrying home billions of dollars of special favors a year, with no public accounting for the sources of their funds, the amounts they spend, the ways they spend their funds. There is no code of ethics that forbids Congressmen to accept free transportation, to remain in law firms doing business with the government, to conceal their finances and their conflicts of interest. Congress is about as ill-organized, ill-staffed, ill-managed as an institution can be, with little capacity for getting information, storing it, sorting it, applying it to legislative problems; consequently, it is hardly in a position to make the kinds of decision that Presidents have been more and more taking it upon themselves to make.

5. Anthropologist Alexander Alland has refuted the much-popularized theory that man is only a "naked ape," dominated by savage ineradicable biological instincts to kill and destroy those who get in the way of his "territorial imperative." It turns out that aggressiveness is not instinctive, because it is not universal to human beings: take, for example, the Semai of Malaya, a culture in which youngsters are not punished, hardly ever see any violence, and so have no aggressive behavior to imitate—hence there is no such thing as murder in that culture. Nor is territorial aggressiveness innate or biologically derived: the most primitive hunters and gatherers are the least possessive about territory; and often share the same territory with very different ethnic groups, who live off the environment in quite different ways. The fact that in our culture children have to be taught to be competitive in sports (and even then a lot of them never come to like it), and that patriotism has to be instilled by repeated ritual (pledges of allegiance, etc.), shows that aggressiveness is a product of culture, not of biological heredity.

Exercise 4

Pick out the main assertions in the following passage; restate them in your own words, keeping as close as possible to the text; number them; and show their relationship in a diagram.

> The most hopeful epitaph for Project Apollo might be: This was the last gasp of a technologically addicted, public-relations-minded society, the last escapade engineered by an industrial-minded coalition seeking conquests in outer space, while avoiding swelling needs on earth.
>
> And what a gasp it was! Never before had so many taxpayers spent so many billions, and so many thousands of talented technologists and scientists labored so hard on a civilian project that yielded so little. Apollo's irrationality stands second only to one—our inclination to get involved in far-off wars, at even greater cost and distraction from our domestic problems.
>
> Both tendencies are part of our difficulty in turning toward self-reform as the ages of exploiting nature and dealing in other people's lands come to an inevitable end. Little wonder the moon was billed as our last potential colony.
>
> The astronauts set out to investigate the moon, but their journey told us more about ourselves than about that arid pile of orbiting rocks. They told us that in the decade in which poverty, social injustice, pollution, mental illness, subquality housing, inadequate education, and crime went untreated, we invested more new public resources and scarce research-and-development manpower, staggering amounts of our muscle and mind, in a combination of a technological superstunt and a geological excavation.
>
> Project Apollo reveals both the how and why of decisions which set the course of the nation. The commitment to put Americans on the moon was made by President John F. Kennedy during a few days in April and mid-May of 1961 following brief staff reviews of the social, economic, and international implications of the project. And a good part of the review available was opposed to the emphasis on expensive, probably unnecessary, manned flights. Among those questioning such a venture was a task force headed by Jerome B. Wiesner and the outgoing President's Scientific Advisory Committee. We do not reflect long before we jump, often disregarding our experts' advice.
>
> The underlying motives for the go-ahead included the public-relations notion that the prospect of a moon voyage would provide a new topic for a nation despondent over the failure of the Cuban invasion; that Apollo would demonstrate to the world that we could match recent Soviet technological feats (the Russians had just put Yuri Gagarin in

space); and that the giant project would help revitalize a recessed economy.

Arguments in favor of other domestic projects were pushed aside, then and since, on the ground that they would not "sell" as well as lunar flights. Mundane, unphotogenic, dispersed activities, such as the collection of garbage in thousands of streets, arrests of muggers on myriad corners, and the reading and writing habits of kids all over America, it was said, do not compare to the Apollo spectaculars on TV.

Once the space coalition was formed, every value dear to man was emblazoned on its banners. Only now we begin to see how absurd most of that razzle-dazzle was. Generals argued that the moon was essential to national security as a "high ground," for observation and fire purposes, disregarding those who pointed out that our reconnaissance satellites would soon be able to gather more detailed information about "the enemy" than we know what to do with, and that it would be rather silly for the Russians to shoot missiles at us from the moon, when they could fire them from much nearer bases.

The promise of economic "spin-offs" from the lunar gear into other areas was touted by NASA, and indeed there were some. If you burn 27-odd billion dollars, you generate some heat, but pitiful little it was. It turned out that most outer-space products, fuels and alloids, geared to extreme temperatures, vacuums, acceleration, and weightlessness, have no use in our earthly schools, hospitals, and bedrooms.

Finally, we were informed Apollo would provide a peaceful outlet for the world's superpower contest, unite the nation, and enrich the human spirit. But at the cost of keeping one of NASA's missiles from catching a cold, Nixon achieved more for peace through his Ping-Pong diplomacy with Mainland China and in SALT talks, than a decade of space jumps.

The nation surely was divided more over these years than in the preceding decade, among other things over the objectives of the space race, which polls show about half of America never came to accept. The notion that this spectator sport, which reaches the people of the world seated before their TV sets, would humanize them, is so simplistic it rebuts itself.

The space coalition is still drawing more per year for its space antics than many domestic missions (most recently, it got us committed to buying Skylabs). The space budget should be cut below the half-billion mark, focused on near space and economical nonmanned efforts (weather control, communication satellites). Every school child, citizen, and inchoate politician should be required to study what Apollo taught us. Then we can cease chasing moons in the quest for a new America. [Amitai Etzioni, *The New York Times,* Dec. 3, 1972. ©1972 by The New York Times Company. Reprinted by permission.]

Exercise 5

In each of the following arguments, the logical connections between the statements are somewhat obscured by the order in which they are presented. Rewrite each argument so that it is orderly. It may be helpful to diagram the arguments before rewriting.

1. Those men who refused to serve in the armed forces to wage war in Vietnam, and who have been in prison, or in hiding, or in exile, have already paid a heavy penalty by separation from their homes and friends and interruption of their careers. It is clear now to anyone who can think objectively about the war that it was unconstitutional, since the President has no power to send hundreds of thousands of American soldiers to invade a foreign country without a declaration of war by the Congress, so a general and unconditional amnesty should be given to all who refused to fight. Such an act of amnesty would be in keeping with our highest historical traditions, with the wisdom and charity of Washington after the Revolution and Lincoln after the Civil War. (It should also be noted that the Vietnamese war was morally wrong; obviously, anyone who refused to fight was acting rightly; and the war resisters were also acting conscientiously, in the light of their duty as they saw it.) The justification for amnesty is also based on the need to heal the wounds of our society and restore our sense of community.

2. In totalitarian societies, especially Red ones, they get the highest voter turnout for all elections: the secret police make sure that 95% to 98% vote, and vote the right way—that ought to be enough to warn us against the proposal to increase voter participation in the United States by fining people who fail to vote (unless they have a medical excuse). No worse idea has been dreamed up in some time. We would be turning what is now a privilege into a painful duty. Since voter apathy is obviously due to lack of confidence in our leadership and in the electoral process, forced voting would only increase the general cynicism and disaffection. We might even have violent protests and a rebellion, if we tried to put it into effect; not to mention the point that the enforcement of compulsory voting would take a vast amount of time and energy, as can be seen from the fact that even trying to enforce laws against drugs costs the country a lot of money each year. To make a blind ritual out of the voting process, driving people into the booths and making them pull any lever in sight, just to avoid a fine, would lead to worse candidates being elected, out of ignorance and carelessness, since obviously if the voters don't care who wins the election, you're going to get worse results.

3. A teacher's strike at this point in time would place a serious new burden on the already hard-pressed School Board, and should not be called by the union leadership. When you consider that the city's

teacher's have made great and deserved progress in the past six years (as is evidenced by the raise in minimum pay for teachers with B.A.'s from $5,300 to $9,000), and that their benefits compare favorably with those of others—which is shown by the fact that their overall pay scale ($8,900 to $24,000) is among the best in the country, and also by the fact that they put in fewer hours (four hours and five minutes a day in high schools) than teachers elsewhere in the state—we must conclude that they are out of order in demanding a raise right now (bearing in mind, too, that the money to pay them is simply not available, even from the state, which the Mayor has hoped to get to increase its $174.5 million subsidy—at least, the Governor has indicated that the funds cannot be forthcoming). (The state provides 54% of the School Board's current operating funds.)

Exercise 6

Which of the following arguments are deductive and which inductive? How do you tell?

1. I realize that the so-called paraffin test (which is supposed to detect nitrates on the hands and cheek of someone who has recently fired a gun) is said by some F.B.I. experts to be utterly unreliable when applied to rifles, and primarily used by police to intimidate suspects. (The rifle is less likely than a pistol to leave traces, at least on some people, since it lacks the pistol's gap between the chamber and the barrel.) And I grant that even when nitrates are found, they may be traces left by tobacco, matches, or urine. I admit also that the rifle said to have been used by Lee Harvey Oswald in the assassination of President Kennedy was fired three times by an F.B.I. agent, who showed no nitrate traces on his hands or cheek. Nevertheless, I believe that the absence of nitrate traces on Oswald is highly significant, and casts doubt on the Warren Commission's conclusion that Oswald was in fact the assassin.

2. Capitalism requires continuing and limitless exploitation of natural resources, to make possible a constantly expanding market and a rising productivity—without this, it must break down. Now ecologists tell us that "space-ship earth," as they call it, is a closed system, whose natural resources are finite and limited. It has been shown often enough that capitalism is the one true and right form of economic system. Therefore the ecologists must be wrong.

3. If you doubt the reality of extrasensory perception, you need only visit the flourishing course in parapsychology that is being taught by Professor Evelyn Monahan at Georgia State University in Atlanta. Breathing deeply, with sealed envelopes pressed to their foreheads, the students "extend their consciousness" into the envelopes, and before long find that they can not only see the colors and shapes of the papers in-

side the envelopes, but even read the words printed on them. This is surely enough evidence to convince even the most arrant skeptic.

4. Witnesses told police they saw Wilson being beaten with a sawed-off pool cue by a gang of youths before he was stabbed in the heart. He was pronounced dead at Germantown Hospital. One of his pockets had been turned out, indicating his assailants were trying to rob him.

5. The Hague Convention, which is accepted international law, prohibits the mining of "the coasts and ports of the enemy with the sole object of intercepting commercial navigation." But when President Nixon ordered the mining of North Vietnamese harbors, he specifically announced that his purpose was to prevent "North Vietnamese naval operations." Therefore that mining was done in full accord with international law.

chapter two

VALID DEDUCTION

Even if you can see right away that an argument is deductive, you may not be able to decide right away whether it is a sound one.

> Because of the acknowledged importance of the educational process, a student cannot be legally barred from it merely on account of his appearance, however distasteful that may be to some people, unless his appearance does, in fact, disrupt the educational process or constitute a threat to health or safety. Therefore it is unconstitutional for school authorities to prohibit long hair, which clearly neither disrupts instruction nor presents hazards, as is obvious from the wide toleration of long hair on many different kinds of people throughout the country.

To be confident that you know whether such an argument contains fatal flaws, you may have to examine it with some care.

A sound deductive argument satisfies two conditions: First, it is valid; second, its premises are true. A deductive argument cannot legitimately claim to establish its conclusion if it fails either test. If the argument is invalid, it doesn't matter much whether the premises are true, since the alleged conclusion doesn't follow from them anyway. If one or more of the premises are false, the argument might (if valid) still have some interest for us, since it shows us what would follow from the premises if they *were* all true; but false premises give no support for the conclusion.

Truth and validity must always be kept carefully distinct. Statements are true or false; arguments are valid or invalid. Even if a deductive argument has a true conclusion, it may be invalid (and have true or false premises), or it may be valid (and have true or false premises). The only combination that logic rules out is being valid but having all true premises *and* a false conclusion.

It is always in order to ask of a deductive argument whether its premises are true; to find this out, we must check them against our own experience or look for further evidence to support them, or perhaps deduce them from still more basic premises. The problems involved in getting and using evidence are to be considered in the following chapter. If we deduce the premises from others, we have pushed the truth-question one step back; sooner or later, in any case, we are going to have to ask the second question: whether the argument is valid. This is the topic on which we are to concentrate our attention in this chapter. What makes an argument valid? And how do we tell when an argument is valid?

§ 4. Molecular Arguments

What makes possible the systematic study of logic is that every deductive argument has a *form,* and every valid deductive argument is valid because of its form. The distinction between form and content cannot be made wholly precise in a brief discussion, but for our purposes it will be enough to note its essential feature. In any argument we can distinguish various subjects, or what the argument is (in a broad sense) about.

> If the President impounds funds voted by Congress for aid to hospitals, he will precipitate a conflict with Congress. And he will impound those funds. Therefore, the conflict will occur.

This is about the President's impoundment of funds and conflict with Congress. Let the letter "I" stand for "The President will impound funds voted by Congress for aid to hospitals," and let "C" stand for "The President will precipitate a conflict with Congress." Then we can recast the argument this way:

> *If* I *then* C.
> *And* I.
> *Therefore,* C.

The form of an argument is marked out by key logical terms, which we can call *logical operators,* since they operate on other words to give them logical connection. "If . . . then . . . " is one of them; "and" is another. We shall meet several others in this chapter. Notice that the letters I have introduced as abbreviations also play an essential role in indicating logical form. As far as the form of the argument is concerned, it doesn't matter what statements you substitute for "I" and "C", but to preserve the same logical form, you must substitute the same statement *for* the same statement throughout. The statement that follows "and" must be the same one that follows "if"—otherwise you have changed the form. Thus it would not change the form to substitute "V" for "I" (where "V" stands for "The President will veto all bills passed by Congress in its next term"):

> *If* V *then* C.
> *And* V.
> *Therefore,* C.

But of course, the substitution of "V" for "I" might change the *truth* of the premises.

There is one question that may already have occurred to you. I have been treating two verbally distinct statements as though they were the same:

(1) The President *impounds* funds voted by Congress for aid to hospitals.

(2) The President *will impound* funds voted by Congress for aid to hospitals.

It was (1) that appeared in the original argument; it was (2) that I abbreviated as "I." I was taking it for granted that, in this particular argument, the differences between (1) and (2) could be—indeed, were expected by the arguer to be—ignored. This decision was guided by a sense of what a valid argument of this form would have to be like, and it proceeded on the assumption that a valid deductive argument was aimed at by the arguer. Evidently to say "The President impounds funds voted by Congress" is not to talk about a habitual action, but about a (possible) future action; so the force of this statement (as far as this particular context is concerned) is not misleadingly rendered by (2). Still, these substitutions have to be made with caution or we may go wrong in interpreting and appraising an argument.

The argument we have been using as an example has the important feature that the elements which make up its content are themselves statements: "The President will impound funds voted by Congress for aid to hospitals" and "The President will precipitate a conflict with Congress." When you combine statements, using logical operators, you get **molecular statements**. When you make up an argument that includes at least one such statement, you get a **molecular argument**. A molecular argument, in short, is one in which the logical operators operate upon statements to build more complex statements, and the statements are shifted about as wholes in the course of the argument. In other arguments, the logical operators are used to build statements out of simpler elements, and the statements are broken up and their parts shifted about and recombined in the course of the argument. Such arguments may be called *atomic* arguments. Later in this chapter we shall come to those arguments; in this section, we are concerned with some common forms of molecular argument.

Perhaps the most familiar form of molecular argument—so familiar, indeed, that you may often use it without even realizing that you are reasoning—is illustrated by the argument we have been discussing. Its essential ingredients are three. (1) The major (or first) premise consists of a statement built up by the logical operator "if . . . then . . . ." Statements of this sort are called **conditional statements**; the statement preceded by the "if" is called the **antecedent** and the statement preceded by the "then" is called the **consequent**. (2) The minor (or second) premise is the same statement (when the tense has been adjusted) as the antecedent of the major premise. (3) The conclusion is the same statement as the consequent of the major premise. The general rule of inference for arguments of this form might be stated this way:

> Whenever a conditional statement is true, and its antecedent is true, then its consequent is true.

This, remember, is a rule about validity. When you encounter an argument of this form, you can tell that it is valid without knowing whether the statements that it contains are true or false.

Any argument that satisfies this rule is a deductive argument of a certain kind, namely, a **conditional argument** (that is, an argument with one conditional premise and one nonconditional premise). There are three other forms of conditional argument, one also valid, the other two invalid. In the valid form we have examined, by asserting the minor premise we affirm the antecedent of the major premise. Suppose we were to affirm the consequent instead. A letter to *The New York Times* (December, 1971) after the nuclear testing in Alaska—which was considered very risky by physicists and environmentalists for a number of reasons—said:

> General E. R. Quesada's contention in a recent letter that because the nuclear blast on Amchitka did not provoke a catastrophic reaction from nature it was therefore justified is utterly ludicrous. It is analogous to encouraging a person to play Russian roulette and then gloating because the firing pin struck a blank chamber.

The writer evidently attributes to General Quesada the following argument:

> If the Amchitka nuclear test was justified, it did not provoke a catastrophic reaction. It did not provoke a catastrophic reaction. Therefore, it was justified.

Here the *consequent* of the major premise is affirmed, rather than the antecedent, so the conclusion does not follow. Even though the bomb-testers happened to get away with it that time, it might still be the case that they took a fearful risk (like the Russian roulette player), and were more lucky than smart. I don't know. In any case, if that was General Quesada's reasoning, it was indeed fallacious; his argument, and all other arguments having the same form, commit the **fallacy of affirming the consequent.**

To **negate** a statement is to add a "not" to it in the appropriate place, or to subtract a "not" if it is already there; thus these two statements negate each other:

> Violence is evil.
> Violence is not evil.

Of course, some other grammatical shifts may be required to make the transition smooth: to negate "Bird lives," we have to say "Bird does not live." (The relationship involved here will become clearer in the following section.) To affirm a statement is simply to assert it; to *deny* a statement is to assert the statement that negates it.

Now, the minor premise in a conditional argument can negate, rather than simply repeat, one of the statements in the conditional premise. Again, we have two forms of argument. In asserting the minor premise, we may deny the consequent, then conclude by denying the antecedent. That is the valid form.

> If Congress has good leadership, it will override the President's veto.
> Congress will not override the President's veto.
> *Therefore:* Congress does not have good leadership.

Or in asserting the minor premise, we may deny the antecedent, then conclude by denying the consequent. That is the valid form: it commits the **fallacy of denying the antecedent.**

> If Congress has good leadership, it will override the President's veto.
> Congress does not have good leadership.
> *Therefore:* It will not override the President's veto.

This conclusion does not follow from these premises, though it might be true, and would no doubt follow from other premises.

It might seem that not all arguments of this last form commit the fallacy of affirming the antecedent, but that is an illusion. Consider:

> If Congress passes the bill, the President will veto it.

Congress will not pass the bill.
Therefore: The President will not veto it.

The conclusion seems to follow all right, even though the antecedent is denied. But that is because we are assuming another premise, not explicitly stated here: namely, that the President can't veto a bill that hasn't been passed. When we add this premise, and combine it with one we already have, we get a new major premise—and a variant form of conditional argument:

The President will veto the bill *if and only if* Congress passes it.
Congress will not pass the bill.
Therefore: The President will not veto it.

The operator "if and only if" is convenient for showing that the "if . . . then" relationship goes both ways:

I will go *if and only if* you go.
I won't go *if and only if* you don't go.

In such molecular statements, the atomic statements involved are both antecedents and consequents. Therefore, from these major premises a valid conclusion can be drawn by *either* affirming *or* denying either of the atomic statements.

There is a useful form of argument—which we may call the conditional chain argument—that consists of nothing but conditional statements, arranged in sequence so that each links with its predecessor:

If P then Q.
If Q then R.
If R then S.
Therefore: If P then S.

This chain has three links, but evidently it could have any number and still be valid, if the rule of linkage is followed—that the antecedent of the first conditional and the consequent of the last conditional appear in the conclusion, and that, after the first premise, the antecedent of each premise be the same as the consequent of the premise that precedes it. When we happen to know a number of connected conditional statements, this form of reasoning can take us quite far.

If you are careless with campfires on your fishing trip, there will be a forest fire.
If there is a forest fire, there will be nothing to trap the rain.
If there is nothing to trap the rain, the soil will be washed into the river.
If the soil is washed into the river, the gills of the fish will become clogged with silt.

If the gills of the fish become clogged with silt, the fish will die.
If the fish die, there will be no more fishing in that stream.
Therefore: If you are careless with campfires on your fishing trip, there will (eventually) be no more fishing in that stream.

For logical purposes (that is, in order to state an argument in the clearest possible way), conditional statements are cast in the plain "If . . . then . . ." form. This is a kind of standard, or ideal, form for them. But in ordinary discourse we can frame conditional statements in several other ways, each of which has its special uses. We can say:

If Jones is not granted immunity from prosecution, he will not testify.
Jones will not testify if he is not granted immunity from prosecution.
Jones will not testify unless he is granted immunity from prosecution.
Jones will not testify except on the condition that he is granted immunity from prosecution.
Jones will testify only if he is granted immunity from prosecution.

These statements do not have exactly the same meaning—indeed, the differences are of a sort that will interest us in Chapter 5. But they have a common core of meaning, in that they all make Jones's being granted immunity a condition without which he will refuse to testify. This core is most simply and directly expressed by "if . . . then . . . ."

A molecular argument with complex clauses is best recast, and perhaps abbreviated, in order to make its validity or invalidity plain. This is especially true with an argument that is incomplete or elliptical. Senator Sam Ervin, in the Watergate hearings, discussed the claim that was made by some of President Nixon's past assistants that the White House was justified in hiring agents to burglarize the office of a psychiatrist to get information from his files about Daniel Ellsberg. He recalled the time during the Korean War when President Truman ordered the seizure of steel mills by the government, but was overruled by the Supreme Court.

If the President does not have any inherent power under the Constitution to seize steel mills in order that he might carry on a war and furnish the weapons and munitions that will enable the soldiers to fight and prevent the destruction of themselves at the hands of the enemy, I think that is authority that he has no inherent power to steal a document from a psychiatrist's office in time of peace.

The shape of this argument can be shown this way:

If the President does not have a Constitutional power to seize steel mills in time of war, then he does not have a Constitutional power to order the burglarizing of a psychiatrist's office when the country is not at war.

The President does not have a Constitutional power to seize steel mills in time of war (the Court's decision).
Therefore: The President does not have a Constitutional power to order the burglarizing of a psychiatrist's office when the country is not at war.

There is perhaps one feature of the "if . . . then . . . " locution that might make it misleading, unless we explicitly (and purely for logical purposes) rule it out. Quite often, we find it most natural to say "If *P*, then *Q*," when the event or state of affairs referred to by *Q* is later than the event or state of affairs referred to by *P*. For example, the first statement in the list just above is logically equivalent (as will become clearer in the following section) to the statement:

If Jones testifies, then he will be granted immunity.

And this sounds a little odd, because the grant of immunity would naturally come before, rather than after, the testimony. But the "if . . . then . . . " operator is not used in logic to suggest any such temporal sequence, only the dependence of one event or state of affairs upon another. To make this clear we could write instead:

If Jones testifies, then he will have been granted immunity.

Two other logical operators play an extremely fundamental role in our molecular thinking, though their operations are seldom noticed in ordinary circumstances. They are "and" and "or":

The defendent's telephone was illegally tapped *and* he was not informed of his right to counsel.
Either the defendent's phone was illegally tapped *or* he was not informed of his right to counsel.

These two descriptions of a situation lacking in due process of law differ in this important respect: for the first to be true, both violations of due process had to occur, but for the second to be true, only one of them had to occur.

A molecular statement consisting of two statements joined by "and" is a **conjunctive statement** (or **conjunction**), and its two ingredient statements are **conjuncts**. When the conjuncts share the same subject or the same predicate, we generally abbreviate the conjunction. Thus "Dostoevsky and Tolstoy were both Russian novelists" is short for "Dostoevsky was a Russian novelist *and* Tolstoy was a Russian novelist." And "Dostoevsky wrote *Crime and Punishment* and *The Possessed*" is short for "Dostoevsky wrote *Crime and Punishment* and Dostoevsky wrote *The Possessed*." In English we have various ways of expressing conjunction:

Jones was granted immunity, then he testified.
Jones was not granted immunity, but he testified.
Jones testified, although he was not granted immunity.
Jones testified because he believed that to be his duty.

(To this list we could add "moreover," "also," "too," "nevertheless," "despite," "however.") It is apparent that the relationships presented in these statements are rather different. They all include conjunction, and part of what each statement means can be captured by the operator "and"; but each adds to conjunction another notion: that one action is surprising in view of the other, or that one followed the other or was a reason for the other.

Inferences involving "and" are simple. We can go in two directions. Given a number of true statements the conjunction of them is true. Given a true conjunction, each of the conjuncts is true.

Jones was born in Sheboygan, lived in Oshkosh, married at the age of 22, and became a bricklayer.
Therefore: Jones lived in Oshkosh.

This doesn't take us far, but it takes us safely.

A molecular statement consisting of two statements joined by "or" is a **disjunctive statement** (or **disjunction**), and its two ingredient statements are **disjuncts**. The word "or" has a tricky feature, which it is well to be on guard against. In the sense adhered to in logic, it simply indicates that at least one of the disjuncts is true, and leaves open the possibility that both may be true.

"Either the battery is dead or the gas tank is empty" is true if one of these unfortunate conditions exists or if both exist. Thus it is logically correct to argue in the following way:

Either the battery is dead or the gas tank is empty.
The battery (it turns out) is not dead.
Therefore: The gas tank is empty.

But it is a logical error to argue in the following way:

Either the battery is dead or the gas tank is empty.
The battery is dead.
Therefore: The gas tank is not empty.

For the fact that one of the disjuncts is true does not imply that the other one must be false.

These arguments are examples of the **disjunctive argument**: i.e., an argument in which the major premise is a disjunctive statement and the minor premise and conclusion are nondisjunctive. In its valid form, the minor premise negates one of the disjuncts in the major premise, and the conclusion repeats the other disjunct. It is a process of elimination: We know (presumably) that at least one of the two is true, so if one turns out to be false, the other one must be true. In its invalid form, the minor premise repeats one of the disjuncts, and the conclusion negates the other; such an argument commits the **fallacy of affirming a disjunct**.

It may seem that affirming a disjunct is not always a fallacy, because of the contexts in which "or" seems to carry a stronger sense.

> Dostoevsky was born in Russia or Poland.
> Dostoevsky was born in Russia.
> *Therefore:* Dostoevsky was not born in Poland.

This seems perfectly valid. And it would be valid if we took "or" as excluding the possibility that both conjuncts are true. The expression "and/or" is sometimes used to make clear that the joint truth of the conjuncts is not being ruled out. But we do not really need to introduce a second sense of "or" here. What happens is that we know that a person cannot be born in nonoverlapping places (one can be born in both New York City and New York State—and one can be born in a town which is at one time in Poland and at another time in Russia), and we supply this information tacitly as another premise. Once we do supply this premise, of course, the original major premise is no longer needed, and we are reasoning (validly) in the following way:

> Either Dostoevsky was not born in Russia or he was not born in Poland.
> Dostoevsky was born in Russia.
> *Therefore:* Dostoevsky was not born in Poland.

Whenever we find a disjunctive argument that commits the fallacy of affirming a disjunct, but somehow seems convincing, we should consider whether there are not some well-known facts from which we can draw a suitable new major premise. This doesn't make the original argument any less fallacious, but it transforms it into a valid one—which might be what the arguer had in mind all along.

A check-up quiz

Which of the following arguments commit the fallacy of affirming the consequent? denying the antecedent? affirming a disjunct?

Valid

1. If inflation is allowed to continue, the unions will demand a steep rise in wages. And that's what's going to happen, because inflation is sure going to be allowed to continue.

2. The alternatives seem to be that the United States government weakens its NATO commitment by withdrawing troops from Europe or that it meets increasing criticism at home for the enormous funds spent in maintaining these troops abroad. The government will never weaken its NATO commitment; so we may expect that criticism to increase.

3. The streets are no safer today than they were five years ago; yet if the Crime Control Act was effective, we would expect streets to be safer. Hence the Act was not effective.

4. The food service in the cafeteria will not improve unless there is a student strike. A strike is scheduled for tomorrow. It follows that the food service will improve.

5. It looks to me like either the battery is dead or something is wrong with the starter. . . . Yes, the battery is dead. Then there can't be anything wrong with the starter.

6. Granted that if there were no problems on earth, man should explore the moon. But you admit that there *are* problems—plenty of problems—on earth. How can you consistently say that man should explore the moon?

7. If people disagree about whether human beings descended from lower forms of animals or were specially created, California school textbooks in biology should state explicitly that this question has not been settled by scientists. They do disagree, and that's what the books should say.

8. Maybe the Governor did accept kickbacks from the syndicate selected to manage harness-racing in this state. Maybe, on the other hand, these accusations are just vicious rumors deliberately spread by his political enemies—which I for one find incredible.

9. By 1980, either we will institute far-reaching procedures to recycle our trash, or by 1980 we will have to find room to dispose of 440 million tons of junk cars, plastics, cans, waste paper, etc., that will be ground out each year by the great American planned obsolescence mill. But we are assured that somehow such room will be found, so large-scale recycling is not expected soon.

10. If Americans tend to eat, drink, and smoke more than people in other advanced countries, we may expect their life-expectancy to be lower than that in European countries, Japan, Australia, etc. This is exactly true—American men live an average of 67.1 years, women 74.6 years; a good deal below that of Sweden, Iceland, France, Canada, etc. The conclusion? We eat too much, drink too much, smoke too much.

§ 5. Basic Logical Relations

When the truth or falsity of one statement determines, or helps to determine, the truth or falsity of another statement, the two statements are **logically related**. Otherwise they are **logically independent**. Statements that are apparently independent may turn out to be indirectly related through other statements that connect them. Thus it turns out in plane geometry, for example, that the statement "The sum of the angles of a plane triangle is 180°" (a familiar theorem in Euclid) is logically related to the statement "When equals are added to equals, the results are equal" (one of Euclid's axioms). because the latter is used in proving the former—although this relationship is by no means obvious at first glance.

The basic logical relation is implication, which has already been introduced. Other important logical relations based on implication are now to be considered. The network of such relations in any discourse constitutes its most important aspect, from the logical point of view, for unless we grasp it clearly and firmly, we have little chance of finding out whether the discourse is worthy of our assent.

Two statements that imply each other are **logically equivalent.** "The pitcher is half-full" and "The pitcher is half-empty" are so related that if either of them is true, the other must be true; and if either is false, the other must be false. A very important pair of equivalences among molecular statements involves the relationship between "and" and "or." Denying a conjunction is equivalent to affirming a disjunction of denials:

> "Peabody will not both produce the Off-Broadway play and direct the pornographic film" is equivalent to "Either Peabody will not produce the Off-Broadway play or he will not direct the pornographic film."

Denying a disjunction is equivalent to affirming a conjunction of denials:

> "Peabody will neither (= not either) produce the Off-Broadway play nor direct the pornographic film" is equivalent to "Peabody will not produce the Off-Broadway play and he will not direct the pornographic film."

When the truth of one statement implies the falsity of another, then the truth of the second statement also implies the falsity of the first, and they are **logically incompatible**. Since they cannot both be true, anyone who asserts them both must be asserting at least one false statement; and we can be sure of this even if we do not know which of his statements is false. For he is really describing a state of affairs that is logically impossible—not just unlikely or unimaginable or excluded by the laws of nature. A discourse that either contains or implies a pair of logically incompatible statements is **inconsistent**. Its statements cannot all be true together. It is logically self-defeating. Even a single sentence may be inconsistent, if it implies incompatible statements by combining logically conflicting terms: a "female uncle" is a logical impossibility (but we must be careful here: "woman chairman" is not inconsistent, any more than "male nurse" or "female sculptor," in current usage).

Some inconsistencies are so easy to spot that you wonder how they could have been committed. If the Honolulu travel brochure says

> The weather is always warm, with temperatures averaging 80 degrees year-round. The rainy season runs from June to October, the dry season from May to November,

you sense something wrong—though in this case you can also see how the slip should be corrected. In longer and more serious passages, it might take some thinking to be sure whether or not there is inconsistency.

> [President] Washington rejected a request from the House of Representatives that he turn over copies of instructions and other papers relating to the Jay treaty. Though he based his refusal on the narrow ground that the House was not involved in the treaty-making process and that all the papers affecting the negotiations with Britain had already been laid before the Senate, he established a larger precedent that future Presidents used to deny information to the Senate as well. [Arthur Schlesinger]

As *The Nation* pointed out, it's true that later presidents sometimes grasped at any straw, however feeble, to justify their refusal to give information to the Senate, but to say that George Washington "established a larger precedent" seems to contradict what has just been said, since Washington made such a point of *giving* information to the Senate when it was clearly related to the Senate's constitutional power to ratify treaties.

In other cases, we find something like inconsistency, yet we may not be able to show it explicitly. A study of sentencing in Federal courts in the New York City metropolitan area showed enormous disparities in comparable cases, or even in cases where the facts would seem to point in the opposite direction. For income tax evasion, the average sentences for whites was 12.8 months, for nonwhites 28.6; for immigration violations, 9.7 for whites, 27 for nonwhites; a small-time addict-pusher might draw a 30-year term in one court, and a three-year or four-year term in other courts. It seems that there is inequity in these practices; but is there strictly inconsistency? Inconsistency occurs in discourses, not practices. If someone were to defend these disparities, he might do so on various grounds. For example, he might argue that individual judges should be allowed to determine sentences, no matter how bizarre the results, because no one is in a better position to make the determination than the judge who hears the case. Such a defense would not involve inconsistency, though it might have other logical deficiences. But suppose one judge were to argue this way:

> We must make a fundamental distinction between drug-pushers who are themselves addicts and those who are under no such compulsion to support themselves by criminal activity that preys so heavily on others. Addict-pushers should always be given reasonably short sentences, in the hope of helping them; but no sentences are too long for nonaddict-pushers. I have been criticized for sentencing an addict-pusher to prison for 30-years, but he was a very successful pusher who had led a number of young people to become addicted as well.

If the judge's principle is that "Addict-pushers should always be given reasonably short sentences," then he is inconsistent in making the exception in this case. If you pressed him, he would probably withdraw "always" and substitute "nearly always," or something of the sort, thus removing the inconsistency without admitting that the 30-year sentence was unjustified. But so long as the inconsistency stands, neither the universal principle nor the special exception can be said to be soundly defended, since each cancels the other out.

Arguments of this sort—where a universal principle is announced and perhaps applied against others, but not applied to some case that especially interests the arguer—are guilty of **special pleading**. A Texan argues strenuously against Federal aid to states for all sorts of services (for example, free milk for school-children), on the ground that this is Federal paternalism and an unwarranted interference with states rights, but at the same time approves of the fact that Texas, which is sixth in population and seventh in the amount of federal taxes paid, is third in the amount of federal money it receives. This is special pleading. A defender of the Equal Rights Amendment accepts the principle that men and women should be equal in their opportunity to share the benefits and bear the burdens of society, but adds that, of course, he thinks men should fight the wars and women should stay at home. This is special pleading. Perhaps he has another principle that qualifies his principle of sexual equality, and justifies the military exception, but if he doesn't come up with such a qualification, he is simply inconsistent.

When two statements are incompatible, and their denials are also incompatible, they are **contradictories** of each other. One of them must be true and the other must be false—though we may not know which is which. We get clear-cut contradictories by putting "not" in the right place: "The moon is blue" vs. "The moon is not blue." But pairs of contradictories can be more complex:

> "Peabody will both produce the Off-Broadway play and direct the pornographic film" contradicts "It is not the case either that Peabody will not produce the Off-Broadway play or that he will not direct the pornographic film."

The second statement is rather awkward, and is not recommended for its style, though sometimes a little awkwardness is a small price to pay for getting a statement exactly right.

When two statement are logically incompatible, but are *not* contradictories, they are **contraries** of each other. Contraries cannot both be true, though they can both be false: "The moon is blue" vs. "The moon is pink."

> "Peabody will both produce the Off-Broadway play and direct the pornographic film" is a contrary of "Peabody will neither produce the Off-Broadway play nor direct the pornographic film."

A statement's contradictories are all equivalent to each other; but it may have any number of nonequivalent contraries.

In the previous section, I spoke of "denying" a statement. To deny a statement is to assert that it is false. This can be done by asserting a statement that is plainly incompatible with it; the most direct denial is a contradictory. If you say "It's hot," and I say, "It's chilly," I am denying your statement; but my most direct denial would be "It's *not* hot." It is important not to confuse the term "denying" with the term "refuting"—which is unfortunately often used as though it were a synonym. "Mr. Colson's testimony would seem to refute the testimony of Mr. Erlichman," says the newspaper—but what is meant (or at least, all that is known) is that what Mr. Colson said conflicted with what Mr. Erlichman had said: There was a logical incompatibility, so apparently they cannot both be true. To refute a statement, strictly speaking, is not merely to deny its truth, but also to present convincing reasons for disbelieving it. If you say, "It's hot," and I (while shaking my head) produce a working thermometer that shows the temperature to be under sixty, then I am not merely denying, but perhaps also refuting, what you have said.

To illustrate and clarify further all these basic logical relations, we must now turn our attention to statements of a very numerous and important kind. Their essential features are exemplified by the statement

> All snakes are deaf.

(The snake-charmer charms the snake not by his notes but by his movements.) There are various ways of considering this statement from a logical point of view; the one we shall adopt here is among the simplest and most useful. The term "snakes" refers to members of a certain class, or set, of animals. Since it is snakes that the statement is about, the term "snakes" is the **subject-term** in the statement. The **predicate-term** can also be understood as referring to a class, if we take it as a part of a noun-phrase, "deaf animals" or "deaf creatures" or "deaf things." The other two words, "All . . . are . . . " are logical operators: They link the two terms in such a way as to mark a certain relationship between the two classes—namely, that the class of snakes is wholly included, or contained, in the class of deaf things. Since this statement contains exactly two terms, it is a **two-term statement.**

The statement "All snakes are deaf (things)" is an affirmative statement, because it affirms a class-inclusion; it would be a negative statement if it denied a class-inclusion (or, equivalently, affirmed a class-exclusion). The statement

No snakes have ears

(or "No snakes are things with ears") is a negative statement: It says that nothing that is a snake is something with ears, or that no members of the class of snakes are members of the class of eared things.

The statement "All snakes are deaf (things)" is also a universal statement, because it affirms that *every* snake is a thing that cannot hear. But the statement

Some snakes are poisonous (things)

purports to give us information of a more limited sort: It does not rule out the possibility that all snakes are poisonous, is simply says that there is at least one poisonous snake. It is a particular statement. The statement

Some snakes are not poisonous (things)

is also a particular statement, though a negative one: It says that at least part of the class of snakes is excluded from the class of poisonous things. These are, then, the four basic types of two-term statement.

The logical form of any two-term statements can be made very explicit by a diagram. To construct such diagrams we require one further distinction. Given any term, "snakes" or "poisonous snakes that are either rare or dangerous to handle," we can form the negative of that term. The negative term refers to the class of things to which the term does not itself refer. There is the class of snakes, and there is the **complementary** class of nonsnakes. But what shall we include in the class of nonsnakes—how broadly shall we conceive it? Shall we include Secretariat,

Julius Caesar, the Nile, the White House? Certainly none of these are snakes, and we can indeed include them if we wish to. In that case our complementary classes are *snakes* and *things that are not snakes*; and these two classes together make up a universe of discourse that consists of everything. The **universe of discourse** to which a class belongs contains everything in that class plus everything in its complementary class. But for most practical purposes, as will be evident in the following section, we choose a limited universe of discourse, and find that our reasoning becomes more manageable, though no less valid.

Suppose when we got to thinking about snakes we were concerned not with such remote things as the White House and the Nile, but only with the broad class of animals. We may, for example, have been wondering how snakes compared with other animals with respect to hearing ability or dangerousness. Then our conceptual scheme could be represented this way (letting S stand for "snakes" and A for "animals");

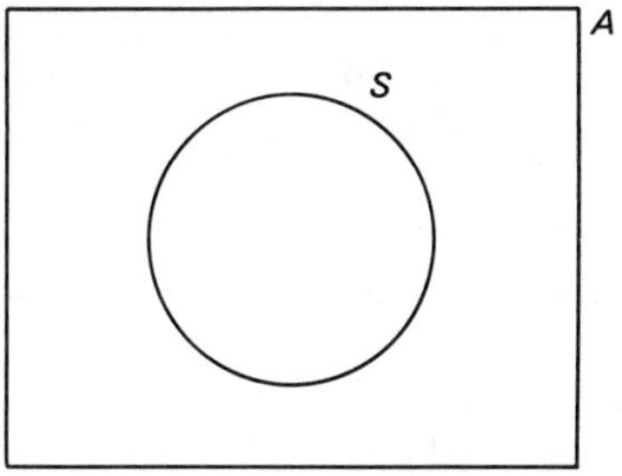

Animals within the circle are snakes; those outside are nonsnakes. To diagram a two-term statement we need only introduce another overlapping circle into our universe or discourse (letting P stand for "poisonous animals"):

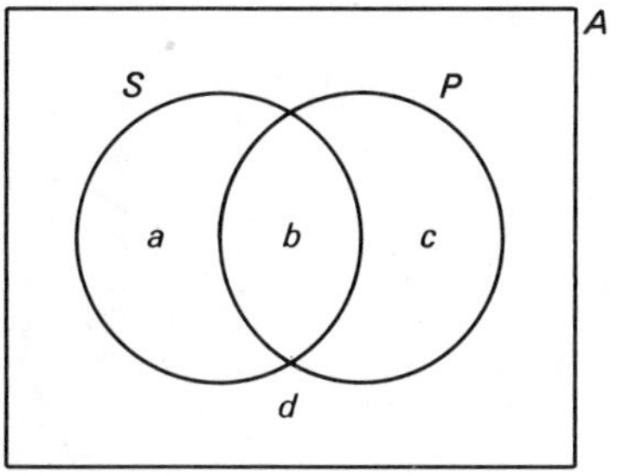

Then we have four subclasses of animals: nonpoisonous snakes *(a),*

poisonous snakes *(b)*, poisonous nonsnakes *(c)*, and nonpoisonous nonsnakes *(d)*. Garter snakes would go in *a*, copperheads in *b*, scorpions in *c*, and (say) lobsters (and Secretariat) in *d*.

Each of the four kinds of two-term statement can be represented on a diagram like this, for each one says that a certain subclass either has no members (is empty) or has at least one member (is occupied). To show that a subclass is empty we shade it out; to show that it is occupied, we put an asterisk in it.

Consider now the four two-term statements that can be constructed with the terms "people who like people" and "the luckiest people in the world"—to borrow from a show-tune of some seasons ago. We can give a name and a diagram to each. The universe of discourse is evidently "people in the world" *(W)*, the subject-term is "people who like people" *(P)*, and the predicate-term has to be taken to refer to a class of very lucky people *(L)*, those near the top of the luckiness-scale if there is such a thing. In abbreviated form:

All *P* are *L*	Universal Affirmative *(UA)*
Some *P* are *L*	Particular Affirmative *(PA)*
No *P* are *L*	Universal Negative *(UN)*
Some *P* are not *L*	Particular Negative *(PN)*

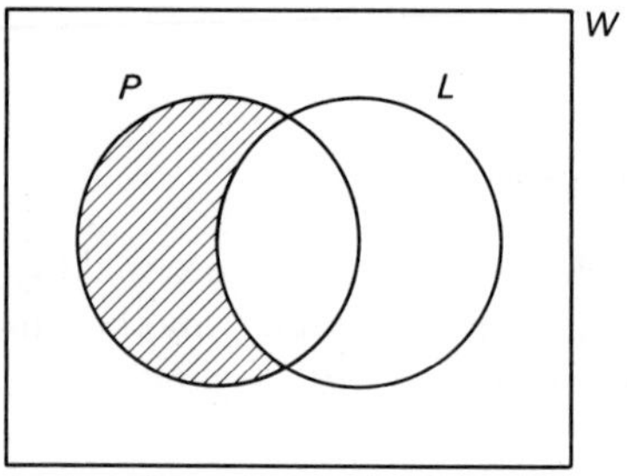

All *P* are *L*.

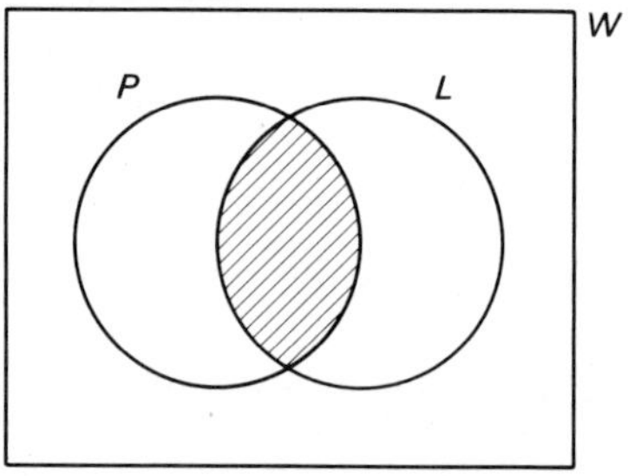

No *P* are *L*.

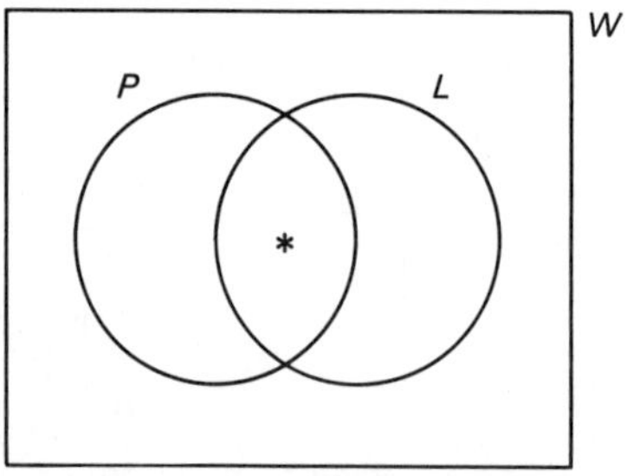

Some *P* are *L*.

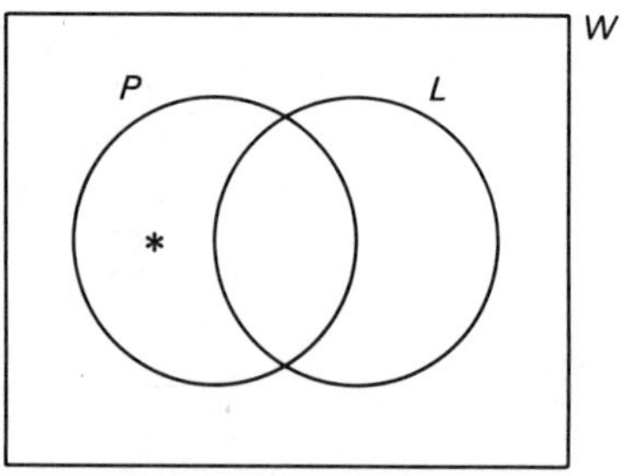

Some *P* are not *L*.

Remember that a logical analysis of a statement does not give us all that is meant, or may be meant, by that statement in every context (I shall say more about this in Chapter 5). It gives us that part of the meaning which enables the statement (and all other statements of the same logical form) to enter into certain kinds of valid deductive argument.

Now, as the diagrams show, there is a very important difference between the universal and the particular statements: The latter tell us that something actually exists, and the former tell us that something does not exist. Many of the things we ordinarily talk about, and argue about, are things that do exist: members of Congress, stolen money, divorces, laws, acts of friendship and of love. But we also talk about, and argue about, things that do not exist, or that we do not know to exist: living things on Mars, corruption in City Council, constitutional amendments ratified in 1983, cures for the common cold. We need a logic that will enable us to think validly about nonexistent or doubtful things sometimes, because we have to decide whether we want these things to exist, and what would be the probable consequences if they did exist. When we say, for example,

> No nonpolluting automobile is (will ever be) powered by an internal-combustion engine,

we don't necessarily want to assume that there are (or will ever be) nonpolluting automobiles. So all that we may commit ourselves to saying can be represented by a diagram that shows the subclass consisting of nonpolluting automobiles powered by an internal-combustion engine to be empty:

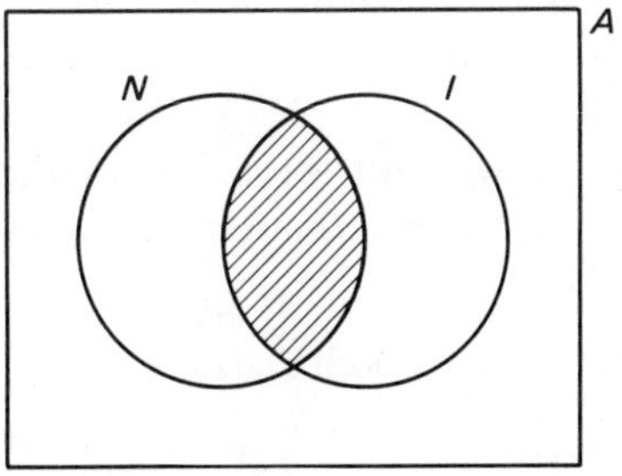

But when we say

> All automobiles powered by internal-combustion engines cause air-pollution,

we are quite ready to assume that there are automobiles powered by internal-compustion engines. And anyone who hears or reads what we say, in ordinary contexts, will be prepared to supply that assumption out of his own knowledge. So what we are saying can be put this way:

(1) All automobiles powered by internal-combustion engines are automobiles that cause air-pollution,
(2) There are automobiles powered by internal-combustion engines;

which may be diagrammed:

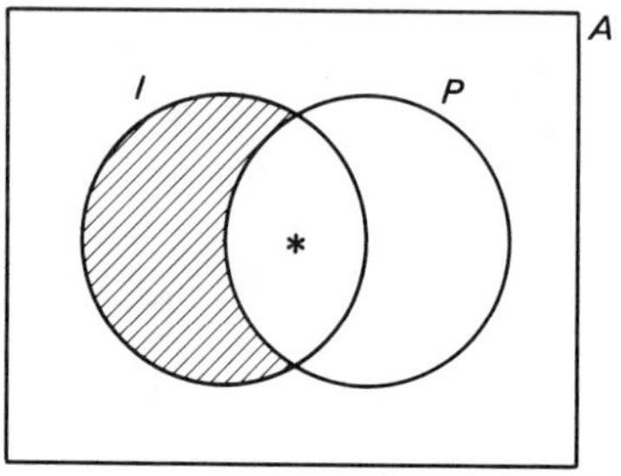

To make the *existence assumption* in uttering a universal (affirmative or negative) statement in a certain context is to take it for granted, and expect the reader or listener to take it for granted, that the subject-term refers to actually existing things. If someone says "Dragons are dangerous," we can safely suppose that he is not making the existence assumption. If someone puts up a sign saying: "NO PARKING. Illegally parked cars will be towed away at owner's expense," we know he *hopes* there will be no illegally parked cars there, but we don't know whether he assumes that there will be or won't be. We can, however, see some of the consequences that follow necessarily from his sign, though we can't be sure of them all unless we know whether the existence assumption is made.

The diagram just above will serve for another kind of statement that we have not yet considered, though it figures prominently in our common reasoning. Take

Wounded Knee is a town in South Dakota.

Since Wounded Knee is not a class, but an individual thing, this statement really does not involve two classes, but only one—the class of towns in South Dakota (the universe of discourse presumably being towns in general). For the purposes of fundamental logical theory, this distinction must be preserved. But for a great many familiar inferences, such as we are discussing here, the statement can be assigned another interpretation. Suppose we think, not of Wounded Knee, but of the class whose only member is Wounded Knee. Everything in the world is unique—that is, it is the only one of *some* kind (in this case, the site of the most recent [1890] mass killing of Sioux Indians). So we can treat the statement as affirming that the class consisting solely of Wounded Knee is included in the class of South Dakota towns. But more than that: You recall from Chapter 1 that this sentence could not be a statement, true or false, unless "Wounded Knee" actually refers to something. So there is an existence assumption built into it.

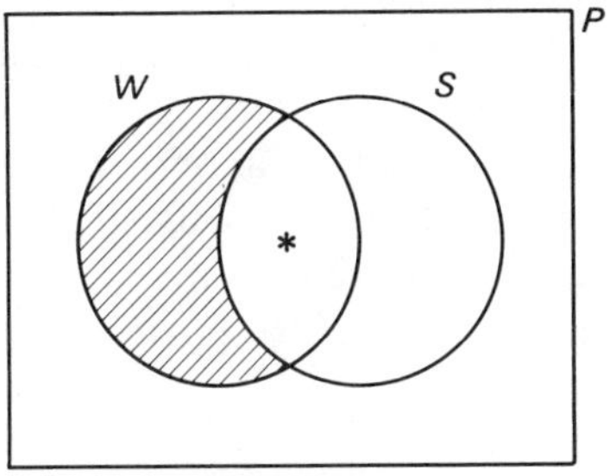

Wounded Knee is a town in South Dakota.

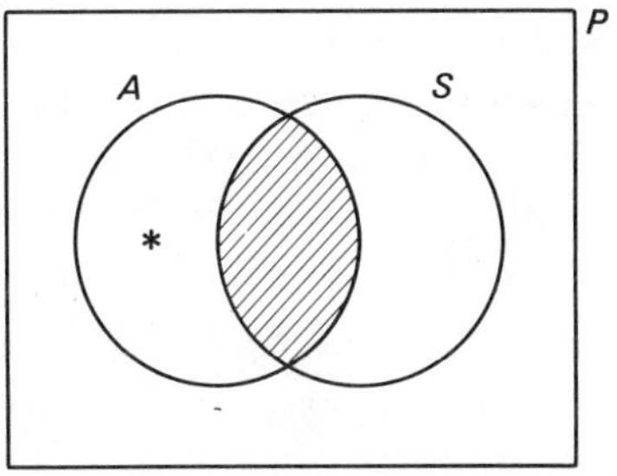

Attica is not a town in South Dakota.

We are now ready to turn to the basic logical relations that hold among two-term statements.

One principle commends itself for adoption at the start: Two statements that have exactly the same diagram are logically equivalent. The same diagram will serve for "No *A* are *B*" and for "No *B* are *A*"; and the same diagram will serve for "Some *A* are *B*" and for "Some *B* are *A*." These equivalences involve a relationship called **conversion**:

> "No snakes are animals with ears" is the converse of "No animals with ears are snakes" (and vice versa).
>
> "Some snakes are poisonous animals" is the converse of "Some poisonous animals are snakes" (and vice versa).

Four other equivalences arise because we have both affirmative and negative statements and we have both positive and negative terms. Take any two-term statement, change its *quality* (from affirmative to negative, or vice versa) and change its predicate-term from positive to negative, or vice versa; and you have an equivalent statement. These equivalences involve a relationship called **obversion**:

> "All snakes are deaf" is the obverse of "No snakes are nondeaf" (and vice versa).
>
> "Some snakes are poisonous" is the obverse of "Some snakes are not nonpoisonous" (and vice versa).

"No snakes have ears" is the obverse of "All snakes are noneared" (and vice versa).
"Some snakes are not poisonous" is the obverse of "Some snakes are nonpoisonous" (and vice versa).

The prefix *non-* doesn't always make for very good English, and when other idioms suggest themselves they may be preferable, provided they are clear—"All snakes are noneared" might better be "All snakes lack ears"; "No snakes are non-deaf" might better be "No snakes are capable of hearing." But sometimes the logical locutions, however artificial, are a useful way of making explicit to yourself exactly how the original statement is transformed into its equivalent.

Logical equivalence, as we have seen, is two-way implication. Are there, then, one-way implications among two-term statements? This depends on the existence assumption. If someone were to reason:

All poltergeists are playful.
Therefore: Some poltergeists are playful,

we might want to disqualify this inference, since if we are not prepared to grant that there are poltergeists, we would agree that the premise is true (in the sense that if there were poltergeists, they would be playful), yet deny the conclusion. Our diagrams of the two statements would show that the inference is not valid. For if the diagram of the conclusion contains information that is not contained in the diagram of the premise, then the conclusion has not been validly deduced.

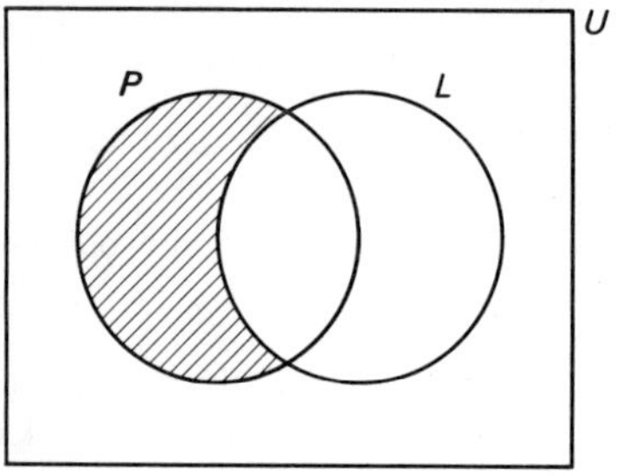

All *P* are *L*.

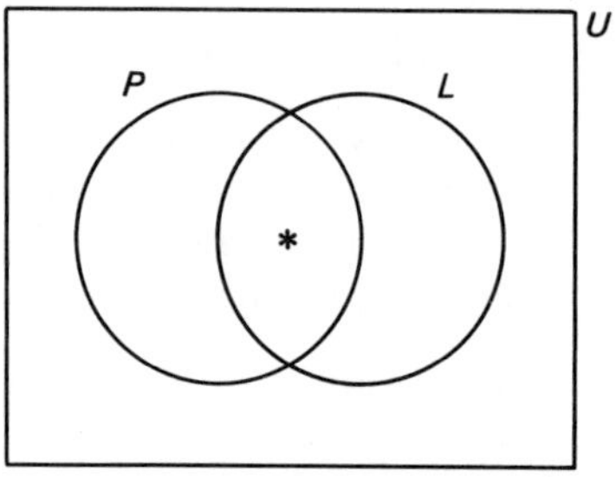

Some *P* are *L*.

On the other hand, if someone were to reason:

All snakes are deaf.
Therefore: Some snakes are deaf,

we would grant the existence assumption; and then the diagram would appear this way:

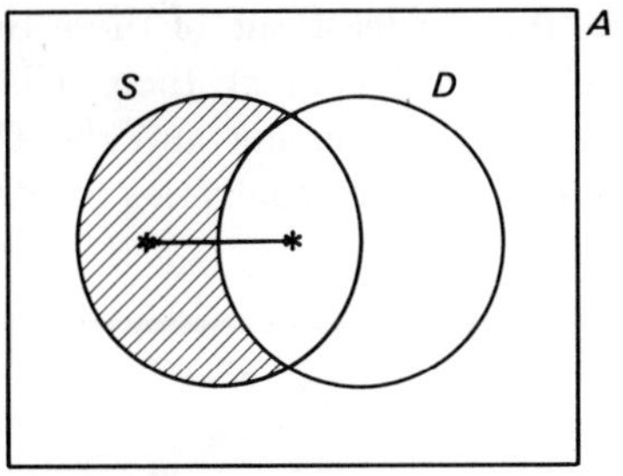

All S are D, and S exist.

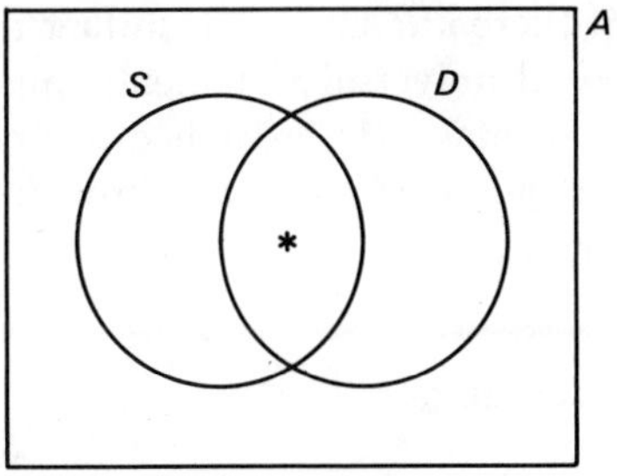

Some S are D.

In the left-hand diagram, we record the existence assumption by placing an asterisk in the S-circle. But since this circle has two parts, and we do not (at first) know whether the existing snakes are in one or the other subclass or both, we put in two asterisks, connecting them tentatively by a line. Next we record the premise, which empties one of the S-subclasses, thus pushing the asterisk, so to speak, over into the other. And so the right-hand diagram gives us part of the information already contained in the left-hand diagram.

When we look for logical incompatibilities among two-term statements, we find two varieties.

First there are the strict contradictories:

"Some snakes are poisonous" (*PA*) contradicts "No snakes are poisonous" (*UN*).

"Some snakes are not poisonous" (*PN*) contradicts "All snakes are poisonous (*UA*).

Second, there are the contraries. Consider "No snakes are poisonous" *(UN)* and "All snakes are poisonous" *(UA)*; evidently they can both be false, for indeed they are both false; but could they both be true? If we diagram them together, we get a curious result, namely that there are no snakes:

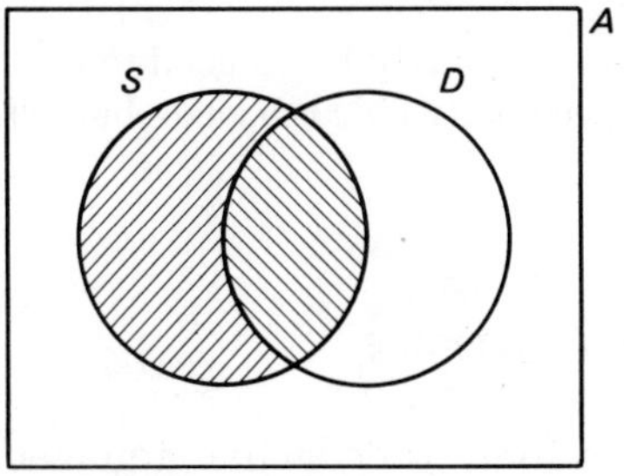

All S are D, and no S are D.

So if there *are* snakes, as in fact there are, then at least one of these two opposed universal statements must be false. In any context, then, where we can make the existence assumption, the *UN* statement and the *UA* statement (with the same terms in the same order) are contraries of each other.

A check-up quiz

Say whether the two statements in each of the following pairs are equivalent, incompatible, or neither (on the existence assumption).

1. (a) The dress is partly wool.
   (b) The dress is partly orlon.
2. (a) The dress is 100% wool.
   (b) The dress is 100% orlon.
3. (a) No one was injured in the accident.
   (b) Everyone involved in the accident came through it unharmed.
4. (a) Perkins is running for governor of the state.
   (b) Perkins is the district attorney of the city.
5. (a) Sarah is smart and witty.
   (b) Sarah is witty.
6. (a) Pileggi, the plumber, is the strongest man in our town.
   (b) Pileggi is the strongest plumber in our town.
7. (a) If the patient has hypoglycemia, he will feel listless before meals.
   (b) If the patient does not feel listless before meals, he does not have hypoglycemia.
8. (a) Susan has three first cousins.
   (b) Neither of Susan's parents has brothers or sisters.
9. (a) Everybody at the party had a good time.
   (b) Nobody at the party had a good time.
10. (a) Everybody at the party had a good time.
    (b) Nobody at the party failed to enjoy himself.

§ 6. Syllogistic Arguments

The **syllogism** is a form of deductive argument that (1) consists of exactly three two-term statements, two premises and a conclusion, and

(2) contains exactly three terms, of which one appears in both premises and each of the others appears in one premise and in the conclusion.

All great works of art are profound works of art.
No pop-art works of art are profound works of art.
———
No pop-art works of art are great works of art.

Taking the universe of discourse to be "works of art," the term that appears in both premises (the **middle term**) is "profound works of art"; the terms that appear both in a premise and in the conclusion (the **end terms**) are "great works of art" and "pop-art works of art." The horizontal line is a useful symbol for "therefore." The whole argument is set out in an orderly way, so that its validity is fairly plain. A single syllogism doesn't take us very far in reasoning, but syllogisms do take us one step forward, and they can be combined with each other, and with molecular arguments, into elaborate structures that yield surprising and significant conclusions.

Valid syllogisms can be decisively separated from invalid syllogisms with the help of a small set of rules. You don't always need such rules, but a syllogism can be confusing, and any dispute about its validity can be resolved by appealing to the rules.

Rule 1. The middle term must be distributed exactly once.
Rule 2. No end term may be distributed only once.
Rule 3. The number of negative premises must equal the number of negative conclusions.[1]

A syllogism is valid if, and only if, it obeys these three rules.

One technical concept requires explanation: Each of the terms in a two-term statement is either **distributed** or **undistributed**. This is entirely a matter of position. When a term (no matter what term it is) appears as the subject of a universal statement, or as the predicate of a negative statement, it is in a *strong position,* and is distributed; when the same term appears as the subject of a particular statement, or as the predicate of an affirmative statement, it is in a *weak* position, and is undistributed. Thus:

UA statement: subject distributed, predicate undistributed.
PA statement: subject undistributed, predicate undistributed.
UN statement: subject distributed, predicate distributed.
PN statement: subject undistributed, predicate distributed.

[1] I have borrowed this formulation of the rules from Wesley C. Salmon, *Logic,* 2d ed. Foundations of Philosophy Series (Englewood Cliffs, N.J.: Prentice-Hall, Inc., 1973), p. 53.

It is not really necessary to define "distributed" further, as far as the rules of syllogistic inference are concerned; you can just think of the positions. But if we ask what makes some positions strong and the others weak, something more can be said by way of answer.[2] A term is distributed in a certain position in a certain kind of statement when the following condition holds: If the statement is true of the class of things referred to by that term, then it is true of every subclass of that class. For example, if "All great works of art are profound works of art" is true, then it is true that all *large* great works of art are profound, and all great *Italian* works of art are profound, etc. But it does not follow that all great works of art are large profound works, or that they are profound Italian works, etc. So (in this *UA* statement) "great works of art" is in a strong position, but "profound works of art" is not. The same criterion of distribution can be applied to the other kinds of two-term statement.

To see how our three rules work out in practice, let us consider some invalid syllogisms.

All religious works of art are profound works of art.
Some modern works of art are profound works of art.

Some modern works of art are religious works of art.

The middle term is "profound works of art," and it appears first as the predicate of a *UA* statement, second as the predicate of a *PA* statement. It is not distributed in either position, so the syllogism violates Rule 1. It commits **the fallacy of maldistributed middle**. We need a term like "maldistributed middle," because there are two ways of violating Rule 1: The middle term may be under-distributed, as in this case (the traditional name of this fallacy is "undistributed middle"); or it may be over-distributed, as for example in:

All great works of art are profound works of art.
All great works of art are formally integrated works of art.

?

No conclusion can be drawn from these premises by the three rules for syllogisms just laid down.

Consider now the second rule.

All religious works of art are profound works of art.
No cubist works of art are religious works of art.

No cubist works of art are profound works of art.

[2]I borrow this explanation of distribution from Stephen F. Barker, *The Elements of Logic* (New York: McGraw-Hill Book Company, 1965), pp. 43–46.

Since the term "profound works of art" is distributed in the conclusion (as the predicate of a *UN* statement) but not in the premise (as the predicate of a *UA* statement), this syllogism violates Rule 2. It therefore commits the **fallacy of unequal distribution**.

The third rule is needed to make the set complete, but the syllogisms it rules out are so obviously invalid that it is not likely to be of frequent practical application. It does eliminate syllogisms with two negative premises, which can sometimes be deceptive if they are stuffed with a large quantity of verbiage. Such syllogisms commit the **fallacy of unequal negation**.

The three syllogistic rules allow all syllogistic inferences that do not depend on making special existence assumptions. You may encounter syllogisms that are apparently valid and yet are not allowed by the rules. And it may seem that the rules must then be faulty. Consider an example in abbreviated form:

No *C* are *B*.
All *A* are *B*.
____
Some *A* are not *C*.

This violates Rule 2, because *A* is distributed in the premise but not in the conclusion. Yet if we are thinking of such things as snakes, coins, laws, or revolutions, the conclusion seems to follow. And it does follow if we make the assumption that there are *A*—that *A* exist.

However, there is another way of deriving the conclusion, one that is quite in keeping with the principles set forth in this chapter. We first draw the *UN* conclusion permitted by our rules:

No *C* are *B*.
All *A* are *B*.
____
No *A* are *C*.

Then we invoke the existence assumption (if the context permits it). and draw the desired conclusion.

No *A* are *C*.
There are *A*.
____
Some *A* are not *C*.

So you see that we are not leaving valid inferences out.

It is true that we are working with a simple model of the syllogism. The three rules clearly admit only syllogisms that are valid under all conditions. And it seems best to set up minimal rules for the syllogism without taking for granted any more than we have to—otherwise we would get into the opposite difficulty and find ourselves allowing invalid syllogisms in contexts where the existence assumption is not permitted. For example:

> No unicorns are fire-breathers.
> All dragons are fire-breathers.
> ———
> Some dragons are not unicorns.

We certainly do not wish to call this a valid syllogism, since both premises are true, yet the conclusion (because it says that there are dragons) is false.

You can test any syllogism—your own or someone else's—by the rules, or by a diagram. Indeed, a diagram will tell you not only whether the proposed conclusion follows validly from the premises, but whether some other conclusions might have been drawn instead.

Since a syllogism involves three classes, the diagram has three circles, overlapped in such a way that every possible combination of subclasses is included.

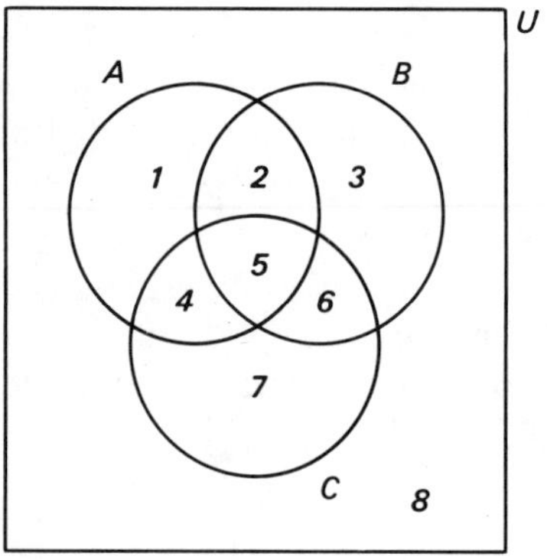

Subclass 2, for example consists of the *U* that are both *A* and *B*, but not *C*. (The numbers are just for reference as we go along; they are not part of the diagram.)

All syllogisms that are valid by our rules divide into two groups—those that consist only of universal statements (universal syllogisms) and those that have one particular conclusion. It is convenient to consider the universal syllogisms first.

The principle of diagramming is this: The conclusion of a syllogism follows necessarily from the premises if the information it presents is already contained in the premises. So if we diagram the premises together, we ought to be able to read off the conclusion from the diagram. Take, for example, the abbreviated syllogism:

All *B* are *C*.
All *A* are *B*.

All *A* are *C*.

To diagram the first premise, we shade out the part of *B* that is outside *C* (subclasses 2 and 3); to diagram the second premise, we shade out the part of *A* that is outside *B* (subclasses 1 and 4). Now according to the conclusion, the part of *A* that is outside *C* (subclasses 1 and 2) is empty, and indeed these two subclasses have already been shaded out by the premises.

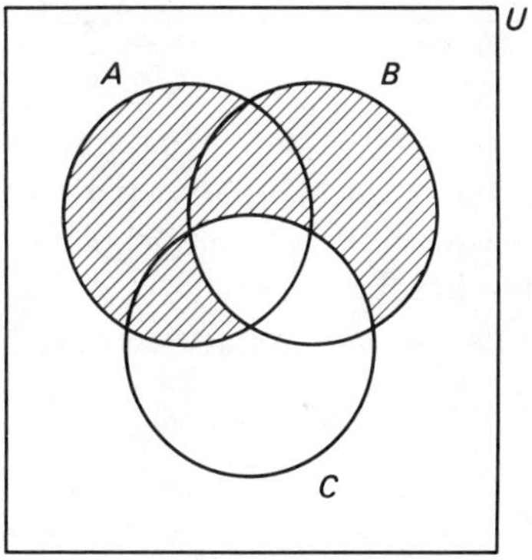

For an example of a particular syllogism, we may take the first one in this section, abbreviating "works of art" *W*, "great works of art" *G*, "profound works of art" *P*, and "pop-art works of art" *PA*.

All *G* are *P*.
Some *PA* are not *P*.

Some *PA* are not *G*.

The diagram of this kind of syllogism is a sort of disjunctive argument, and its logical force is clearest if we begin with the particular premise. This premise tells us that there are occupants of the part of the *PA*-circle that is outside the *P*-circle, though it does not tell us whether they are in 4 or 7 or both. So we put an asterisk in both of these subclasses, connecting them by a bar to show that we are still in doubt as to the exact location of these *PA*. When we then add the shading to represent the other premise, subclasses 1 and 4 turn out to be empty. But if 4 is empty, then the *PA* must be in 7, hence outside *G*—they are, as it were, pushed outside *G* by the universal premise. So we can now read off the proposed conclusion, "Some *PA* are not *G*."

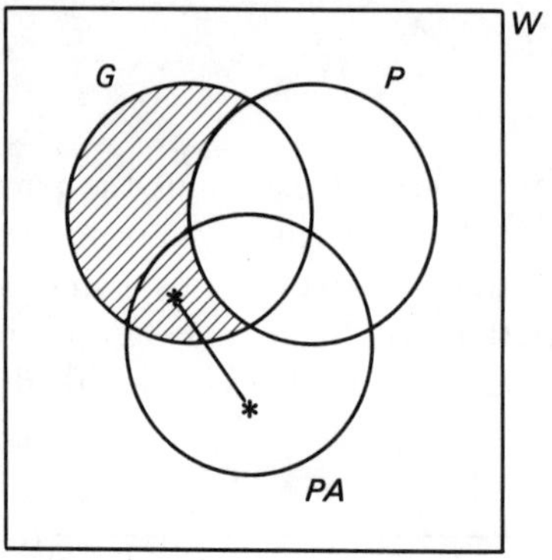

We can see from these diagrams what sorts of syllogism are going to be unsuccessful. A syllogism with two particular premises will obviously not enable us to read off any new conclusion. A universal syllogism in which two premises fail to shade out four subclasses will also give us nothing. Take this example of unequal distribution:

All *B* are *C*.
No *A* are *B*.

No *A* are *C*.

Its diagram is this:

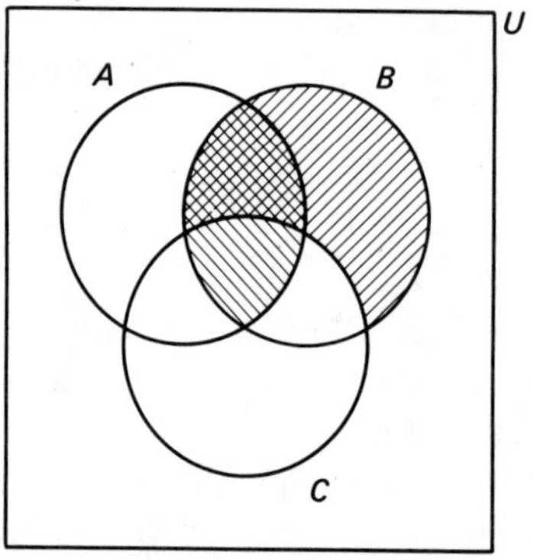

The cross-hatchings go different ways here to bring out the overlapping of the two premises, both of which tell us that subclass 2 is empty, so that between them they fail to give us enough information to draw any conclusion about the relationship between *A* and *C*.

A particular syllogism is invalid if the universal premise and the particular premise fail to intersect in such a way as to specify the location of those things whose existence is affirmed in the particular premise. Taking our earlier example of maldistributed middle, and abbreviating "religious works of art," and "modern works of art," we get:

All *R* are *P*.
Some *M* are *P*.
———
Some *M* are *R*.

and the diagram:

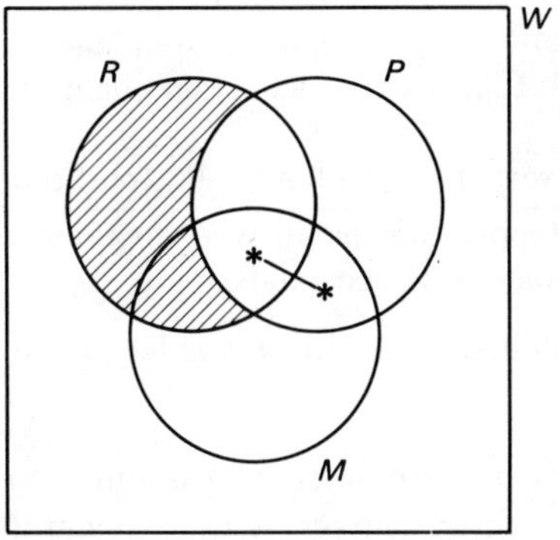

The premises simply don't connect.

The syllogisms we have been discussing so far are in fairly tidy condition, that is, *standard form*—in which the statements are clearly separated and marked as premises or conclusion, and the terms are properly framed. But those we are more likely to encounter in ordinary life present us with various difficulties that have to be overcome if we want to be quite confident that we know whether they are valid or invalid—and whether their premises are true or false. They may be couched in the casual, elliptical, and sometimes careless language of journalism, or (more troubling) in the intense, emotional, and often confusing language of persuasion. We need an orderly procedure by which syllogistic arguments in their natural state, so to speak, can be logically appraised.

I suggest the following seven steps for sizing up a syllogism. Not all of them are called for in every case, but most arguments require a little attention to some of these points.

Step 1. Read it carefully (of course).

Police have a constitutional right to stop a car only when they have reason to think a crime has been committed by one of its occupants.

> Hence some cars are stopped without such a reason, since sometimes cars, as we know, are stopped without valid constitutional justification.

This might be part of an argument against police insistence on random car-stoppings as a technique for catching intoxicated drivers, tracing stolen cars, or just frightening people into being more law-abiding. Never mind how you feel about this practice; the task at hand is to check the argument's validity.

Step 2. Separate premises from conclusion. The logical indicator, "hence," tells us how to do it:

> Police have a constitutional right to stop a car only when they have reason to think that a crime has been committed by one of its occupants.
> Sometimes cars are stopped without valid constitutional justification.
> ___
> Some cars are stopped without (reason to think that a crime has been committed by one of its occupants).

The phrase in the conclusion has to be spelled out to make the argument fully explicit.

Step 3. Identify the universe of discourse and the three classes. A syllogism connects three classes with one another, but it can only connect classes within the same universe of discourse. Sometimes there are two or three reasonable ways of interpreting one of the statements, and each gives it a different universe of discourse; but when the statement appears in a syllogism, we must try to find a single universe of discourse that will accommodate all the classes. The mere effort to see exactly what these classes are can give us a much better understanding of what the argument is all about. Our example is about police actions (*P*). Within this universe of discourse we have the class of car-stoppings (*S*), the class of constitutionally permitted police actions (*C*), and the class of police actions done with reason to think that a crime has been committed by someone whom the action affects (*R*). Quite often you find that a deductive argument appears to involve more than three classes. If this turns out to be the case, you don't have a syllogism—though you may have two syllogisms mixed up together, as we shall see shortly. But two of the classes may be complementary, and then you can reduce them to one. Take for example the abbreviated syllogism:

> All *C* are *B*.
> All *A* are *nonB*.
> ___
> All *A* are *nonC*.

This has five terms, and yet it is valid. To show its validity according to the syllogistic rules, we transform two of the statements into equivalents, by obversion:

All *C* are *B*.
No *A* are *B*.

No *A* are *C*.

Step 4. Analyze the logical forms of the three statements. This step can give us trouble when the style of the argument is ornate or legalistic or just clumsy. In our first premise, the word "only" is the important clue to logical form: "Only *A* are *B*" is equivalent to "All *B* are *A*." In our second premise, "sometimes" refers to times, but we can reinterpret it so that it refers to actions. The conclusion has "cars" for its subject, but it can be recast as a statement about car-stoppings—without too much distortion. The first premise is a *UA* statement, the other two most readily and naturally framed as *PN* statements.

It may be well to pause a moment to consider more generally the problems of recasting statements so as to bring out clearly their logical form. It is not hard to go wrong at this stage if one is hasty. All such recasting must take the context into account and must be sensitive to nuances of meaning, even though the transformed version leaves out some of the original meaning. Perhaps it will be most helpful just to note some common transformations. "Roses are never purple" can be recast as "No roses are purple"; but "Jones is never angry" can be recast as "No feelings of Jones are angry feelings." "There have been some extrovert painters" can be recast as "Some (past) painters are extrovert painters." "All bonds are taxed except municipal bonds" can be recast as "All non-municipal bonds are taxed bonds." "Apologies are of no avail unless they are sincere" can be recast as "No insincere apologies are availing apologies." "All aspirin is not alike" can be understood in two different ways, and so this "All . . . is (are) not" construction is to be avoided; instead, we may write "Some aspirin is unlike (some) other aspirin" or "No aspirin is like (any) other aspirin," to make clear which is meant.

Step 5. Put the whole syllogism into standard form, using slanted lines to separate the terms when they are fairly complex.

All / constitutionally permitted police actions / are / police actions done with reason to think that a crime has been committed.
Some / car-stoppings / are not / constitutionally permitted police actions.

Some / car-stoppings / are not / police actions done with reason to think that a crime has been committed.

The shape of the argument is clearer in an abbreviated version:

All *C* are *R*.
Some *S* are not *C*.

Some *S* are not *R*.

We might have done it differently, using not the terms we chose, but their negatives; but if we did well, we would have come out with an equivalent syllogism—not one with the same logical structure, yet one that would be valid if ours is valid, and invalid if ours is invalid.

But is our syllogism valid?

Step 6. Test the syllogism by the rules. We do not have to look far, for the very first rule is violated: *C* is distributed in both premises. And the second rule is also violated: *R* is distributed in the conclusion, but not in the premise. Of course one violation is enough to sink a syllogism, but for practice it is well to check it against all the rules.

Step 7. Diagram the syllogism. This will give you another check, in case you have overlooked a violation of the rules. It will also help you to understand how the argument goes astray.

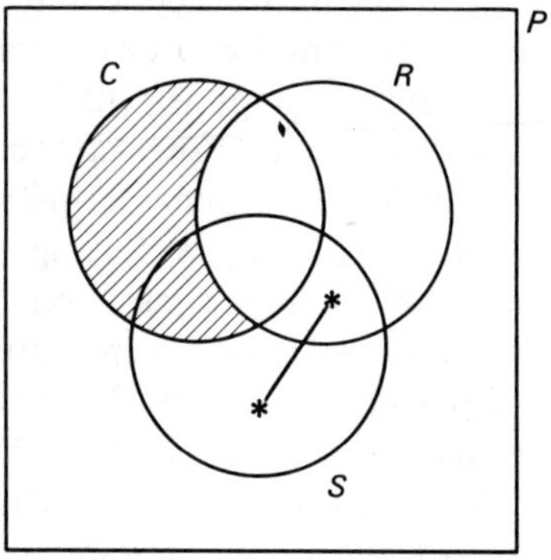

Though single syllogisms do not yield very striking results, syllogisms can be combined in a **syllogism chain**: that is, a series of syllogisms so linked that the conclusion of one syllogism is a premise of the next. Suppose we knew, for example, that

(1) Unprincipled persons are never capable of acting altruistically.
(2) Some members of the President's staff are so-called pragmatists.
(3) Only people who are capable of acting altruistically are morally mature.
(4) So-called pragmatists are always unprincipled.

Maybe you can see right away what conclusion follows from these four premises; even so, it may be just as well to review the deduction in an orderly way. Take any pair of statements that have a common term, say the first and third. From them we can infer syllogistically that

(5) No unprincipled persons are morally mature persons.

Combine this statement with the fourth, and get:

(6) No so-called "pragmatists" are morally mature persons.

Combine this statement with the second, and get:

(7) Some members of the President's staff are not morally mature persons.

This is the final conclusion of the syllogism chain.

The rules of the syllogism not only tell us what conclusion we may draw from a pair, or series, of premises, but what is required to complete a proof. Often we are given a conclusion and one premise; the missing premise is tacitly assumed.

Some American products certainly need to be protected by tariffs, since they are at a disadvantage in competing with foreign products.

If we may take this to be a deductive argument, it is clearly incomplete. And we are in no position to judge its soundness until the missing premise is supplied. First we set out the argument formally:

Some / American products / are / products that are at a disadvantage in competing with foreign products.

Some / American products / are / products that need to be protected by tariffs.

The rules tell us that, given a *PA* conclusion and a *PA* premise, the other premise has to be a *UA* statement; and we know what the middle term is and what the missing end-term is:

[All / products that are at a disadvantage in competing with foreign products / are / products that need to be protected by tariffs.]

The square brackets show that we are supplying this premise ourselves, but in the effort to make explicit what the arguer is taking for granted. Maybe his suppressed premise is open to some criticism—and maybe that is why he was skipping over it so lightly, hoping we would not pay too much attention to it.

An extended deductive argument will have many premises, including some tacit premises. We have discussed one way in which it can go astray: It may be invalid. There is a second kind of flaw that we find in some deductive arguments, though they are perfectly valid: They take for granted what they purport to prove, and so fail to get us anywhere in our thinking. When the conclusion of an argument, or some statement logically equivalent to it, is already contained among the premises (explicit or explicit) of the argument, the argument is said to be **circular.** It assumes what it claims to establish and commits the **fallacy of begging the question.**

The most deceptive circular arguments are rather long ones; circularity is easiest to conceal when the distance between premise and conclusion is great. But consider this example:

> The importance of preventing revolutionary changes of government wherever possible throughout the world, as a prime goal of American policy, has been well established—though the neo-isolationists refuse to understand it. For if the United States failed to live up to its world responsibilities by refusing to allow leftist governments to take power in underdeveloped countries, the stability of world order would be threatened. And that would unfortunately but inevitably lead to a weakening of the power of the United States—not only its actual and comparative military power, but the credibility of its threats—thus making it far more difficult for us to prevent revolutionary changes in distant parts of the world.

This writer sets out to argue for the thesis that it is desirable for the U.S.A. to prevent revolutionary changes of government in any country. Why? Because such changes would upset the stability of world order. Why would this be a bad thing? Because it would weaken the relative power of the U.S.A. Why would this be undesirable? Because that would make it more difficult to prevent revolutionary changes of government in other countries. But if we then ask why *that* would be undesirable, we see that the writer is taking it for granted that it is desirable for the U.S.A. to prevent revolutionary changes of government elsewhere. And this is just what he set out to prove.

Another common form of circular reasoning involves asserting a generalization of some kind—say about all members of a certain race or religion, or some social group—hard-hats or college students or people supported by welfare payments. "Hard-hats are all ignorant and intolerant," says the confident arguer. We reply, "What's your evidence? Have you made a study? I know a number of construction workers who are willing to allow dissent and who understand the Bill of Rights." "Well, I wasn't talking about them, but about real hard hard-hats." Words like "really," "genuine," "truly," "essentially"—though they also have their legitimate uses—often become *weasel words* in such contexts, and serve to dismiss arguments against the conclusion, by ruling them out of court. But a conclusion that is protected from counter-criticism in this way is really being held as a dogma, not reasonably defended. It is a basic premise of the argument, masquerading as a final conclusion.

The only protection against circularity is to keep a firm grip on the logical structure: what is asserted as a conclusion, what is asserted as a premise, and by what steps the argument moves from one to the other.

A check-up quiz

What fallacies (maldistributed middle, unequal distribution, or unequal negation) are committed by the following syllogisms?

1. All burglars are unsocial.
   All burglars are enterprising.
   ____
   All enterprising persons are unsocial.

2. No credit-card holders are deprived persons.
   No credit-card holders are slum-dwellers.
   ____
   All slum-dwellers are deprived persons.

3. No saints are egoistic.
   Caspar is not egoistic.
   ____
   Caspar is a saint.

4. All con artists are amiable.
   All car salesmen are amiable.
   ____
   All car salesmen are con artists.

5. All readers of the *National Review* are conservative.
   Some members of the student senate are not readers of the *National Review*.
   ____
   Some members of the student senate are not conservative.

6. Some stamp-collectors are unmarried.
   No unmarried people are good credit risks.
   ____
   Some people who are good credit risks are not stamp-collectors.

7. Some bail-bondsmen are kind-hearted.
   All kind-hearted people are easy touches.
   ____
   Some easy touches are bail-bondsmen.

8. Some involuntary actions are utility-maximizing.
   Some actions by public officials are not utility-maximizing.
   ____
   Some actions by public officials are not involuntary.

9. No poems by Wordsworth are obscure.
   All poems by Wordsworth have some merit.
   ____
   No poems with some merit are obscure.

10. All deliberately cruel acts are unforgivable.
    Some selfish acts are not unforgivable.
    ____
    Some selfish acts are deliberately cruel.

OUTLINE-SUMMARY: chapter two

Deductive arguments may be divided into (1) molecular arguments, in which whole statements are combined and recombined in various ways; and (2) atomic arguments, in which parts of statements (namely, terms) are rearranged in the course of the reasoning.

Two forms of molecular argument are very common and fundamental: (1) In the valid form of the *disjunctive argument,* the first premise is a disjunctive statement ("Either Jane closed the window or it rained in"), the second premise negates one of the two disjuncts ("It did not rain in"), and the conclusion repeats the other disjunct ("Therefore Jane closed the window"). In the invalid form of the disjunctive argument, the second premise repeats one of the two disjuncts ("It rained in") and the conclusion negates the other disjunct ("Jane did not close the window"); this commits the *fallacy of affirming a disjunct.* (2) In the *conditional argument,* the first premise is a conditional statement ("If the pitcher is dropped, then it will break"); in one valid form, the second premise repeats the antecedent of this conditional premise ("The pitcher will be dropped"), and the conclusion repeats the consequent ("Therefore, the pitcher will break"); in the other valid form, the second premise negates the consequent ("The pitcher will not break"), and the conclusion negates the antecedent ("Therefore, the pitcher will not be dropped"). In one of the invalid forms, the second premise repeats the consequent, and the conclusion repeats the antecedent (this commits the *fallacy of affirming the consequent*); in the other invalid form, the second premise negates the antecedent, and the conclusion negates the consequent (the *fallacy of denying the antecedent*).

A *conditional chain argument* is a series of conditional premises linked in such a way that the antecedent of the first one and the consequent of the last one can be combined in a conditional statement that is a valid conclusion.

One statement *implies* a second one if the second necessarily follows from the first, and two statements that imply each other are *logically equivalent.* When one statement implies the falsity of a second statement, they are *logically incompatible;* if their denials are also incompatible with each other, then they are *contradictories;* if they are incompatible without being contradictories, they are *contraries.* A discourse that either contains or implies a pair of incompatible statements is *inconsistent.*

There are four types of two-term statement: (1) universal affirmative ("All *A* are *B*"), (2) particular affirmative ("Some *A* are not *B*"), (3) universal negative ("No *A* are *B*"), and (4) particular negative ("Some *A* are not *B*"). The *UA* statement and the *PN* statement are contradictories; the *UN* statement and the *PA* statement are contradictories. If we make the *existence assumption* (that is, assume that there actually are members of class *A*), then the *UA* statement and the *UN* statement are contraries.

The most common type of atomic argument is the *syllogism*, which involves (1) three two-term statements, of which two are premises and one the conclusion; and (2) three terms, of which one (the middle term) appears in both premises and each of the others (the end terms) appears in the conclusion and in one of the premises. A syllogism is valid if and only if it satisfies the following three rules: (1) The middle term must be distributed (that is, it must be either the subject of a universal statement or the predicate of a negative statement) exactly once; (2) No end term may be distributed only once; and (3) The number of negative premises must equal the number of negative conclusions. A syllogism that violates Rule 1 commits the *fallacy of maldistributed middle;* Rule 2, the *fallacy of unequal distribution;* Rule 3, the *fallacy of unequal negation.*

When the conclusion of a deductive argument (or its logical equivalent) appears as one of its own premises, whether explicit or implicit, the argument is *circular* and commits the *fallacy of begging the question.*

Exercise 7

What fallacies, if any, are committed by the following molecular arguments?

1. Regrettably the report of Harvard's Center for Educational Policy Research has a serious flaw as a policy guide for educational reform: It proceeds on the false premise that there is an inherent contradiction between the belief in equality of opportunity for all and the acknowledgment of great individual differences in competence, aspirations, and effort; therefore, its conclusion that schools cannot significantly reduce inequality of opportunity must be false.

2. If the President could legally be subpoenaed, then he could be hauled into court for trivial offenses by prosecutors aiming only to subject him to political harassment, which of course cannot be considered to be allowed by the Constitution. From which it follows that the President cannot legally be subpoenaed.

3. If the President cannot be legally subpoenaed under any circumstances, he is placed above the law. And surely we can see (especially in the light of many shocking examples of Presidential abuse of

power) that the Constitution does not place the President above the law. Therefore he can legally be subpoenaed.

4. Judge Morrit's proposal to allow Congress to veto unpopular Supreme Court decisions either is the result of poor research into Constitutional history, such as the earlier attacks on the Court reflected in Marbury vs. Madison (1831) and ex parte McCardle (1869), or it is a calculated demagogic attack on the court. Further study of his statement shows that he is indeed quite ignorant of Constitutional history, so I guess we must acquit him of the charge of demagoguery.

5. If the Metropolitan Museum's bronze horse is a genuine ancient Greek work, it was cast by the lost-wax method (since the sand-casting method was not invented until the fourteenth century). But it was not cast by the lost-wax method, so it is not authentic.

6. American citizens did not know until the press revealed it in 1971 that American warplanes intervened in the war in Laos between Souvanna Phouma and the Pathet Lao from 1964 on, that the CIA had been supporting the Mao army before that time, and that American sabotage in North Vietnam began in 1954, when there was supposed to be a peace settlement. If the government security apparatus was working well during that time, we would expect these sensitive facts to be kept secret. We may conclude that the apparatus was indeed working well.

7. Either we will resist the spread of the so-called school voucher system, under which parents are given funds to shop around for schools, or we must be prepared to accept increasing racial and economic segregation, a weakening of the church-state wall, and the destruction of the public school system. But we will not resist the movement, and so these consequences will follow.

8. If the danger to the public posed by hijacking of airplanes were adequate ground to justify such a wholesale violation of the Fourth Amendment as is involved in making every airline passenger submit to search, in the absence of any reason to think he has committed a crime, then the sharp increase of serious crimes in our major cities could equally be used to justify similar searches of persons or houses in high crime areas, based solely upon the "trained intuition" of the police, rather than probable cause. This is absurd, and consequently so is the supposition.

Exercise 8

Examine the following pairs of statements and determine in each case whether (1) one of the statements implies the other, or they are (2) equivalent, (3) contradictory, (4) contrary, or (5) independent.

1. (a) More Democrats than Republicans voted to override the President's veto.
   (b) More Republicans than Democrats voted to override the President's veto.

2. (a) Only those who are confident of their own ability are capable of exercising political leadership.
   (b) Only those who are capable of exercising political leadership are confident of their own ability.

3. (a) Abercrombie is a friend of mine.
   (b) A friend of Abercrombie is a friend of a friend of mine.

4. (a) People who live in suburbs rarely have a deep understanding of the problems of the inner city.
   (b) People who have a deep understanding of the problems of the inner city rarely live in suburbs.

5. (a) There are morally impermissible actions that are, however, perfectly legal.
   (b) Legal actions are without exception permissible from the moral point of view.

6. (a) Unless we reach an arms agreement, we shall neither cut the cost of military spending nor lower international tension.
   (b) Unless we reach an arms agreement, we shall not lower international tension and we shall not cut the cost of military spending.

7. (a) If the witness is lying, he is one of the best actors I've seen.
   (b) If the witness is one of the best actors I've seen, then he's lying.

8. (a) Some liberal newspaper columnists have been sternly critical of government attacks on the press.
   (b) There are people who have been sternly critical of government attacks on the press and are not liberal newspaper columnists.

9. (a) There were at least six survivors of the accident.
   (b) There were seven survivors of the accident.

10. (a) The writing of history can be considered a science only if there are genuine historical laws.
    (b) History-writing is not a science unless there are historical laws.

Exercise 9

Put the following statements into standard logical form.

1. Sorry her lot who loves too well.
2. Unsolicited manuscripts will be returned if accompanied by a stamped, self-addressed envelope.

3. Not every dog has its day.
4. All those who testified before the committee were granted immunity, except those who had already been convicted.
5. You won't find any wild-eyed radicals in this student body.
6. No one was admitted to the convention floor without an identification card.
7. She never does it on Sunday.
8. She never does it on Sunday, unless the horoscope is favorable.
9. Those who were on the scene were arrested unless they were recognized by the officer in charge.
10. Into each life a little rain must fall.
11. There are those who have dropped out of college and returned to get a degree.
12. If a person can't stand the heat, then he ought to stay out of the kitchen.
13. Not through Eastern windows only / When morning comes, comes in the light.
14. Honest politicians? Certainly, they exist.
15. All that glitters is not gold.

Exercise 10

Cast the following syllogisms into standard form, and test their validity (a) by the syllogistic rules and (b) by a diagram.

1. Foreign affairs is inherently a game of strategy, and will always be so. Like all games of strategy, it requires secrecy for success.
2. Those who paid their dues were without exception charter members, but no members have served on committees except the charter members. Therefore, none of the dues-paying members have served on committees.
3. Some poems are sincere, and therefore good; for it is a fundamental truth that all good poems are sincere.
4. All who both know Communist teachings and respect the truth should teach Communism; therefore, none who believe in Communism should teach it, since none who believe in it both know Communist teachings and respect the truth.

5. Apparently there is no way of combining political talent with modesty. But we know that Clarence is not at all modest, so we can be confident that he has political talent.
6. The tenured faculty members are all conservative; the untenured faculty members are all skillful teachers; it follows that none of the skillful teachers are conservative.
7. We are told that the cuts made in the proposed budget have been confined to nonessential government services, while only essential services have been insisted on by the opposition party; hence those insisted on have not been cut.
8. We must recognize that not all of those who are ineligible for election will find it possible to be appointed, while none of those who have worked hard will fail to be appointed; it follows that some who have worked hard are not ineligible for election.
9. Actions performed pursuant to orders of a higher authority are coerced, and so a person is not responsible for such acts, since responsible acts are uncoerced.
10. People who are deeply involved in transcendental meditation must be very happy people, since they are evidently not concerned to be rational persons, and we all know that those who are concerned to be rational persons are by no means happy.

Exercise 11

Supply the premise that is missing from each of the following syllogistic arguments.

1. Some of the College trustees are alumni, and consequently cannot be expected to welcome changes in the dormitory visitation rules.
2. There is no point in studying philosophy, since it is well known that "philosophy bakes no bread."
3. Jones will never be a success in business, for he is just as concerned about the social impact of his operations as he is about the earnings of his stockholders.
4. Being large and heavy, the official City Council cars must not be very economical to use.
5. We believe in the inherent worth of all human beings, and therefore in their inalienable right to privacy.
6. Clearly some investors did not know about the discovery of the new oil fields, because they sold their stock last month.

7. There must be some members of the Club who are willing to serve as officers. They can't all be lazy.
8. Certainly it should be made a criminal offense for a newspaper to publish confidential White House memoranda concerning secret deals with the milk producers. Such publication can only undermine confidence in the American system of government.
9. The Mayor has implicitly admitted that some members of his administration are not politically sophisticated, by repeatedly denying the charge that no honest people are members of his administration.
10. How can you question the moral rightness of capital punishment? Lacking moral rightness, it would not be constitutional.

Exercise 12

Explain all inconsistencies and circularities of reasoning in the following passages.

1. Some of the butterflies, tagged by scientists in Canada, have been found in Mexico, their wings tattered and torn. They fly against heavy winds, completely unaffected by the weather.

Year after year, they will return to a certain tree for rest, even though they have never been there before. [Chicago *Sun-Times*]

2. There is a strong case for parochaid, and especially for insuring that private schools obtain a significant share of the funds that are to come to the states under the Federal Government's "revenue-sharing" plan. And private schools should get help in transporting their pupils as well as in supplying textbooks. Up until now the public schools have had it their own way, but the time has come when they must be subjected to careful critical examination. First, with the demands of defense and the need to support our largest industries when they are in financial difficulties—not to mention the budget problems of our cities—there just is a shortage of funds for public schools: They can no longer expect to get as much money as they have been getting. Second, recent social-science research has cast much doubt on the claims of the schools to improve their pupils' social and economic status; the fact it that the quality of schools cannot really be improved by these vast infusions of money. Finally, despite the efforts to prevent it, there will be more and more bussing of pupils to public schools, in order to try to reach the will-o'-the-wisp goal of racial desegregation—thus violating the basic principle of neighborhood schools for our youth.

3. Women should continue to be treated different than men in employment—in opportunity for jobs, in promotion, and in pay—for they

simply do not have the qualifications of stamina, strength, powers of concentration, and ambitiousness required. This is shown by their poor record in the past, when it comes to jobs and professions. For very few have made the grade in medicine or law or construction work or upper-level management.

4. I am opposed to a Federal program for day-care centers to take care of the children of working mothers. My reason is that nothing is more important, more vital, even more sacred to preserve than the American family, and day-care centers would lend the vast moral authority of the government, and of this Administration, to the side of communal approaches to child-rearing, as over against the American family-centered approach. We must enhance, not diminish, parental authority and parental responsibility for, and involvement in, the rearing of their children, at all costs. That is why I have recommended to the Congress a very limited program for day-care centers, merely enough to provide mothers of small children who are now supported by public tax funds, to get them off the relief rolls and on to the payrolls, where they can make their contribution to the productivity of this great country, without draining its resources, knowing that their children will be well taken care of during their working hours.

5. Mr. Carpenter's testimony before the Special Committee may be difficult to believe, since some of the events he has related appear to involve culpability at very high levels of government, but I am convinced that he is telling the truth. The evidence we have shows that he is a truthful and honest person: We know—from his own testimony—that he was brought up strictly by strait-laced parents, that he was indoctrinated with a strong moral revulsion against lying, and that he has a "deep contempt" (his own words) for those who would perjure themselves before a court or government agency.

6. *Sir:* If a fetus is classed as human life, as claimed by the anti-abortionists, why is an aborted fetus not accorded the burial that a full-term dead baby receives? Likewise, why does a dead fetus, the result of a miscarriage, not receive burial as a human? The answer would seem to me to be that a fetus, aborted by accident or design, is not properly considered a human life until it is fully formed, for until then it cannot live as a human being. [Frieda Smith, Aukland, N. Z., in a letter to *Time*]

7. Some people believe that it's really all right to disobey the law if you do it openly, conscientiously, for a high moral purpose (like remedying an injustice, not like getting elected), and with a willingness to accept the legal consequences (rather than try to cover it up). They call that "civil disobedience." I say it's wrong. If you follow this principle, you will find yourself doing things like having sit-ins at businesses that refuse to hire women, or blocking workmen who are trying to tear down

a fine old house now used as a neighborhood health clinic—in short, you will find yourself doing things that are clearly illegal.

8. Probably the most inconsistent of all Federal Communications Commission rulings is that which concerns cigarette advertising. The Federal government spends between 600 and 800 million dollars a year to promote and sell tobacco. It subsidizes tobacco growers to the tune of at least 400 million dollars a year. Yet the government prohibits the advertising on TV of cigarettes. If tobacco is harmful, then the growth and manufacture of tobacco should be prohibited by law. But so long as the government itself encourages the growth and development and sale of tobacco, it certainly has no business telling manufacturers and TV stations they cannot advertise tobacco. This is only one more instance of how powerful the Washington bureaucrats have become.

The so-called "fairness doctrine" has nothing whatever to do with fairness, but it has everything to do with the power of government to harass people whose opinions the bureaucrats don't like. [*Arizona Republic*]

9. I am totally opposed to so-called "public broadcasting," because it is a serious threat to our civil liberties. This may strike you as peculiar, when everyone is always talking it up, and praising *Sesame Street*, and so on. But the fact is that under present economic conditions, public broadcasting (because it carries no advertisements) cannot survive without government aid, in some form or another. Now what does that mean? It means, first, that you and I have to support it, through our taxes, whether we like it or not, and whatever the programs may be; it means, second, that in the last analysis some bureaucrat in Washington, no doubt acting under orders from some assistant at the White House, is going to pull the strings, and make sure that the programs are favorable to the government, and its policies and personnel, even when the government is mistaken, the policies dangerous, and the personnel dishonest; we will, in short, get a slanted broadcasting instead of free speech. We may take it as a fundamental axiom that government control inevitably means government propaganda. The evidence for this is everywhere: "leaks" of favorable secrets, the President's "non-political" broadcasts, the publications of the Government Printing Office, the so-called "statistics" doctored up for the press by the Labor Department, the Agriculture Department, the F.B.I., etc.—and, of course, public broadcasting.

10. It burns me up when the government declares some old broken-down building a "National Landmark," because it was designed by some forgotten architect; the owner then is not allowed to alter it or sell it, without permission. This is an unwarranted interference with property rights: It takes away another man's property, like a common thief, by in effect denying him its use and disposal. Property rights are inalienable and absolute; no motive justifies their violation; and keeping these old

buildings is a way of blocking progress, using the force of law to freeze society at the technological level existing at the time of creation. Instead of wasting its time with these old buildings, the government should be getting on with the essential tasks of progress, laying out new highways to speed transportation, using its power of eminent domain to take over farms and slums and clear the ground for those vast arteries of concrete that bind the nation and its people together.

chapter three

WEIGHING THE EVIDENCE

Most of the questions we want to ask, and must ask in order to cope with our circumstances, cannot be answered by deductive reasoning—that is, we cannot deduce the answers from what we already know. The answers must be obtained and supported by a different kind of argument, which uses, not premises of necessary inference, but *evidence*. If we are troubled, say, about whether our state legislature should respond to the rising crime rate by reinstituting capital punishment, or whether the Mayor (as report and rumor have it) is systematically favoring large real estate interests at the expense of middle-income home-owners, we need certain kinds of relevant information, and we need to know how to draw reasonable inductive conclusions from that information.

Of course, the information may not be available. Despite the best efforts of the press (which does not always make its best effort), much that we would need to know to reach a sound conclusion, may be successfully concealed. But part of being a good inducer, so to speak, is knowing when to stop: that is, knowing when you *don't* have the evidence you need, so that the reasonable thing to do is suspend judgment for the time being.

Inductive arguments can be extremely complex, like deductive ones, but ultimately they rest on basic reasons, too. These are the *data* of the argument, the *facts* with which we begin. The word "fact" is used in different ways; I mean by it, simply, a statement that is known to be true. The data of one inductive argument may have been the conclusions of an earlier one; but in any particular argument it is essential to distinguish clearly between the statements that are taken as established, and hence not questioned on this occasion, and those it is proposed to establish here and now.

The data of an inductive argument may come from *observation*, as when we look out of the window and notice the clouds or read the outdoor thermometer. When an observation is made under controlled—that is, specially arranged—conditions, as in a laboratory, it is an *experiment*: planting two different varieties of corn in the same soil to see which does best, or introducing a new method of teaching reading in school to see whether it is more successful than the one we have been using. When we are not ourselves in a position to make observations, we must rely on the *testimony* of others: the astronaut returned from the moon or the witness at a trial. Testimonial evidence is observation at second hand, and of course it introduces another risk of error or deception. So when we are serious about getting facts, we may have to check to make sure that there is no reason to suspect that the witness really did not observe what he claims to have observed—for example, that he was not present at the scene, or was in no condition to see what was going on, or that his memory is unreliable, or that he is lying.

When we are considering the strength of an inductive argument, then, we will always ask: What are the data? Where did they come from? Do we have sufficient reason to accept them? If we are in doubt, we may have to undertake another induction to check the data. For if they let us down, any conclusions based on them will lack support. But suppose the data are reliable. The next question concerns the relation between those data and the conclusion we have at hand. A deductive argument is either valid or invalid, but an inductive argument is more or less strong. We must ultimately make a judgment, however rough, about the amount of support the data can provide. To put it more technically, the evidence is said to *confirm* the conclusion of an inductive argument to some degree, rendering it more or less probable or acceptable. There are two very different ways in which evidence can do this, and we shall deal with each in turn.

§ 7. Dependable Generalizations

When we believe something about an individual object, person, or event, we can express our belief in a *singular statement*, whose subject-term refers to that individual, and that only: "The dog next door is rough on flower-beds," "The record throw of a hen's egg without breaking it (303 feet, 6 inches) was obtained (on their 119th try) by Rauli Rapo and Markku Kuikka at Rilhimaki, Finland, on October 28, 1971." When we believe something about the members of a class of objects, persons, or events, we can express our belief in a *general statement,* which is a statement about the distribution of some property among the members of some class: "All snakes respond to vibrations transmitted through the ground," "Five per cent of Americans dream in color" (so one study concluded a few years ago, but that was before color television was as widespread as it is now; the percentage may be out of date).

A general statement that is offered as the conclusion of an inductive argument is a **generalization.** What makes an argument inductive is that the conclusion takes a leap beyond the data that support it; to generalize is always to take off from information about some members of a class and make an inference about other members of the class (though not necessarily all of its members). It is this leap that can make induction risky, but also rewarding—when it works.

The ingredients of a generalization argument, then, are three. Consider:

Snake S_1 responds to ground vibrations.
Snake S_2 responds to ground vibrations.
Snake S_3 responds to ground vibrations.
•
•
•
•
- -
All snakes respond to ground vibrations.

(The broken line means "therefore"; not "therefore, necessarily," but "therefore, probably.") First, in a generalization argument there is always the class we are concerned to generalize about: the **target population.** Here it is the class of *snakes.* Second, there is a subclass of the population, containing those individuals that have actually been observed, examined, or tested, and that furnish the evidence on which our generalization is based; this subclass is the **sample** of the target population. In our example it contains those snakes, S_1, S_2, S_3—and any others we may have had the opportunity to study—from whose behavior we are trying to learn something about the class of snakes in general. Third, there is the **projected property** (in this case, *responsiveness to ground vibrations*) which we are trying to extend from the sample to the population at large. We want to know whether this property, if found in the sample, is also to be found in all, or most, or few, or nine out of ten (or whatever) members of the total population. Each member of the sample that possesses the projected property is an **instance** of the generalization in question.

We may begin with a tentative generalization and seek to discover what available data would support it, by sampling the population generalized about; or we may begin with a sample, and some information about its properties, and wonder what generalization about the population we may safely base upon it. The logic is the same in both cases: The question is what generalization is warranted by what evidence. Now a sample of a population is a *representative* sample when the distribution of the projected property in the sample approximates the distribution of that property in the whole population. We would like, if we can, to choose our sample in such a way that it turns out to mirror the whole in miniature: If five percent of our sample American citizens dream in color, the same is true of American citizens whom we have not sampled; if all our sample snakes respond to ground vibrations then all snakes respond to them. So the basic problem in generalizing is how to make our samples representative. Or, since we cannot be certain that they are representative (at least, until we perhaps learn, later on, more about the whole population), how can we at least increase as much as possible our chances of having a representative sample?

A precise answer to this question can only be given in terms of the mathematics of sampling theory, which has been carried to a very high degree of sophistication. Sampling problems that arise in government, in industry, in the social sciences, require this careful, quantitative, and systematic treatment. But even if we do not command these techniques, as ordinary citizens, and even if we do not have the mass of data that might be required to use them, we can still take precautions in generalizing, or in accepting generalizations proposed by others. We can, in fact, save ourselves a good deal of tribulation by questioning generalization arguments—without necessarily becoming so skeptical that we are unable to believe anything but singular statements. (This would be paralyzing, for we cannot possibly get along without generalizing from our experience and the experience of others, and trying to build up—though constantly re-evaluating—a repertoire of dependable general statements on which to base our actions.)

Consider the following news item:

> LONDON.—"Coeducation is clearly associated with marital happiness," wrote Barnarr Atherton, head of an all-boys school, in the publication *Educational Research.*
>
> He concluded from a two-year study of 2,536 couples that people who go to single-sex schools and have less contact with the opposite sex dur-

ing adolescence are more likely to end up unhappily married, separated, or divorced.

The questions to raise about any generalization argument can be illustrated by this one.

The first question is whether the target population is clearly defined, so that we know exactly what group is being generalized about. Here there might be some confusion; the generalization seems to be about *married people in general,* but since the investigator is headmaster of a British school, it is a fair guess that he is concerned with *married British people,* rather than married people in general. Certainly we must be definite about this (and no doubt he was in the original article, here very briefly reported), for a generalization about *people* as such would be far more ambitious than a generalization about *British people.*

The second question is whether the scope of the generalization is sufficiently clear—whether the conclusion is supposed to be true of all, or most, or a specific fraction of the class under investigation. Our report is not informative about this. Clearly it involves a comparison between two different populations: *married British people who have attended coeducational schools* and *married British people who have attended noncoeducational schools.* Two generalizations are involved: (1) that a certain percent (*X%*) of the coeducationally-educated group have been unhappily married and (2) that a certain percent (*Y%*) of the noncoeducationally-educated group have been unhappily married. It is a simple (arithmetical) deduction that *Y%* is larger than *X%*. We can understand the logical structure of the argument, and raise questions about it, even though we don't know the actual percentages. In any case, the argument would not be complete unless they were explicitly given.

The third question is whether the projected property is clearly enough defined so that we can tell with reasonable confidence whether something has it, and consequently whether something is an instance of the proposed generalization. The property is *being unhappily married,* and this may require some critical examination. How is it defined, at least for the purposes of the present investigation? It is easy enough to count divorces and separations—at least, legal separations. But how are we to judge domestic unhappiness so that marriages divide clearly into happy ones and unhappy ones? This difficulty may not be impossible to overcome, though we shall not stop to deal with it now. The point is that any generalization argument must involve a property that is projected, or extrapolated, from the sample to the target population, and a good generalization argument takes pains to make that property fairly definite.

The fourth question is whether the sample is adequate to support the generalization. There are three factors to consider: *size, spread,* and *randomness*. All we learn about Mr. Atherton's sample from this news story is its size—2,536 couples (i.e., 5,072 individual people—for it is individuals, not couples, who are being generalized about). This size is impressive, considering that nation-wide Gallup polls of public opinion are based on samples far smaller than this—although we must bear in mind that these people presumably divide into two samples, one for each of the two generalizations involved. Absolute size counts, of course, especially at the lower end; if Mr. Atherton had examined, or interviewed, six couples, we would pay little heed to his conclusions. Relative size also counts, and that we do not know here, for the report does not tell us how many married couples there were in England during this period. Neither absolute nor relative size can be laid down as an exact requirement; we have to make an estimate—and our estimates get better as we acquire more experience in generalizing about certain kinds of things, learning from our successes and our failures.

Since we know that people differ in an enormous variety of ways, and since our own common-sense observations give us some reason to suppose that marital happiness may well be affected by a great many factors (such as money problems, sex hang-ups, personality strains, immaturity, social ambition, attitudes of relatives and in-laws, etc., etc.), we cannot assume that even a sample of 5,072 persons is adequate unless we have assurance also that the sample is spread over a range of other variations. If the persons studied all came from the North of England, well, perhaps things are different in the South. Or suppose they are all or mostly upper class and well off—suppose that Mr. Atherton used only graduates of his own boy's school and of a nearby coeducational school that is equally expensive. Then his conclusion might be true of upper-class persons, but not of others. Such a sample would be *biased*, in putting undue (or exclusive) emphasis on certain subclasses of the population. The freer from bias the sample, the more confidence we should repose in the argument. This is one of the main reasons for having a sizeable sample, since a very small sample will not be large enough to include instances of all the significant variations in the population.

When everything possible has been done (in the light of current knowledge) to insure a sample with adequate spread, we must fall back on another fundamental method for avoiding bias—that is, choosing our sample as randomly as possible. A random sample is one that is chosen by chance—by a method that gives every member of the population an equal opportunity (so to speak) to be included. Of course a random sample may turn out to be unrepresentative—as a hand dealt from a well-shuffled deck once in a long while turns out all spades—but it has the greatest probability of being representative, if the sample is made relatively large. If we want to generalize about the vibration-sensitivity of all snakes, we would insure spread by including specimens from various species; but in choosing which specimens, say, of garter snakes to use, it would be best to select them in such a way that we are not likely to get only sick or starved or dull or particularly nervous ones. And if we are generalizing about married couples, it would be smart to pick their names out of a hat or get a computer to select them in some equally random fashion.

To accept a generalization on the basis of a sample that is not sufficiently large, or well spread, or random, is to commit the **fallacy of hasty generalization**. It is a common enough mistake. Many are the useless or harmful pieces of friendly medical advice, the misguided theories about bringing up children, and the widespread myths about important social problems that begin with someone's seizing upon a few instances from his own experience and then generalizing freely. Once a superstition gets started, it is difficult to dislodge. Many tunnel workers, for example, believe that if a woman walks into a tunnel while it is under construction, a worker will shortly be killed; women are just bad luck in tunnels. This could easily be tested by letting a woman walk through a tunnel unannounced and unrecognized on randomly-selected days, and seeing whether there is any rise in the accident-rate shortly afterward. But who wants to take chances? Isn't it safer just to keep them out, so the jinx can't operate? This problem arose in Silver Plume, Colorado, in November, 1972, when a woman with impeccable credentials was hired by the Highway Department as an engineer on a tunnel project; she was hired by mail under the impression that she was a man. Of course they were distressed when she turned up for work, because the Department and the contractors had been firmly upholding the no-woman rule. But the Colorado state constitution had recently been amended to give women equal rights, so they had to take her. I don't know whether the superstition has been dented by her employment; some of the most alarmed male workers did not wait around to see what would happen but fled at once.

A particularly important kind of generalization is that which does not merely associate a property with the members of a class, but claims a causal relationship between one property (or group of properties) and another. A *causal generalization* may come in a rather loose form, and one of our tasks in coming to grips with it may be to get it straightened out enough so that we can see how well it is supported. "Massive doses of vitamin C (250 to 10,000 milligrams a day) prevent the common cold." Only the context, if there is one, can tell us whether the claim is (1) that *everyone* who takes massive doses will succeed in warding off the common cold or (2) that, even if they don't work in every single case, these massive doses have a causal connection with cold-immunity, and thus *tend* to prevent colds. I don't pursue this particular medical principle further (although it has been widely popularized in recent years), because the kind of evidence required for a definite decision can only be obtained by qualified medical researchers using carefully controlled experiments. But it is important to note, and bear in mind, the two sorts of causal claim: the stronger one, which is that taking much vitamin C is sufficient to prevent colds; and the weaker one, which is that taking much vitamin C increases one's immunity or renders one less susceptible to colds.

There are both singular and general causal statements. We say that Johnny's touching a poison ivy leaf caused him to have poison ivy rash; here we are speaking of a particular sequence of events. But even this singular causal statement depends on a general one, for unless we have reason to believe that there is a general causal connection between touching poison ivy leaves and developing the rash we could not call this more than a coincidence. After all, on that unfortunate picnic Johnny also ate six hot dogs and fell into the brook, but we don't say that either of these events caused his rash, because we don't subscribe to any such general statement as "Eating six hot dogs always causes a rash" or even "Eating six hot dogs makes people rash-prone." Not that all contacts with poison ivy leaves cause a rash (your first contact has no outward effect, but sensitizes you for later contacts). But when such a contact is followed by the characteristic rash, and no other possible causes appear to be present, we have to conclude that the contact probably caused the rash.

It is always illegitimate to suppose that just because *B* follows *A* on one occasion, *B* must be the effect of *A*. This inference commits the ***post hoc, ergo propter hoc*** ("after this, therefore because of this") **fallacy**. It amounts to basing a generalization on a singular instance. Take for example this letter to the editors of *Newsweek*:

> Your statement that Philadelphia's streets "look cleaner and better repaired" under Mayor Rizzo's administration overlooks one fact: In 1972-73 there was, for the first time, absolutely no snow or freezing rain in Philadelphia. Thus the potholes and other damage caused by normal winter weather did not appear. . . .

If *Newsweek's* story (April 23, 1973) did claim that the better-looking streets were the effect of the new municipal administration, the reproof was apt. Politicians, more than most people in other walks of life, are fond of the *post hoc* argument, either to puff up their own accomplishments (though they may have had a lot of luck on taking office) or to damn their opponents for the misfortunes that befell shortly after *they* took office. I do not wish to suggest, of course, that improvements and deteriorations in city services can never be attributed to municipal administrations, but only to remind you that it takes more than a single succession of events to justify the attribution.

Causal connections in fact require rather careful marshalling of evidence to establish. For we are not just saying that *A* and *B* always, or generally, or always under certain conditions, go together, but that *A* makes *B* happen or appear. Therefore, for one thing, we must always test a causal claim not only against the positive cases (where *A* and *B* are present), but against the negative cases as well. There are two kinds of negative case, and two principles to keep in mind. First, there are the *negative-cause* cases, from which *A* is absent. And the first principle is that if *B* happens no more frequently when *A* is present than when *A* is absent, we don't have good evidence that *A* causes *B*. It was suggested somewhere a few years ago that swallowing tadpoles would be an effective method of birth control, but the suggestion was withdrawn when experiment showed that the fertility of tadpole-swallowers was not noticeably different from that of non-tadpole-swallowers. I call this an "experiment," however crude it may have been, because it involved deliberate comparison of positive and negative cases. The negative cases (non-tadpole-swallowers) constitute the *control group*, against which we are matching the *experimental group*, in our effort to discover whether tadpole-swallowing makes a difference to fertility. If the fertility of the two groups is exactly the same (and assuming that they have been selected with adequate size, spread, and randomness), we have no evidence of a causal connection. If there is a slight difference, it may have been due to chance, or error in recording the data, so it is not "significant"; but a large difference would certainly be rather strong evidence. How much of a difference is significant? That is a delicate technical question that we won't take up here.

Second, there are the *negative-effect* cases, from which *B* is absent. And the second principle is that if *A* is present just about as frequently when *B* is absent as it is when *B* is present, we don't have good evidence that *A* causes *B*. This principle would usefully apply when we are trying to answer a question like: "Does smoking marijuana cause people to become addicted to heroin?" We could use the first method, with randomly-selected groups of marijuana-smokers and marijuana-nonsmokers: If there is a causal connection here, we would expect a significantly greater proportion of the first group than of the second group to become addicted to heroin. Or we could use the second method, with randomly-selected groups of heroin-addicts and non-heroin-addicts: If there is a causal connection, we would expect a significantly greater proportion of the first group than of the second group to have smoked marijuana at some time in the past.

When someone claims to know a causal connection in a particular case, we must always try to examine the causal generalization on which the claim must be based (considering the reliability of that generalization in the light of the evidence for it)—but it is also always relevant to stop and consider the possibilities. Could the effect have been caused by something else? And is there something about the effect that perhaps could only have been caused by something else? The civil liberties dangers of the commonest form of "lie-detector," the polygraph, illustrate this problem. Although several hundred thousand people (mostly employed in private industries) are given polygraph tests each year, there is still much question about the reliability of such tests, and even more about the invasion of personal privacy and of constitutional rights that may often be a consequence of their use. The reliability problem is a causal one. There is no doubt that the test indicates certain physiological responses (changes in respiration, blood pressure, and galvanic skin response) when the subject answers a question that is put to him. But the claim that the polygraph test indicates when the subject is lying (i.e., asserting a statement that he knows to be untrue) rests on a sequence of assumptions: that lying causes psychological conflict in the liar, that conflict causes fear and anxiety, that fear and anxiety cause those measurable physiological changes that the polygraph records. So the basic causal generalization is: "Lying causes polygraphable physiological changes."

Actually, it is more complicated than that. It is widely conceded by the polygraph operators that the tests generally do not work unless the subject is convinced that they do work (otherwise he may feel no anxiety about being detected). There is a rather elaborate ritual that must be gone through before the test, in order to impress the subject with the infallibility of the machine (including often a rigged pre-test in which the subject is asked to lie, and is shown that his lies are instantly detectable). So the generalization is: "Lying by someone who believes in the reliability of polygraphs causes polygraphable physiological changes." It is an interesting question in itself how this generalization could be well confirmed. If we had some other (sure) way of determining when people are lying, we could then test the polygraph test by seeing whether it picks out the mendacious answers from the truthful ones. But an enormous number of the statements made by polygraph subjects must remain untested. Someone is fired from a factory for stealing transistor radios (though he maintains his innocence to the end), because the polygraph showed physiological responses. There is no hearing, no trial, no further investigation. But if this is put down as one more "success" for the polygraph, we have an interesting kind of circular reasoning.

Nevertheless, it may be true that there is reasonably good evidence that lying while believing in the polygraph can cause polygraphable physiological changes. The problem, then, is what to believe in individual cases. Suppose we ask the employee whether he stole the radios, and he denies it. The polygraph records a rise in pulse rate, blood pressure, perspiration, etc. Are these physiological changes caused by his lying, or by something else? It is known that exactly the same changes can be produced in subjects who are highly nervous even when they are telling the truth, because they fear that they will not be believed. (It is known that some people who have no sense of guilt and no troubling conscience feel no conflict in lying, and can lie without any detectable physiological changes at all.) Still, if we can show that *most* people who undergo the physiological changes are lying, that would be *some* (though not conclusive) evidence that our employee is lying. Here is where the civil liberties questions come in again: Since nothing has been proved beyond a reasonable doubt, is it fair to fire him, or deny him a government job, because he fails a polygraph test, or to present the test results to a jury to shore up a sagging criminal case? Of course these questions go beyond our concern with logic; I mention them to underline this point: that causal generalizations come in all degrees of reliability, and how much reliability you demand depends on what you are planning to do with it.

When *A* causes *B*, and *B* causes *C*, we can speak of *A* as the indirect cause of *C*: A causal chain links one event, or state of affairs, to another. By reasoning along causal chains, we are able to reconstruct the distant past and, more importantly from a practical point of view, predict the future. In recent years, the mounting problems of ecology have brought home to us very sharply the remote consequences of our actions—sometimes disastrous—and the crucial importance of trying to foresee what series of causes and effects will unroll if we interfere in certain ways with the environment. Consider this example from an essay by Peter A. Gunter in *The Living Wilderness* (Spring 1970):

> In Malaysia recently, in an effort to kill off mosquitoes, American technologists sprayed woods and swamplands with DDT. Result? Cockroaches which ate poisoned mosquitoes were so slowed in their reactions that they could be eaten by a variety of tree-climbing lizard which, sickened in turn, could be eaten by cats, which promptly died of insecticide poisoning. The cats having died, the rat population began to increase; as rats multiplied, so did fleas: *hence the rapid spread of bubonic plague in Malaysia.* But this is not all. The tree-climbing lizards, having

died, could no longer eat an insect which consumed the straw thatching of the natives' huts. So as Malaysians died of plague, their roofs literally caved in above their heads.

Closely connected with the notion of cause are the notions of *necessary* condition and *sufficient* condition, which are often misused in everyday, especially in political, disputes. A necessary condition of an event is a condition without which it does not happen: say, Johnny's touching the poison ivy leaf. Of course, it is not true that the only way to get poison ivy rash is to touch a poison ivy leaf; but given the conditions at the picnic, where no other children or pets had touched poison ivy, no one was burning ivy leaves, etc., Johnny would not have gotten poison ivy if he had not touched a leaf. A sufficient condition of an event is a condition under which it will happen. Oxygen is a necessary condition of human life, but hardly sufficient: We need food, shelter, and other things—it would be hard to draw up a complete list. But again we can talk about sufficient conditions in a particular context. Assuming that Johnny had been sensitized by previous contact, was not coated with a zirconium cream, and did not wash his skin immediately after the contact, then his touching the leaf was sufficient (on top of the other prevailing conditions) to give him ivy poisoning.

Confusions about necessary and sufficient conditions often appear in disputes: One person says that *A* is a necessary condition of *B*, and someone else replies heatedly that *A* is not a sufficient condition of *B*. This is a kind of logical irrelevance, but it is often successful in confusing issues, as in President Nixon's famous statement that we cannot cure poverty by throwing money at it. *The New York Times* editorialized about this form of argument:

> Let us suppose that a man is drowning thirty feet from shore. A rescuer throws him ten feet of rope. He drowns. It would scarcely be logical to conclude: "Rope is of no use in the prevention of drowning."
>
> Yet that is the kind of logic enshrined in President Nixon's budget and set forth over the weekend in his radio talk on "Human Resources." Once again, the President blandly asserts that the Federal programs enacted in the last decade were "based on the assumption that any human problem could be solved simply by throwing enough Federal dollars at it." Money flowed from Washington, according to Mr. Nixon, "in a seemingly inexhaustible flood."
>
> There was no such assumption and no such flood.

The assumption in the minds of those who once tried to help the poor and ill and unemployed in this country was surely that Federal funds were a necessary condition of success. To reply that they are not a sufficient condition is beside the point.

X: As the late Professor Chafee, America's outstanding civil liberties scholar, said, the right of habeas corpus is the most important in the Bill of Rights, and the foundation of all the others.

Y: But surely this is a mistake, even if said by an authority. There is no single magic measure that can be counted on to produce justice without fail.

Y's reply is, of course, a serious misrepresentation of *X*'s statement.

A check-up quiz

Here are some generalizations and the samples on which they are based. In each case, give a reason why the sample may not be representative of the target population.

1. *Generalization:* Thirty-nine percent of the cars in this city are Volkswagens.
   Sample: The cars in a parking lot next to the Spectrum during a concert by Alice Cooper.

2. *Generalization:* American citizens are more concerned about the rising cost of living than about any other social problem.
   Sample: American citizens questioned at a large suburban shopping center.

3. *Generalization:* Bussing elementary school children to schools outside their neighborhoods tends to arouse anxiety and tension.
   Sample: 200 black children from a Boston ghetto bussed to a suburban school for two months.

4. *Generalization:* The names given to children affect their tendency to win out, or become a loser, in life.
   Sample: Four compositions written by fourth-grade and fifth-grade students, which were graded by 80 elementary-school teachers and student-teachers, and which were in most cases graded higher by the experienced teachers when they were attributed to pupils named "Michael" and "David" than when they were attributed to pupils named "Elmer" and "Hubert."

5. *Generalization:* Hitch-hiking in a large city is easier for women students than for men students.
   Sample: Two men students and two women students, who each thumbed five rides at different times of day from a university to Center City, keeping a record of the length of time that passed before a ride was offered, and calculating that the men waited an average of four minutes and forty seconds more than the women.

§ 8. Appraising a Hypothesis

When we find ourselves puzzled about how some event or state of affairs came about, we may ask for an *explanation* of it. Why has your favorite cactus plant begun to droop and look pale? Perhaps the explanation is that you have been watering it too much. Why are there fragments of greenish glass lying about the desert at White Sands, New Mexico? Their presence can be explained: The first test of an atomic bomb took place here in the damp dawn of July 16, 1945. These explanations may not be the *only* explanations that could be given, but they do explain what we want explained. And if we accept them as the correct explanations, our original puzzlement or bafflement is relieved.

When we look closely at some typical explanations, in order to see more clearly what is involved in explaining, we find three essential elements. First, there is the event or state of affairs that puzzles us: The cactus is ailing; there are fragments of green glass here. In short, there is a fact to be explained. Second, there is a **hypothesis**—the explaining statement, or set of statements: "The cactus is being watered too much," "An atomic bomb was exploded here in 1945." Third, there must be some connection between the fact and the hypothesis: a generalization that relates cactus-watering with cactus-ailing, or atomic explosions with the conversion of sand into glass. An **explanation**, then, is a set of statements of which at least one is reported as a fact and at least one is offered as a hypothesis to account for that fact in virtue of one or more generalizations connecting the events or states of affairs referred to in the fact and the hypothesis.

These two examples just given differ in an important way. When we observe the fragments of glass, we may already know (from our study of history) about the atomic explosion—it just takes a while to put the two bits of knowledge together and see how one explains the other (and of course to do this we have to know something about what happens in an atomic explosion and how glass is formed). We did not, so to speak, discover any new facts, but came to understand the relation between facts we already knew. In the case of the cactus, we made a discovery, for it had not occurred to us before that we were giving the plant too much water. Our reasoning is thus an inductive argument of a simple sort:

The cactus is ailing.
- -
The cactus is getting too much water.

We are taking the cactus's ailing as *evidence* of over-watering. It is not overwhelming evidence, of course, and we don't have to put a great deal of stock in the conclusion until we cut down on the water for a while (say, to a couple of tablespoons a week), to see if the plant revives —and even that may not be conclusive, for if the plant still dies, it may be because we had already fatally harmed it.

It might seem that the cactus inference could easily be transformed into a deductive one by adding a suppressed premise: "All cases of ailing cactus are cases of over-watered cactus." If this premise were true, we could indeed deduce the conclusion. But of course it is not true, for other things make a cactus ill. It might be getting too little sun, for example. It might be under attack by mealybugs or red spider mites. Now we have three possible explanations of the original fact, and since we have not eliminated the other two, we cannot enthusiastically embrace one of them—at least, at this stage—even if we may have good reason to think that over-watering is the most likely explanation. We have here, then, another form of inductive argument, in which the conclusion is a hypothesis which is suported by one or more facts that are explainable by that hypothesis; the hypothesis gets its convincingness from its capacity to account for things we already know. And if we get to the point where the hypothesis explains enough facts and does a good enough job so that we can now claim to know that the hypothesis is itself true, we can say we have discovered a new fact (that the plant was over-watered), and use that fact, if we have occasion to, in other inductive arguments.

A legitimate claim to know is not necessarily an insistence on certainty. No matter how strongly a hypothesis argument is built up, no matter how convinced we may be that the hypothesis is true, two possibilities remain (at least theoretically) open. First, the hypothesis could always, or nearly always, be made even more probable by further evidence. When we cut down on the watering, and the cactus revives, we are so cheered by this result that we are quite certain we know what was wrong. But it is just possible that we moved the plant a little, without noticing, and that that is what improved its health; or that some temporary change in the usual atmospheric pollution did in the mealybugs. Suppose we were more interested in science than in the cactus itself; we might deliberately go back to watering the cactus frequently, as we did before, to see if the cactus turns sick again—and to see if it revives when the over-watering is stopped again. A certain number of such trials will make us just about as convinced as we could be that our hypothesis was right; it would be neurotic to demand more evidence. And yet, if we tried one more time . . . .

Second, a hypothesis, no matter how well established, is always in principle open to refutation. Some evidence we had never imagined might turn up to refute it, or at least to require it to be seriously modified. Suppose the cactus becomes healthy when watered less, but after a week begins to droop again. It may have a totally new ailment, of course; or maybe it wasn't the over-watering after all, but some other malady (temporarily suspended) that was at fault. That would not refute our hypothesis, but it would raise difficulties, since we now have to explain how, if our hypothesis correctly accounts for the first illness, the second illness came about. Or suppose we found out that someone else with access to the cactus, hating to see it so dry and parched, had all along been secretly watering it, while we were cutting down on the water; that would explode our theory.

It is helpful in understanding hypothesis arguments to see them as the culmination of a process of *inquiry,* or of some stage of such a process. An inquiry is the systematic and persistent attempt to answer an explanation-question; it is systematic because it involves a differentiation of phases, and moves in an orderly way from one phase to another.

Inquiry begins when someone wants an explanation. Phase 1 consists in formulating the question we want to answer, as clearly and specifically as we now can (what we learn later may lead us to go back to Phase 1 and start over with an improved version of the question). Sometimes we cannot be very exact at the start, but the more clearly we have in mind what we want to know, the better our chances of discovering it. Consider, for example, the famous bronze horse at the Metropolitan Museum of Art in New York City, acclaimed for many years as "one of the finest bronzes of classical Greece," then convincingly attacked (in 1967) as a twentieth-century forgery, then finally (or is it final?) shown (in 1972) to be an "irrefutably genuine work of antiquity." We can distinguish several inquiries here, or consider them as parts of a single continued one. We can also distinguish different questions that the many experts involved were asking, but let us try the following one: "When (that is, in what period) was the bronze horse made?"

Phase 2 consists in devising a hypothesis. In this case, the first and most obvious hypothesis, which was no doubt strongly set forth and was certainly accepted at the time the Metropolitan acquired the sculpture in 1923, is Hypothesis H_1: *The horse was made in the classical Greek period* (probably fifth century B.C.). The hypothesis must answer the question, and it must be testable.

Phase 3 consists in drawing logical consequences from the hypothesis, seeing what else must be true (in the light of known generalizations) if the hypothesis is true. For example, Joseph Noble, who exposed the horse as a forgery in 1967, reasoned that *if* it was made in the classical period, *then* it must have been cast by the lost-wax method, since the alternative method, sand-casting, was not invented until the fourteenth century A.D. He further reasoned that if it was cast by the lost-wax method, hence in one piece, it does not have seams running up and down its nose, mane, and belly. But when he examined the horse, he found it does have such seams. By an ordinary conditional argument (denying the consequent) it follows that Hypothesis H_1 is false. Thus Phase 4 consists in confronting the consequences with experience, to determine whether they are true.

Noble had a number of other items of evidence against Hypothesis H_1, some of them merely making it seem implausible, others coming into direct conflict with it. We cannot follow the details of this complicated controversy; our concern is to illustrate the basic logical features of inquiry. In any case, when Noble rejected Hypothesis H_1, he went back to Phase 2 and offered his own alternative Hypothesis H_2: *The horse was made in the nineteenth or twentieth century.* When, at Phase 3, we derive consequences from this hypothesis, we see, for example, that from Hypothesis H_2 (together with other assumptions about the popularity of sand-casting in modern times) it follows that the horse will have been sand-cast and will have the seams actually observed. So the fact that it has seams, which counted against Hypothesis H_1, helps to confirm Hypothesis H_2.

When the later experts began to reconsider Hypothesis H_2 (back to Phase 2), they were able to derive consequences from it (Phase 3) that did not match the observations (Phase 4). One of them involves the thermoluminescence test for determining the age of archaelogical objects (and also lunar rocks). This test had shown, for example, that the Metropolitan's admired Euphronius vase and Etruscan warriors are forgeries. Phase 3: If Hypothesis H_2 is true, the horse is not 2,000 years old. Phase 4: The thermoluminescence test showed that it is at least 2,000 years old. Therefore Hypothesis H_2 is false. Stylistic evidence, and evidence of other sorts, have been brought forth to support this conclusion.

We do not go back, however, to Hypothesis H_1, for the date cannot be more than vaguely fixed. The evidence does not say whether the horse was cast in classical times or in the Hellenistic period. So we have Hypothesis H_3: *The horse was made in ancient (pre-Christian) times.* Given this hypothesis we would expect the thermoluminescence test to come out as in fact it did. A difficulty remains however: "What about the seam? For the seam counts against Hypothesis H_3 just as much as it counts against Hypothesis H_1. Here is one of the odd features of the story. Since the horse was first put on display fifty years ago, thousands of plaster casts have been made of it, including one for the 1936 Olympics. It was also customary early in this century to wax bronzes to preserve them. Kate Lefferts and Lawrence Majewski wondered whether the fact that could not be accounted for by Hypothesis H_3 was really a fact, so they cleaned the horse with cotton swabs. The seams disappeared; they were apparently wax ridges caused by the various casts made to reproduce it. Here is a fine example of an important aspect of inquiry. It is dogmatic to cling to a hypothesis in the face of incompatible facts; but it is far from dogmatic, when a hypothesis is well-supported by solid facts, to reconsider very carefully the apparent conflicts. Sometimes it is the assumed generalization that gives way before further examination: For example, it was assumed by the defenders of Hypothesis H_2 that no ancient bronzes (but only modern sand-casted sculptures) contain an "armature," or sausage-shaped core which X-rays and gamma rays revealed inside the bronze horse. But investigation turned up several examples of well-authenticated fifth-century bronzes with just such armatures. Thus one consequences that was thought to follow from Hypotheses H_1 and H_3 did not follow after all.

It might be possible to revise Hypothesis H_2 so that it could still be maintained. But it would have to be drastically revised. It might also be possible to think of other hypotheses that will also account for what we know about this horse. And, of course, Hypothesis H_3 is very broad, and could be broken down into any number of narrower hypotheses specifying shorter periods of time. In any case, it is well to think of the acceptance of a hypothesis as an act of choice between that hypothesis and others that we may already have before us for consideration, or that might be thought of by someone with sufficient ingenuity. When an inquiry comes to a halt, as when the prosecution and defense have rested their case at a trial, we must make up our minds on the evidence we have. And since we cannot eliminate finally and conclusively all hypotheses but one, we ask whether the hypothesis we are considering is good enough to warrant acceptance.

How do we decide whether one hypothesis is more acceptable than another one which explains (let us assume) the same facts? Disputes continue to this day about the Warren Commission report on the assassination of President John F. Kennedy—about the guilt or innocence of Ethel and Julius Rosenberg, convicted of giving Russia atomic secrets and executed in 1953—even about the Sacco-Vanzetti case back in the 1920s. Every bit of physical evidence and of testimony can be explained in a number of ways: For example, in the Rosenberg case there is the hotel registration card supporting the account of Harry Gold (who gave the most damaging testimony against the Rosenbergs) that he was in Albuquerque on June 3, 1945. The jury accepted this as genuine; others who have reviewed the case with great care have concluded that it was forged by F.B.I. agents. Perhaps few of us can expect to be in a position to make an independent judgment in such a case; we have to fall back on our general beliefs and experience about the F.B.I., about the criminal trial system, about the climate of opinion in 1951, at the time of the trial, and so forth.

But we do have two principles to go on when we have enough evidence to apply them; and though they are far from precise, they can help us make reasonable judgments about the comparative acceptability of alternative hypotheses.

First, every hypothesis describes a certain (hypothetical) state of affairs or event or sequence of events, and we can ask about the *frequency* of states or events of this kind. Say a man opens a can of tuna and begins eating it voraciously; suddenly he bites on something very hard, which looks like a good-sized piece of glass, breaking two teeth. Disgusted, he rushes off to his dentist to get his teeth capped, and then to his attorney to press a damage suit against the cannery. If the object in the can is really glass, which got there through the negligence of the cannery's employees, then the cannery may be financially liable. If, on the other hand, it is a struvite crystal formed by certain chemical processes that can occur in canned seafoods after they are sterilized, the cannery may not be legally responsible. Of course chemical analysis can tell the difference and decide the issue. But even in advance of analysis (or if, say, the object got lost before it was analyzed), we would be justified in assigning a higher probability to one hypothesis than to the other if we knew how often such particles in canned seafood are pieces of glass and how often they are struvite crystals. If struvite crystal formation is twice as frequent as glass pollution, then the struvite-crystal hypothesis is rather more likely to be true. Sometimes we have to rely heavily on this kind of appraisal—as when we say of a friend just arrested on some surprising charge that "He couldn't possibly have done that; it's not at all in keeping with his character." Even our confidence in fingerprints as a means of identification rests on the same principle. Two fingerprints are considered identical if they are so classified in the usual Henry system. We do know it to be impossible for two people to have identical fingerprints, but only that the odds against their having one fingerprint in common are 60 billion to one, and against having ten in common, 250 trillion to one (according to official calculations).

Second, every hypothesis, we might say, tells a story, and some stories are more complicated than others: they have more characters, more going on. Thus we can ask about the *simplicity* of a hypothesis: whether it tells a less complicated story than its alternatives. Consider the recurrent disputes about the authorship of those plays and poems which are generally attributed to William Shakespeare. We know there was a William Shakespeare who was born in Stratford, lived in London for many years, did various things, and retired to Stratford again. There are people who just cannot believe that someone with a humble lower-middle-class background, and such limited schooling, could have become one of the greatest poets of all time. So they constantly devise other hypotheses to avoid this one. In recent years a number of books have defended the hypothesis that the plays and poems were written by Edward de Vere, Earl of Oxford—who did write some poetry on his own, and some plays (now lost) for private performance. The details of all these Shakespearean disputes are far too many to do justice to here, but one feature of the disputes is worth noting. Nobody seems to have discovered any fact that is sharply incompatible with the Shakespeare-hypothesis. The Oxford-hypothesis supposes that Oxford wrote the poems and plays, but did not wish to acknowledge them publicly because association with the stage would mar his social status (and because they contained attacks on living people—Portia, for example, being a reference to Queen Elizabeth I); that he bribed William Shakespeare to let his name be used, and to go off to Stratford and keep the secret, and later paid others to issue the First Folio with Shakespeare's name on it. This hypothesis involves a far more complicated story than the Shakespeare-hypothesis. If it could explain something the Shakespeare-hypothesis cannot explain, the complexity might be justified; if not, it is simply otiose.

The acceptable hypothesis is the simplest one that can explain the facts we want to explain—but of course it must actually explain.

> When Orval Faubus left the governorship of Arkansas, he was asked how he had managed to build a two-hundred-thousand-dollar house after having earned only ten thousand dollars a year during his twelve years in office, and he said he owed it all to thrift. [*The New Yorker*, June 17, 1972]

That's a bit too simple.

We cannot say that the simpler of two alternative hypotheses is always the true one; further evidence may turn up to prove that it will not do. But at a particular time, given the evidence at hand, we want to know what it is reasonable to believe, or to act on, or at least to accept provisionally. And it is never reasonable to accept an elaborate hypothesis to explain something that can be explained just as well by a hypothesis that makes fewer assumptions about what happened, or involves fewer persons, places, or things.

There is no term in common use for the logical error of choosing a hypothesis that is less acceptable than its rivals, in terms of frequency or simplicity or both: Let us call it the **fallacy of far-fetched hypothesis.** It is not an all-or-none fallacy—a hypothesis is more or less far-fetched depending on how good the available alternatives are. Nor can we always apply the two criteria very easily and decisively—we may not know enough to judge frequency, and we may find the two hypotheses about equally simple, as far as we can tell. Still, the criteria have their uses, and there is a fallacy that we do well to keep in mind and try to steer clear of.

A check-up quiz

Here are some (assumed) facts and hypotheses to explain them. In each case, suggest an alternative hypothesis that would explain the fact, and suggest an observation that would decide between the two hypotheses.

1. *Fact:* The President has appointed a lawyer whose clients have included oil and gas producers and who has long been a spokesman for the interests of the energy industries to the position of chairman of the Federal commission on energy.
   Hypothesis: The President wishes the Commission not to interfere with the interests of the fuel producers.

2. *Fact:* When the two Pennsylvania state policemen were arrested in the motel room, they were listening in to a bugged conversation between members of the Governor's Corruption Commission investigators, which was going on across the hall.
   Hypothesis: The two state policemen were bugging Commission investigators.

3. *Fact:* It is the custom in the United States to drive on the right-hand side of the street, but in England to drive on the left.
   Hypothesis: Originally Conestoga wagon drivers rode the left lead horse on a team of horses because horses were trained to be mounted from the left so the right hand would be free to draw a gun quickly; while early English horsemen drove on the left so the right hand could draw a sword quickly against an approaching enemy.

4. *Fact:* The stairway door in the Watergate office building has tape across the bolt to keep it from locking automatically when it is closed.
   Hypothesis: A burglary is now in progress in one of the offices upstairs.

5. *Fact:* Reports of corruption among police have increased in recent years.
Hypothesis: There has been a general decline in morality.

§ 9. Classification and Analogy

From the discussion of the syllogism in the previous chapter and the discussion of generalization in this chapter it is evident that the idea of *class* plays a very fundamental role in much of our thinking, deductive and inductive. We have seen how one class may be part of another, how classes may or may not overlap (that is, have members in common), how conclusions may be drawn about the relationship between two classes from knowledge about the way each is related to a third class, how under certain conditions we may legitimately infer something about a class from one of its subclasses (a sample). There remain to be considered in this section some other important ways of thinking that involve classes.

A class is formed in either of two ways: *collection* or *division* (we could adopt terms from physics and call them *fusion* and *fission*). Take any property, such as *having four legs*: We can think of all the things (if any) that have that property as constituting a class. (If nothing had that property, the class would be empty.) It is not necessary to lay hands on things and put them in a pile or a pen; the kind of collecting that creates classes is purely a matter of thought. (A class of first-graders is more than a class in the purely logical sense, when they are assembled in one room.) The members of the class may be scattered all over the world, or the universe, but they are tied together by their common property—which can be as complex as we wish to make it. When we have formed one or more classes, we can proceed in the opposite direction to break them down into subclasses, dividing, say, the class of quadrupeds into those that are brown, those that are white, those that are gray, etc.—or into those that are not more than a year old, those more than one year but not more than two years old, etc. As long as we can bring in other properties that cut across the one we started with (*quadrupedicity*), we can continue the division—though, again, some of the subclasses we wind up with may turn out to have no members (purple quadrupeds over 1,000 years old).

Division not only generates new classes out of an old one, but also relates the new classes to the old one: They are *subordinated* to it. We can relate classes to each other in three ways: by division, by subsumption, and by coordination. Subsumption goes in the opposite direction from division. We start with a class, say, old stripped-down abandoned cars, and ask: Of what larger class shall we consider this a subclass? We have various alternatives to choose among. I don't suppose these objects can be called cars any more, strictly speaking, since so much is missing and they have no hope of working again. But they all belong to the class of metal objects, of abandoned objects, of objects in streets, of junk-objects, etc. For certain purposes, we may decide to regard them as a subclass of the class of junk-objects; this is subsumption.

When we divide a class into subclasses, the subclasses themselves have a parallel status: they are *coordinate* classes. When we subsume one class under another, the subsumed class is at least implicitly contrasted with other subclasses that could also be subsumed coordinately with it.

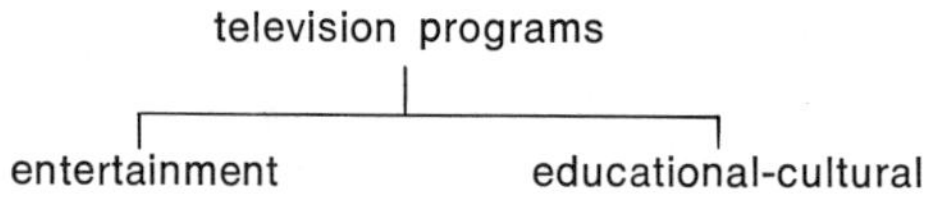

This schematic diagram exhibits a certain relationship among three classes, of which the second and third are coordinately subordinated to the first. Choosing a different universe of discourse, we might have proposed, instead:

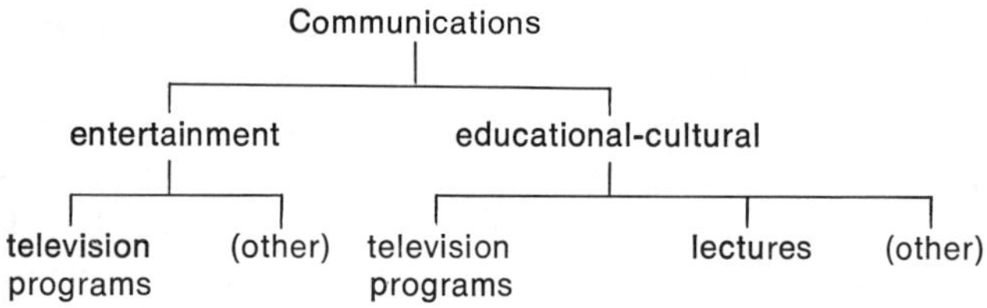

Each of these diagrams represents a **classification** of certain things, the first one of television programs in general, the second of communications (for want of a better term). That is one difference between them: change of scope. Another is inversion of relationships: The first scheme subsumes entertainment television programs under television programs in general; the second subsumes entertainment television programs under entertainment communications in general (no doubt, along with such coordinate subclasses as staged musical comedies, nightclub comedy acts, etc.). Neither of these differences is a matter of truth or falsity; a classification is not a statement, but a proposal, and each of these classifications might be appropriate and acceptable for certain purposes. Nevertheless, as we shall see shortly, a classification rests upon, or presupposes, certain statements, in that the classification cannot be a good one if the statements happen to be false.

Our first classification might be extended, or elaborated:

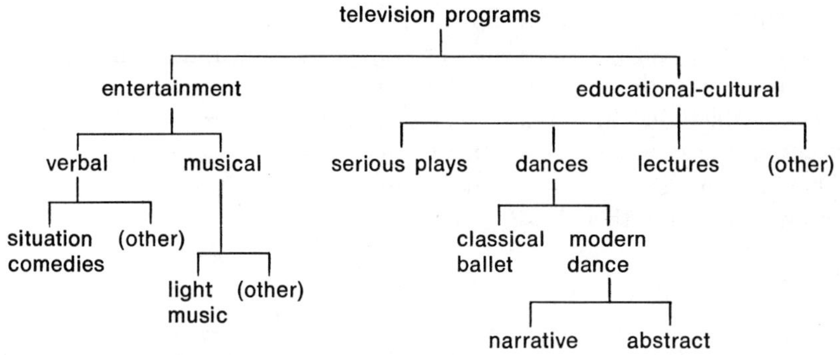

A few more special terms will be useful. The classes named in the diagram are called **categories**, to suggest that they are to be treated like pigeonholes which we have made available, whether or not they turn out to have actual members. The categories are ordered on various levels, or **ranks**, from the most general to the most specific. Within each rank, the coordinate categories are distinguished by reference to a particular property, which is the **basis of division.** When we divide cars, for example, into red and green, the basis of division is *color*; when we divide people into male and female, the basis of division is *sex*. It is not so easy to specify the basis of some of the divisions in our classification just above. At the second rank, it might be said to be *primary value* or *dominant function*—which would mean that the division is not very sharp, and there are bound to be borderline cases: that is, television programs that have considerable aesthetic or intellectual value, and are at the same time highly entertaining, so that we are not sure in which category to place them. The division of entertainment programs into verbal and musical seems to have *medium* as its basis of division; that of verbal programs into situation comedies and others, something like *genre*. Obviously this classification of television programs is not well thought out; it is only a rough start.

The two main troubles to watch out for in a classification, whether your own or someone else's, are confusion and triviality.

The rule that guards against confusion is this: In each rank the categories are to be distinguished according to one and only one basis of division. If you want to use more than one basis of division, use them at different ranks, one at a time. For instance, an essay on economics says "In the social sciences, one speaks today of three kinds of resources: human resources, natural resources, and man-made resources." Do these three categories belong on the same rank, as the quotation suggests? We may have to be clearer about the meaning of "human resources" before we can be wholly sure. If we are referring to capabilities and talents that are genetic endowments, they are not man-made; if we are talking of abilities and skills developed by education and training, these are man-made, in a sense. There is also some question about "resources," which in the context seems to include everything that contributes to the creation of wealth (in the economist's sense of what has utility). In any case, there do seem to be two distinct principles of division involved in this classification:

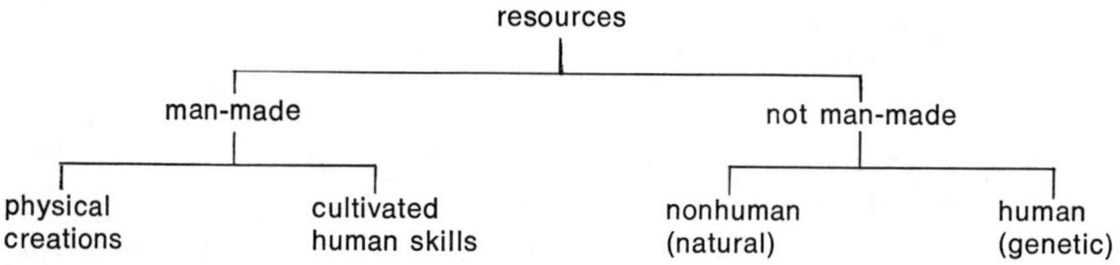

In the second rank, the basis of division is something like *causal relationship to human activity* (machines *vs.* oil deposits); in the third rank, it is something like *dependence on human beings for existence* (machines *vs.* ability to write shorthand under one main category, oil deposits *vs.* the inventor's genes under the other main category).

A classification that violates the single-basis rule commits the **fallacy of cross-ranking**. Sometimes it can easily be straightened out, as we can see right away that "men, women, and children" really involves two distinct ranks lumped together. Sometimes the task of straightening out the classification involves just the kind of hard—and fruitful—thinking that the original confused classification avoided. Unless we know pretty clearly just what it is that we are classifying (physical objects? human actions? works of art? ways of cooking potatoes?), and just what distinctions we want to make at each stage (are we dividing by sex, by age, social status, by conformity/nonconformity with the law?), we can get into serious difficulties in our thinking.

A classification that commits the fallacy of cross-ranking will not necessarily be defective in other ways, but it is quite likely to be. Sometimes the categories in a given rank will fail to be exclusive of each other, so that the same thing belongs in both of two overlapping categories. This means that we have not thought things through far enough, and we had better not work with our classification until we separate the categories by using better bases of division. Sometimes the categories in a given rank will fail to be exhaustive, so that we find we have no pigeonhole for some of the things we want to classify. Of course we can always make a rank exhaustive by adding a box for "other," or "miscellaneous." But if we find we are tossing a good many things in that category, probably we need to introduce more categories and sort things out more fully. A classification is a preliminary, not necessarily final, way of sorting things, and as our knowledge of a class increases, as we find out more about the things in it, the ways in which they differ, we may be continually revising our classification-scheme, adding new categories and scrapping some bases of division in favor of others.

In this way our classification becomes more *significant.* A classification brings together some things and separates others; when (to put the point pretty roughly) the things brought together really belong together, the classification is a significant one. Significance here is not just a matter of special interests. Some years ago, when the Food and Drug Administration disclaimed any jurisdiction over tobacco as a hazardous substance on the grounds that it is neither a food nor a drug, the tobacco industry, headed by former Senator Earle Clements of Kentucky, insisted that tobacco be classified as a food for the purpose of the Food for Freedom program, which was designed to buy up surplus American foods and send them abroad. This is classification for a practical purpose—though the classification of tobacco is not really that arbitrary, the function of tobacco being to make certain drugs (such as nicotine) ingestible. But what I have in mind by "significance" is something more closely related to our knowledge and understanding, rather than our wish to promote special interests. True, a philosopher must be concerned with different distinctions from those that are important to an astronaut, a social worker, or a medical researcher. But whatever the field may be, certain distinctions will turn out to be more fundamental than others, in the light of what is discovered about that field; and if the resulting classification is orderly, the more fundamental distinctions will appear at the highest ranks.

The notion of fundamentalness is not hard to illustrate, but it cannot be made fully explicit without a more elaborate discussion than will be provided here. Think of it in this way: If you were classifying people, in the light of what you know about them (or you can take any other class of things that you happen to know something about, such as paintings, board games, computer programs, sports, or theories about the origin of the moon), some bases of division would seem more promising than others. Hair color is one way of dividing people, but it is superficial, because nothing else seems connected with it—when you know that someone has brown hair, you can't infer very much else about him.

Religion is more fundamental, in that there is a good deal of knowledge, at least of a statistical sort, about the ways in which one's religion might affect one's voting habits, one's likelihood of going to jail, one's income group, etc. Grouping by religion brings together people who have (or tend to have) much more in common than just the property by which they are classified. And a classification with *religion* as a basis of division would, to that extent, be more significant than one limited to *hair color*.

Sponsoring a proposed constitutional amendment prohibiting abortion except to save the life of the mother, Senator Mark Hatfield once said that he considered abortions part of a wave of "depersonalization and violence" spreading throughout the nation, his other examples being the war in Indochina, with its body-counts; the denial of amnesty to those who would not violate their consciences and fight in the war; and the conditions that led to rioting in the Attica prison. Here is a proposed category, with examples of the sorts of thing that are to be placed in it. Is it a significant category? Are abortion, the Vietnam war, the denial of amnesty, and evil prison conditions all examples of the same significant property? Or do they differ so much in their causes, in their social effects, in their moral and psychological aspects, that they don't actually go together? Of course I'm not proposing to discuss such deep and far-reaching questions here, much less consider the merits of arguments for and against abortion, but only offering an example of a kind of dispute in which a good deal of careful thinking, as well as knowledge, would clearly be required to decide how significant this classification is.

One special, and familiar, form of classification is *grading*. Suppose we wanted to set up a simple grading system for ears of corn to be sold at retail (not converted into corn syrup, etc.). We might want to have three grades, A, B, and C. First we must single out those features of corn that we consider desirable, and that are generally acknowledged to be desirable (if we wish others to adopt our system): say, size of ear, fullness of ear, evenness of rows, tenderness, sweetness. Next, we must set standards for our three grades: for example, we would require that, to be Grade A, an ear of corn must have at least a certain size and degree of tenderness and sweetness, be filled out and have even rows. For Grade B we set the standards lower, and for Grade C lower still (or perhaps let Grade C cover all the rest). Now we have a classification-scheme, but of a special sort: a *normative one*. For we are assuming that the qualities chosen as our basis of division are desirable qualities, which confer value on corn to the extent to which they are present, so that we want Grade A to be a higher grade, to mark out better corn, than Grade B. Similiar considerations, of course, apply in the far more complex matter of grading students' work in specific courses A, B, C, etc. And the difficulties loom up: Can we get reasonable agreement on the qualities that are to be considered desirable? Can we be sure that we have measured them accurately in each case? Can we sensibly lump together a variety of performances (as in tests, papers, classroom discussions, creative work, etc.), which may in fact represent very different skills and talents? I am not arguing for or against grades in schools and colleges here, but emphasizing the point that, though grading is classifying, it brings in new problems that ordinary classification does not present.

Sometimes grading is done not by selecting minimum standards for each grade, but by setting up a number of diverse criteria for each grade, so that, for example, an ear of corn might still be Grade A even if the rows were a bit crooked, providing it were extremely sweet and tender. In such cases we do not have classes, strictly speaking, but something a little looser which might be called *clusters*. We shall say more about criteria in Chapter 6.

Each of us carries around an elaborate and constantly growing classification-scheme for sorting out experience—if we did not, we would find life even more confusing than it is. True, sometimes we encounter objects or people or events that don't fit our categories, and thus we are led to construct new ones; and we have to readjust our categories and their relationships as we learn more about how objects and people behave. Some of the categories in such a classification-scheme are fairly close together; others are rather remote: fish and traffic laws, revolutions and chromosomes, poems and sunflower seeds. Now, given any two categories, we can always compare their members in search of hitherto unnoticed similarities, and when the categories are remote, and such similarities less likely, the discovery of common properties is especially interesting and striking. It is the comparison of members of remote categories that gives rise to a kind of thinking that we have not yet considered: drawing an *analogy*.

An **analogy**, then, is a comparison between rather different kinds of things: To say that two pigs are both fat is not to analogize, but to say that the structure of a novel has something in common with the shape of an hourglass may be the start of an analogy. An analogy is also a somewhat complex comparison, not just in one respect but in several: The old analogy between the state, or "body politic," and the human organism was carried through elaborately, with political institutions and functions taken as parallel to the brain, heart, liver, digestive processes, etc. Some analogies are richer than others, in that they expose, or claim to expose, more common properties (and perhaps more interesting ones). Finally, an analogy nearly always involves not merely qualitative similarities (as when two things are both green), but structural or formal similarities as well: To liken the American economy to a delicate piece of machinery is to suggest that the relations among elements of the economy are the same sorts of relations as those between parts of a machine.

Analogies can often be exceedingly helpful to our thinking. They put an object in a new light, and suggest new hypotheses or generalizations that we might otherwise not have thought of. The oceanographer, puzzled about the discontinuous ridges and strange faults in the ocean floor that develop as the ocean floors slowly shift, may study a small tray of molten candle wax that is cooled by an electric fan. What happens to the wax does not prove anything about the ocean floor, but it helps him to develop better theories to test. When we speak of "noise pollution" (although this can be regarded as a metaphor, in a way we shall consider in Chapter 5), we suggest an analogy, even if we don't pause to work it out: The relationship between (a) the constantly-increasing and both psychologically and physically dangerous noisiness of our cities and (b) the optimal level of quiet required for work and comfort is in various ways like the relationship between (c) the hazardous chemicals introduced into the atmosphere by factory smoke, car exhausts, etc., and (d) the optimal level of air purity required for health. We must be careful not to push this analogy too far, by claiming similarities where none exist; but as far as it safely goes, the analogy may be fruitful in our thinking, and may encourage appropriate action, by getting us to consider noise in this way.

The logical problem about analogies appears when they are used in another way:

> Pornography has spread rapidly in recent years in this country, as smallpox would if there were no vaccination and no control by public health authorities. Like a disease, it brings no one any good (except the way a cold lets a lazy person "enjoy ill health" by giving him an excuse for not going to work, so he can stay home and waste his time). Like a disease, it does insidious harm, not only to the moral fibers of the person exposed to pornography, but to his character, for he can never completely recover. Those who have fallen victim to the infection of pornography need our help, as do people who have come down with pneumonia or diphtheria; and those who are deliberately spreading pornography for profit need to be quarantined at once. The conclusion is obvious and unassailable: pornography must be eliminated.

Here the writer is not merely presenting an analogy between pornography and disease: that each is harmful (he claims), that neither has positive value, that one can be "infected" by either, that both "infections" can be spread, etc. He is presenting the analogy to support a conclusion about pornography; in short, the passage is an **argument from analogy.**

The pattern of analogical argument is this:

X has properties $a, b, c, \ldots$
Y has properties $a, b, c, \ldots$
X also has the further property p.
- -
Y has the property p.

The principles underlying this form of inference are two: (1) Whenever X and Y (however remote the categories to which they belong) have a number of properties in common, if X is found to have a further property then probably Y has that property also. (2) The more properties X and Y have in common, the more likely it is that any further property found in X will also be found in Y. In the present case the property p is perhaps somewhat unusual: It is the property of *being something that ought to be eliminated.* The argument is supposed to be an inductive one, yet the conclusion does not seem to be either a generalization or a hypothesis; was I mistaken, then, in saying earlier in this chapter that there are only two forms of inductive argument?

I don't think so—but I must admit that there is some difference of opinion among logicians about the nature of arguments from analogy. The account I shall give seems to me the soundest, but dogmatism would be uncalled for. The argument from analogy, in my view, is indeed a distinctive form of argument, as I have formulated it; but is it not a cogent form of argument, and does not in fact give the conclusion any probability at all. It is plausible; it is a favorite in debate and polemic writing. It is something that you have to know how to handle. And it often contains the seeds of a really good argument, though to make those seeds grow we need to recast it in a more accurate form.

That the argument from analogy proves nothing by itself is easily shown. Suppose we happened to find that all diseases had names ending in the letter "a," that they all involved pain or discomfort to some degree, that they all attacked at one time or another some resident of Peoria. Does it follow that pornography, or pornographic works, have these characteristics? Indeed, since by definition an analogy compares rather fundamentally different objects, there *must* be many properties that each has and the other lacks—so no matter how many we find they have in common, we know that sooner or later we are going to find some others that they don't have in common. What makes an analogical argument plausible is always a hidden generalization; but when we make that generalization explicit, we can throw away the rest of the analogy. Suppose that to our abstract pattern above, we add a further assumption:

Everything that has *a* also has *p*.

Without that assumption, we have no good reason to conclude that *Y* has *p*. But *with* that assumption, we can forget about properties *b*, *c*, . . . , and reason as follows:

Y has property *a*.
Everything that has *a* also has *p*.

Y has property *p*.

This is clearly a *deductive* argument of a familiar sort. In the pornography case, most of the remarks about disease are colorful and interesting, but they make no logical contribution to supporting the conclusion. The relevant point is that pornography (allegedly) does harm but no good, and there is a suppressed premise:

Pornography does harm but no good.
[Whatever does harm but no good should be eliminated.]

Pornography should be eliminated.

There is much to question about this argument. Whether the first premise is true is a question that was gone into rather extensively by the Commission on Obscenity and Pornography that was authorized by Congress in 1967, was appointed by President Johnson in 1968, and presented its report in 1970—and the report casts a good deal of doubt on claims that this premise has been proved. The second premise could also be debated: It ignores, for example, enormous civil liberties problems, and seems to entail that cigarette smoking, gambling, and many other things should be prohibited. But one thing is sure: The conclusion follows necessarily from the two premises—and without any assistance from the analogy with disease.

In dealing with an argument from analogy, then, the first thing to point out is that it is no proof. Next, it may be in order to see whether the conclusion can be supported with the help of available generalizations: Perhaps the argument is miscast as an analogy, and there is a well-known and perfectly acceptable generalization that will give the same result without the analogy. Third, we can try to show the arguer, if he is still attached to his argument, why it won't work. There are various ways of doing this. One is to caricature his argument by extending it to the breaking point—as when I suggested above that all sorts of strange and implausible things might be proved about pornography by the same argument. This reduces the argument to absurdity. Another is to try to get him to withdraw the argument by showing that it can be used equally well to establish other conclusions that conflict with his own beliefs: For example, if he smokes cigarettes, we can show that cigarette smoking is like a disease, too, and should be eliminated. Another is to work on the significant points of divergence between the two things analogized, noting how different they are in what would seem to be relevant respects, so that the analogy cannot be relied on even to be very illuminating, much less a convincing reason for accepting the conclusion. For example, a person's choosing to read pornographic books or see pornographic films (unless he inadvertently tunes in on a cable TV channel that happens to be featuring them at the time) is a voluntary action, but whether he gets the measles is not; and if a person refuses vaccination or medical attention and as a result spreads some dread disease around to others, he is doing social harm, and is a public menace, but one who reads a pornographic book in the privacy of his own home is not thrusting his own tastes on others. This sort of rebuttal is not strictly necessary to destroy an analogical argument, but it may be necessary to help others understand why the argument will not work and why better reasons need to be given for the conclusion, if it is to stand.

A check-up quiz

Which of the following class-divisions (1) use more than one basis of division, (2) produce overlapping categories, (3) leave gaps?

1. Books: paperbound books and hardcover books.
2. Pretzels: soft pretzels and hard pretzels.
3. Pies: one-crust pies, two-crust pies, and mud pies.
4. Buildings: primarily business buildings and primarily residential buildings.
5. U. S. Presidents: great presidents, fair-to-good presidents, and bad-to-poor presidents.
6. Days: sunny days, rainy days, foggy days, cloudy days, and snowy days.
7. Pens: fountain pens, ball-point pens, and felt-tip pens.
8. Sources of energy: atomic fusion or fission, fossil fuels, and water.
9. Planets: those whose orbits are between earth and sun, and those whose orbits are beyond earth.
10. Clocks: electric clocks, mechanical clocks, dial clocks, and digital clocks.

OUTLINE-SUMMARY: chapter three

There are two basic forms of inductive argument: (1) generalization, (2) hypothesis.

In a *generalization argument,* the conclusion is a general statement, describing the distribution of some property among the members of a class; and the evidence supports the conclusion by reporting instances of it. (Each red barn is an *instance* of the generalization "All barns are red.") The class referred to in the generalization is the *target population;* the subclass which has been examined as a basis of the generalization is a *sample* of that population; the property in question is the *projected property.* The more assurance we have that the sample is representative of the whole population, the more probable the conclusion is; and this assurance is increased by the *size* of the sample, relative to the whole, and by the *spread* and *randomness* of the sample. To generalize from too small or biased a sample is to commit the fallacy of *hasty generalization.* A special case of this fallacy, in dealing with causal generalizations, is the inference that because one event follows another it must be an effect of it *(post hoc, ergo propter hoc).*

In a *hypothesis argument,* the conclusion is a singular statement, describing an event or state of affairs; and the evidence supports the conclusion by reporting other observed events or states of affairs that can be explained by the hypothesis. (The hypothesis, or explaining statement, "Someone left the freezer door open" explains the condition reported in the statement to be explained, "The freezer is heavily frosted.") The more superior a hypothesis is to alternative explanations of the same available facts, the more acceptable, or probable, it is; and the criteria of superiority are *frequency* (the statistical frequency of events of that sort) and *simplicity* (the fewness of the events and objects involved in the hypothesis). To accept a hypothesis when a more frequent and/or simpler one can readily be found is to commit the fallacy of *far-fetched hypothesis.*

To make a *classification* is to set forth the relationships among various classes, showing which are parts of, or subordinate to, others, and which are coordinate with others (as tablets and capsules are coordinate subclasses of pills). The principle of good classification is to insure that at every rank there is one and only one *basis of division* (that is, a single characteristic, such as race, color, or creed, in terms of which the division is made). A classification that violates this rule commits the fallacy of *cross-ranking.* A classification is *significant* if it brings together things that have a number of notable properties in common.

An *analogy* (as between organized crime and an octopus) is a complex similarity between two things that belong to basically different categories.

The *argument from analogy* reasons that because two things have a number of common characteristics, it is probable that a further characteristic found in one is also present in the other (because organized crime is like an octopus, and because an octopus has a single brain, then organized crime is directed by a single leader.) Such an argument is always fallacious as it stands, but it may suggest a valid deductive argument, if we already know a generalization that connects one of the common characteristics with the inferred one.

Exercise 13

Discuss the dependability of the following causal arguments. What weaknesses, if any, can you find? What important precautions may not have been taken? How could the arguments be strengthened?

1. Dear Dr. Steincrohn: I believe that my wife and I have discovered how to prevent colds. I was plagued with them for years. So was my wife. What we have been doing during the "cold" season for the past few years is taking two aspirin tablets before bedtime. We haven't had a cold since we started. Shouldn't doctors be recommending this procedure to their patients?

2. An eighth-grade science pupil conducted an experiment which seems to show that primroses thrive on classical music, though hard rock stunts their growth. Sue Jean Condon, 13 years old, said that every day for a month she played three hours of classical music to one primrose, rock music to another, jazz to a third, and country and Western to a fourth. A fifth, control primrose, had to make do with silence. Miss Condon reported that the plant nurtured on the classics grew better than the one reared in silence; the jazz and country and Western listeners experienced "slightly hampered growth," while the one subjected to rock suffered stunted height and fading blooms. Meanwhile, Mrs. Dorothy Retallack of Denver has been growing plants to music at Temple Buell College. Her experiments indicate that the plants respond favorably to Bach and to Ravi Shankar's classical Indian music. But when they hear acid rock, they cringe. They lean sharply away from the sound and die in a few weeks. Even their roots grow aslant, rejecting the music. Here is substantial evidence that growth of plants can be affected by music, and differently by different musical styles.

3. It is often argued by self-serving academics that academic freedom is indispensable for maintaining a good environment for learning and teaching, because unless different opinions are permitted to be expressed and defended, the truth, which is often elusive, will not emerge into the light of day. Moreover, it is claimed that in order to have academic freedom, university faculties must have the right to determine the qualifications for recruiting and promoting their members, since they are the "peer group" with the best qualifications to recognize talent in research and teaching, and are in the best position to defend freedom of inquiry

and freedom of discussion when it is threatened. But nothing could be farther from the truth than this hoary myth. For experience tells us over and over that giving faculties power over hiring and firing is no guartee that their members will teach or defend the truth, or even find any truth to share with the rest of us.

4. Do poor people living in the inner city pay more for groceries than people living in higher-income areas? Donald F. Dixon and Daniel J. McLaughlin, Jr., Professors of Marketing, conducted a study during the week of November 13, 1967, to settle this question. (They reported in the *Economic and Business Bulletin.*) Low income neighborhoods were defined by median income falling into the lowest eighth; in the selected inner city areas, 81 small neighborhood stores and 3 supermarkets were sampled, and in the higher-income areas 72 neighborhood stores and 84 supermarkets were sampled. A standard "market basket" list was set up, containing staple items of all kinds, from one pound of pork chops to a 12 oz. jar of peanut butter. The average prices for the market basket were as follows:

Area	Type of Store	
	Supermarket	Small Store
Higher income	$8.63	$9.38
Inner City	$8.54	$9.01

The nine cent difference in supermarket averages was judged too small to be significant since supermarkets in the higher-income area varied more than that amount. The thirty-seven cent difference in small-store averages is enough to suggest a slight tendency for small-store prices to rise with income of clientele. In any case, the researchers concluded that the inner-city poor are not charged higher prices by food retailers.

5. In South Africa, for example, a campaign was waged against hippopotamuses. Deemed useless beasts that merely cluttered up rivers, they were shot on sight. Result: the debilitating disease called schistosomiasis has become as great a public health hazard in certain areas as malaria was 50 years ago. As usual the missing links in the chain of events were discovered the hard way. It turns out that hippos keep river silt in motion as they bathe. When they heave themselves up riverbanks to dry land, they also go single file and act like bulldozers, making natural irrigation channels. Without the animals, the rivers quickly silted up; without the overflow channels, periodic floods swept like scythes over adjacent lands. The altered conditions favored a proliferation of schistosomiasis-carrying water snails. [*Time,* February 2, 1970]

6. I welcome this opportunity to testify before this Committee as an acknowledged authority on television and its psycho-behavioral effects. When the major networks, a few years ago, became concerned about

possible untoward effects on children of watching television violence, whether in dramatic form during the week, or in cartoons on Saturday morning, they felt that it would be a public service to allay the fears of parents about this matter, if the programs were really quite harmless. I was called in to conduct the research. I conducted interviews with 866 boys from seven to eighteen years of age, from different socio-economic levels and from both cities and suburbs. I selected several weekly story programs in which some shooting, fighting, and like forms of violence frequently occur, and I found subjects who watched them regularly for a month. After each watching, I sent them outdoors to play, but kept them under observation. Of course there was a good deal of scuffling and horse-play, as is natural to young boys who have been sitting still for a time, and occasionally someone would strike a belligerent pose in imitation of a hero of the video screen—thus suggesting the sublimating power of imaginative projection into dramatic fiction. But I found no evidence of excessive violence or violence-proneness.

Since these subjects were not engaged in criminal activities, or coming into the hands of the police, like so many boys, I concluded that, far from producing violent behavior, violent television programs may even inhibit it.

7. Sixty blue collar workers in a Kansas pet-food plant have been participating in an experiment with potentially enormous implications: Instead of specializing in assemblyline fashion, each gets a chance to shift around and do every major job in the processing plant, from unloading with a fork lift truck to making tests in the quality control laboratory. Each determines how to spend his time, free from supervision, and each is constantly learning new jobs or new aspects of jobs as he changes around. The workers are not bored, not alienated, not disaffected like so many American workers; the turnover rate is low and there are none of those random acts of spiteful sabotage that plague much American industry. Morale is excellent, This has been going on now for four months, and the conclusion is plain: rotation of jobs in this way significantly decreases worker boredom, and saves money, and it should be instituted everywhere.

8. Psychiatrist Glenn Wilson and Professors James Ausman and Thomas Mathews have demonstrated a close connection between conservatism of outlook and artistic taste. They asked an art expert to select twenty paintings in four categories: simple representational, simple abstract, complex representational, and complex abstract. Thirty young men and women were asked which paintings they would like to hang next to the favorite snapshot of Mom. After their artistic tastes were established, they were tested on a scale of conservatism with questions about the death penalty, evolution, abortion, the Bible, etc. Most conservatives preferred simple representational paintings, while most liberals preferred the more complex paintings.

Exercise 14

Examine the following pieces of inductive reasoning. Discuss the frequency and simplicity of the hypotheses in comparison with available alternatives, and give examples of evidence that would, if obtained, decide between them and their alternatives.

1, The Mayan Empire, an advanced and complex Central American civilization, collapsed about six centuries before the Spanish conquistadors came across the Atlantic; why it collapsed has long been a mystery. Dr. Frank Saul, a professor of anatomy, conducted an examination of bones from 90 skeletons unearthed by a Harvard University expedition to Guatemala, and identified numerous lesions due to specific disease, such as syphilis and vitamin deficiencies. He found a great variety of disorders, including several types of bone inflammation, indicating malnutrition, parasitic infestation, and childhood infections. He concluded that the decline of the Mayan civilization is to be explained by the ravages of malnutrition and disease.

2. The sudden upsurge of the student radical movement during the 1960s has bewildered many unintelligent people, but the explanation is obviously that given by Lewis Feuer in his brilliant book, *The Conflict of Generations: The Character and Significance of Student Movements.* It all goes back to the primal Oedipal conflict between sons and fathers, leading to a continued generational conflict that bursts into violent rejection of the older generation when the older generation "de-authorizes" itself and destroys its own authority, first by blundering, second by refusing to cover up its blundering, and third by failing to tough it out—instead, accepting blame and tearing its hair out in guilt over its failings. The student movement was basically a revolt against established authority, as symbolized in the father-figure. It was essentially violent, as the TV news reports have consistently shown us; for the student movements inevitably tended toward irrational ends and irrational means, in their desire—not to better the world—but to humiliate the older generation. The issues that the students claimed to fight for are of slight importance, which shows that they were only pretexts; and they always operated on the verge of fascism and authoritarianism, which are always symbolic attempts to grasp parental authority and power.

3. Why does the United States, of all Western democracies, have the lowest voter participation in its national elections? Although 139 million Americans were potentially eligible to vote in 1972—that is, they were at least eighteen years old and were not disqualified by criminal convictions or mental illness—around 30 million did not even bother to register, and another 24 million were registered but did not vote. There are, of course, many differences between the European democracies and the United

States, with its size and diversity of population, its decentralized governments, and the many difficulties it places in the way of registering to vote. But the basic explanation is a crisis of confidence: a widespread sense among the poor, the neglected, the disillusioned, and those, young and old, who are cynical about their government and their leaders. Only this could account for the continuing and serious voter apathy.

4. Although black major league baseball players have made enormous progress toward equal treatment since 1948 when Jackie Robinson broke the color line, the evidence is that persistent prejudice and discrimination are slowing further progress. In 1953 there were 20 black players; today there are about 100. But over all these years the mean batting average for black players has remained about 20 points above that of white players; the number of black pitchers has remained disproportionately small, compared to the numbers holding other positions; there have been extremely few black coaches, managers, and front-office executives. It seems that blacks who are box office stars can get fair treatment, but the average black player still has to be better than the average white player to get a chance, and there is pervasive unwillingness to let blacks occupy positions of leadership and responsibility.

5. Forty-five balloon flights were undertaken in 1971 to investigate conditions in the upper atmosphere that would indicate possible dangers in the operation of supersonic airplanes (the SST). One curious discovery was that during October, there was a sudden increase in the dust content (or "aerosol," as it is called) of the northern stratosphere to two and a half times its normal amount. This was explained by some experts as probably due to the eruption of a large volcano so remote from civilization that it escaped notice; some of the stratospheric aerosol consisted of sulphates, which could be of volcanic origin. More likely, it was due to a hurricane or (as they are called in the Pacific) a typhoon. Typhoons can sweep particles up into the stratosphere, and it was noted that the aerosol declined rapidly after October, during a hurricane season when there were almost no hurricanes.

6. The parallels between Lincoln's assassination and Kennedy's assassination are frightening. Both men furthered civil rights and were elected to office exactly a hundred years apart (1860, 1960). Lincoln's secretary, a man named Kennedy, advised him not to go to the theater the night he was killed; Kennedy's secretary, a woman named Lincoln, advised him not to go to Dallas, where he was killed. Booth shot Lincoln in a theater and fled to a warehouse; Oswald shot Kennedy from a warehouse and fled to a theater. The names "John Wilkes Booth" and "Lee Harvey Oswald" have the same number of letters; Booth was born in 1839; Oswald in 1939; and both were killed before coming to trial. The man who succeeded Kennedy was a Southern Democrat Senator named Johnson, born in 1908; the man who succeeded Lincoln was a Southern

Democrat Senator named Johnson, born in 1808; neither served a second term; and "Andrew Johnson" and "Lyndon Johnson" have the same number of letters. Some Power greater than we ordinarily are willing to acknowledge is clearly giving us a message which we fail to heed at our peril: we must do far better at creating full justice for all people in this country, or we shall have to undergo this traumatic experience every century.

7. Canada abolished the death penalty on December 29, 1967, and that explains the increase since that time in the number of murders in Canada. The recent figures are as follows:

1961–185	1967–282
1962–217	1968–315
1963–215	1969–346
1964–218	1970–432
1965–243	1971–425
1966–221	

True, the 1970 figure is inflated by a fire that killed 40 persons, and that was attributed to arson; but the increase since 1967 is surely significant.

8. Not many people have talked with the departed, even among alleged psychics; but the Rev. Arthur A. Ford, subject of a recent biography *The Man Who Talked With the Dead,* certainly did. It is now freely conceded that occasionally Ford would research his subjects, pasting up clippings which he memorized, checking in libraries, etc., so that he could bring out in his seances little-known facts and impress those who came to be put in touch with their dead husbands, wives, and friends. But this was only part of the story; he also brought back many genuine messages. In his famous platform appearance in London, introduced by Sir Arthur Conan Doyle, he brought many messages to people in the audience: "They send greetings and love"; "She says hold on and all will be well"; "Yes, the child is growing well in heaven, and asked me to tell you not to worry." In his famous seances with the late Bishop Pike, putting the latter in touch with his son who had recently committed suicide, Ford mentioned a nickname that a friend, Bishop Block, used to apply to himself ("ecclesiastical panhandler"), and the fact that he died during a church rite. As Mr. Allen Spraggett writes in his biography, "I think the evidence supports a hypothesis that Arthur Ford was a genuine gifted psychic who, for various reasons, scrutable and inscrutable, fell back on trickery when he felt he had to."

Exercise 15

Select a class of things that you happen to know something about (say, cars, furniture, rock songs, jokes, ways in which the government invades the privacy of citizens). First, draw up a list of several bases of division that could be used in classifying the members of this class. Second, select those bases of division that you consider the most significant, and explain briefly why you consider them significant. Third, choose a guiding purpose or point of view and explain why certain categories would be of special interest from that point of view. Fourth, make a classification with at least four ranks, taking care to avoid the fallacy of cross-ranking, and to make the categories on each rank mutually exclusive and as exhaustive as possible.

Exercise 16

Examine the following arguments from analogy. Exactly what does each assume, and what does it purport to prove? How would you reply to each of them?

1. Biologists are familiar with a "balanced aquarium." It is one with a sealed glass cover, which maintains itself for years without food being added and without being cleaned. It has plants to capture sunlight and produce energy-rich food, a rich bacteria flora in the sand, a few snails to graze. In perhaps five gallons of water, it can support only two tiny fish. If more are added, it falls into irreversible decay, the plants die, the water is fouled and the bacteria take over in massive numbers until their food, too, is depleted. Our world is that aquarium. We have too many fish in the tank, there is too much waste being produced, and the bacteria will likely reap a brief benefit if we don't act quickly. [Kenneth S. Norris, *The New Republic,* May 9, 1970]

2. Judge Michael A. Musmanno [of the Pennsylvania Supreme Court, which ruled in 1967 that Terry Southern's novel *Candy* could not be banned for obscenity in that state] also dissented and took his colleagues to task for saying that, although they allowed *Candy* to circulate, they did not approve of the book [the court's opinion said the book was "revolting and disgusting"]. "This is like saying," Judge Musmanno wrote, "that the court does not approve of a snake entering a nursery, but forbids anyone to build a fence around the nursery to keep the serpent out." [*The New York Times,* October 1, 1967]

3. Speaking as a representative of the National Funeral Director's Association, against certain increasingly common, but distressing, funeral practices, such as cremation, may I say that I agree wholeheartedly with our Executive Secretary of a few years back, who said, "A bodiless funeral is like a baptism without the baby, a wedding without the bride, or a birthday celebration without the birthday child."

4. The controversy over the sanctity of Stephen Girard's will as it applied to the acceptance of Negroes in Girard College [Philadelphia] brings to mind my great grandfather's last will and testament, dated November 10, 1859.

He wrote in his will, among other bequests, that Sam, his Negro slave, and all his children, grandchildren, and great grandchildren were bequeathed in trust, first to my grandfather, then to my father, and then to me. After my death, all descendents of Sam were to be free.

On December 18, 1865, a constitutional amendment was passed abolishing slavery within the United States. As a result of this amendment, my great grandfather's will was set aside as it applied to Sam, and my grandfather, my father, and I were deprived of our property rights.

If the provisions of Stephen Girard's will restricting admission to Girard College to white male orphans can be enforced today under our present antidiscrimination laws, I insist that all of Sam's progeny be turned over to me as my property. What is right for Stephen Girard is right for my great grandfather. [Letter to the *Philadelphia Bulletin,* November 19, 1966.]

5. The new safety automobile, which can (at least theoretically) leave you unharmed after a crash at fifty miles per hour, was designed by the Cornell Aeronautical Laboratory on one basic principle: a car is like a package which is supposed to deliver its human contents unharmed despite rough handling. From this they concluded that (1) the shipping case must be strong (i.e., the body of the car able to withstand crashes and roll-overs), (2) the lid of the package must be fastened tightly (i.e., the doors must be closed with three bolt bars so that no passenger can be thrown out), (3) the contents must be tightly packed (i.e., there must be bucket seats with a maximum support, and plenty of padding), and (4) hard objects must be removed from the packing (i.e., knobs, mirrors, and such protruding objects are to be removed).

6. As the famous criminal lawyer Edward Bennett Williams has remarked, "I think perhaps as lawyers we have done a bad education job in failing to get across to the public that lawyers should not be identified ideologically with their clients. Certainly doctors are not. Nobody says that Dr. Paul Dudley White is a Republican because he treated the President [Eisenhower] for his coronary trouble. Nobody would identify a doctor who treated Eugene Dennis for heart trouble as being sympathetic to Marxism. Nobody would criticize a clergyman because he gave counsel to the worst sinner.

"But when a lawyer gives his counsel to someone who has had the condemnation of society, people point and say what a shocking thing that this lawyer should be giving his counsel and services to this man who is so scorned and degraded."

7. Life, as we know it within the terms of our earthly prison, makes no ultimate sense that we can discover; but I cannot, myself, escape the conviction that, in terms of a larger knowledge than is accessible to us today, it does make such sense. Our position is simply that of the in-

telligent creatures confined to the ocean deeps. Now, however, that we are at last beginning to escape from our native confines, there is no telling what light we may find in the larger universe to dissipate the darkness of our minds. There is also the possibility that we may begin to populate new planets as, after 1492, we began to populate a new continent. Suddenly man's future seems boundless.

Of course we don't know what space exploration might lead to, or even whether it can come to anything at all. Would such uncertainty, however, provide a sufficient argument to justify the fish in remaining at the bottom of the ocean, once they had acquired the means to rise above it? I can imagine the debate that might go on in a deep-sea society between the traditionalists and the adventurous, but to me it is clear which side would represent progress, and the hope of the future. [Louis J. Halle, *The New Republic,* April, 1968.]

8. The security of a nation is comparable to the health of an individual. Though what counts as good health may vary to some extent, as from athletes to college professors, depending on the chosen life-style (and what counts as national security depends on the nation's life-style), still there are norms in both cases. Health and security are necessary conditions for success in any undertaking, whatever it may be; and the greater the ambition—in the individual, to succeed at great tasks; and in the nation, to take a vital part, meet vital challenges, provide vital leadership among other nations—the greater the need for soundness. We do not call a person who takes care of his health, who sees his doctor at regular intervals, takes his medicine, watches his diet, etc., a hypochondriac, but praise him for due care for the important basis of his life. So we should not condemn the Administration's great concern for protecting national security against threats from without and from within; but rather we should encourage it to take the greatest precautions against violations of secrecy (as in the unauthorized publication of the Pentagon Papers), to maintain its security classification (if the present system of forty or fifty distinct security classifications, such as "Top Secret," is not enough, more should be added), and to use any means necessary (whether wiretapping, bugging, burglary, etc.) to go after those whose words or actions make them a potential threat to national security.

chapter four

SOME PITFALLS OF LANGUAGE

Principles of deductive and inductive logic, which we have been studying up to this point, have to do with macrostructure of argument—the main connections that hold an argument together and give it its basic shape. Turning from logic to language, we must now consider the microstructure, or texture, of argument—the subtler, though no less important, connections among its smaller parts. We have to see how the wording of an argument helps or hinders its course, and how language can be managed so that it does not trip up our thinking, but enables it to be clear and cogent.

Some fallacies, as we have seen, are flaws of argument that arise from a wrong grasp of logical connections or a misapplication of logical principles. Others creep into discourse when we fail to realize the difference in meaning between one word and another, or when we confuse two concepts that ought to be kept distinct, or when we think we understand a piece of discourse but in fact misread it. These troubles can befall us when we try to construct arguments that can convince other people—or when we have to make up our minds about the convincingness of arguments presented by others. Only by careful attention to certain features of language can we avoid these errors; and the habit of noticing those features of language is something the critical thinker must acquire.

§ 10. Ambiguity

Most words in our language, except for technical terms that have recently been coined for special purposes, have a number of meanings, or senses. The word "joint," for example, can mean—among other things —(1) *place where two things are joined,* (2) *cut of meat for roasting,* (3) *hangout* ("Harry's joint"), (4) *small electric shock-producer* (applied by a jockey to a horse's neck to make it run faster in the homestretch), and (5) *marijuana cigarette.* There is very little danger of confusing these five senses, because the circumstances in which they would appear are so diverse. In the meat market, "joint" is practically certain to have sense (2); in the doctor's office, where tennis elbow or arthritis is being discussed, it will have sense (1). To use a word in a particular sense is to make part of an utterance of such a sort (and in such circumstances), that it can reasonably be understood in only one way.

Thus the senses of a word are subject to control by *context*—the words that precede or follow it in a particular discourse. The word "context" is itself deliberately vague here. Sometimes only a few other words are needed to fix the sense of a word: "joint of lamb." Sometimes the sense is affected by the whole discourse. The word "induction" means one thing in discourse on scientific induction (or a chapter like the preceding one), something quite different in a physics book dealing with electromagnetic induction, something still different in a Central Committee for Conscientious Objectors pamphlet dealing with induction into the armed services. There is a thread of meaning that runs through all three senses—which helps to explain how the same word got to be used for all three—but the overlap is thin. When we speak of induction into the armed services we refer to a particular procedure, which, taken as a whole, has very little in common with inductive arguments. So we do not speak of three *kinds* of induction here, as though we had a classification; rather, we speak of three *senses* of the *word* "induction."

The distinction between senses (of words) and kinds (of things) is not always easy to apply, but when in doubt approach it this way: If you can think of a clear-cut and reasonably restricted class to which all the things belong (for example, the class of joints of meat, of which lamb joints, beef joints, pork joints, etc., are subclasses), then you are confronted with kinds of things; but if you cannot find such a class (for example, a class that would include elbows, marijuana cigarettes, lamb joints, and neighborhood pool halls), then you are confronted with different senses of the word. A wooden board and a board of directors have too little in common to belong in the same classification-scheme—

the word "board" simply means different things in the two contexts.

A word can change its sense from context to context, within the same discourse—even quite rapidly. A speaker says, "If a manufacturer is not competent to make a profit without treating his workers badly, then he has no *business* being in *business*." The second "business" clearly means *commercial and/or industrial activity,* but the first "business" has to mean something like *proper or suitable activity.* Here the context has to be taken very narrowly, if we are to say that "business" is placed in two contexts, in the very same clause. More usually, such shifts of sense are caused by larger contextual pressures, from sentence to sentence, from paragraph to paragraph, or from chapter to chapter. We shall consider further examples in the following section.

Contexts may themselves roughly be classified according to their main subjects of discourse or the dominant interests of those who construct them: There is butcher-shop talk and there is counterculture talk (or rather there are several kinds of sub-counterculture talk). There is the technical discourse of computer specialists, police officers, surfers, racetrack habitués, rehabilitation counselors. A word that has different senses in different kinds of context is said to have **variable meaning.** The dictionary records various senses of a word, and often indicates the context in which some of the senses are operative: as law, mathematics, falconry, heraldry. And it distinguishes the senses by providing synonyms of the word. A synonym of a word is another word or phrase that has a closely similar meaning in a certain kind of context. "Husband" is synonymous with "male spouse" in nearly all English noun contexts; "pot" is synonymous with "pan for boiling food" in kitchen talk, but not always elsewhere.

Synonyms enable us to mark clearly similarities and differences of meaning. Although statements do not have senses, in the way words (or phrases) do, they do have **truth-conditions**; that is, we can specify what facts about the word would make the statement true, rather than false. "*X* is *Y*'s husband" is true if (1) *X* and *Y* have been legally wed and (2) *X* is a man. "It is now exactly three o'clock" is true if the official chronometer in the National Bureau of Standards now reads three o'clock. When we remove a word from a statement, and substitute another word, we get a second statement; and the second statement may or may not have the same truth-conditions as the original statement. If we have preserved the truth-conditions, we have substituted a word with the same meaning; and if we have substituted a word with the same meaning, we have preserved the truth-conditions.

Thus suppose we have two statements, and the same word appears in each. Perhaps we can think of various synonyms of that word. If we find one synonym that we can substitute for it in one of the statements without changing its truth-conditions, but cannot substitute for it in the other sentence without changing its truth-conditions, then we have good reason to think that the original word was used in different senses in the two statements.

(1) The *conclusion* of the argument was surprising.

(2) The *conclusion* of the play was surprising.

A conclusion of a play has something in common with a conclusion of an argument, but, after all, one is a happening of some kind (the kindly old man turns out to be the multiple murderer after all), and the other is a statement. Suppose we try the following substitutions:

(1′) The *statement alleged to follow from the premises* of the argument was surprising.

(2′) The *statement alleged to follow from the premises* of the play was surprising.

Sentence (1′) is fine, but (2′) makes little or no sense, since plays don't contain premises. We could go the other way:

(2″) The *final event* of the play was surprising.

(1″) The *final event* of the argument was surprising.

Again, the second substitution won't do.

This procedure is not an unassailable proof that the senses of "conclusion" in (1) and (2) are different, because it is just possible that the synonyms we hit upon were hypersensitive to these very changes of context, and changed their own meanings as they moved from one context to another. And it is even harder to show that a word has the same sense in two contexts. Consider:

(3) The *conclusion* of the play was surprising.

(4) The *conclusion* of the novel was disappointing.

If we can find a synonym of "conclusion" that is an equally satisfactory substitute in both sentences, we have some reason to think that the word is being used in the same sense in both:

(3′) The *final event* of the play was surprising.

(4′) The *final event* of the novel was disappointing.

This synonym seems to work: The original truth-conditions remain. But again, the proof is not assailable. We might have hit upon a synonym whose sense happens to vary in the same way as the original word. However, if we try two or three plausible synonyms, and they all work, we can be fairly sure that we have established close similiarity of sense. And this is often very obvious: When we say a car is blue and a dress is blue, we are clearly not changing the sense of "blue," though when we add that a piece of music is blue and that a person is blue, we surely are changing the sense of "blue." This will all be clearer in the light of distinctions to be made in the following chapter.

So far in this section, the contexts we have examined have exerted enough control over the word we were interested in to insure that it had one and only one sense in that context. Only one of its senses was demanded, or permitted, by the context, so that sense was picked out from its repertory of possible senses, and the others were set aside. But it also commonly happens that this contextual control is not complete, and more than one alternative is still left open. When a word can have either (but not both) of two (or more) distinct senses in a certain context, we shall say that the word is **ambiguous** in that context. And, more broadly, we can say that the sentence that contains that word is an ambiguous sentence.

The ambiguity of a word (or a phrase, though I shall not stop to emphasize this at every point) is always relative to a context: no word is ambiguous in itself. Ambiguity is quite a different thing from variability of meaning (multiplicity of senses). Some words with variable meaning are also ambiguous in some contexts, or in some kinds of context; but there are many other words whose meanings vary considerably from one kind of context to another, but which are hardly ever ambiguous ("bolt," "fix," "frame"). Take "joint": You can construct a very short sentence in which it is ambiguous, but just by adding a word or two (such as "body," "lamb," "Harry's," "jockey," or "smoke") you will eliminate the ambiguity completely.

Ambiguity presents a choice: We are invited to decide between two available senses, and we can't have it both ways. If we are told that "Jones was a poor street-cleaner," we can interpret the statement as saying (1) that he was a street-cleaner living in poverty, or (2) that he was an incompetent street-cleaner. But we do not assume that he was *both* poverty-stricken and incompetent. Ambiguity is ambivalence of meaning. We have **multiple meaning**, on the other hand, when the word, or the sentence in which it occurs, has more than one sense in a particular context. Puns exploit this possibility: "How to make a sponge cake: borrow all the ingredients." That may not be much of a pun (what pun is?), but it has the essential element: to grasp it, we must keep in mind both senses of "sponge" and try to enjoy the pun's taking advantage of the fortuitous conjunction of these senses in the same word. This is a case of double meaning—a *double entendre* without the sexual wit.

Poetry, of course, makes the most of multiple meaning; when Hamlet says

> The time is out of joint; O cursed spite,
> That ever I was born to set it right!

we cannot understand his metaphor unless we bear in mind the literal sense of his words (as when a bone slips from its socket) as well as a number of metaphorical senses Hamlet applies to the situation he faces in Denmark: that the natural junctures holding the social fabric together have been violated, that the result is paralysis of the state's functions, that drastic surgery or at least stern measures will be needed to "set it right." (More will be said of metaphor in the following chapter.)

It is a pity that we are up against a certain variability of meaning in the term "ambiguity" itself, which is often used as a synonym of "multiple meaning." Since you and I are in no position to legislate other people's uses of words, but can only make recommendations of obviously sensible uses, you will have to be on guard. If you read William Empson's *Seven Types of Ambiguity* (1930), for example, you will note that what he is concerned with is, by and large, what I am calling "multiple meaning." Two such very different linguistic phenomena as unsettled meaning and extra meaning surely deserve to be marked by clearly distinct terms. For ambiguity is an infirmity in almost any discourse, though it counts more heavily against some kinds of discourse than others; but multiple meaning is one of the chief glories of poetry, and indeed is a value in many kinds of discourse, so long as it is managed well.

The varied ways in which a context can fail to fix meaning decisively are classified under two general and convenient headings to yield two types of ambiguity, which are well worth distinguishing because their causes and cures are so different. Words have two fundamental aspects, in being essentially related both to each other and to things that exist, or that might exist, in the world outside of language. When we say that a word means something, or refers to something, or has various senses, we are talking about the *semantical* aspect of the word. When we say that a word is an adverb or preposition, that it takes a direct or indirect object, or that it is singular or plural, we are talking about the *syntactical* aspect of the word, in short, its grammar. Contextual control, when it is weak, can make us doubtful about either of these aspects of a word—its sense or its syntax.

A word (or any piece of language) is **syntactically ambiguous** in a certain context if there is more than one way, consistent with that context, of construing its grammatical relationships. Syntactical ambiguity arises in several familiar ways. Any attempt to condense information through elliptical syntax takes a risk—which is why so many headlines are ambiguous. Was Richard Nixon the first president to visit China? Yes and no; he was the first to make a presidential visit (i.e., visit while he was president); but not the first person who was president and who also visited China (that was Ulysses S. Grant). A "small college faculty member" may be (1) a faculty member of a small college, (2) a member of a small faculty of a college, (3) a small member of a college faculty. There's no way to tell unless it is spelled out more fully. When a celebrated civil liberties lawyer who has been for years active in the cause of abolishing capital punishment remarked some years ago that he and his colleagues were "very pleased that 1968 marked the first year that no person was executed in this country," we know what he wanted to say, but we also can see that he didn't quite succeed in *not* saying something else he didn't want to say. Recasting:

> We were very pleased that no person was executed in this country in 1968, the first year in which this was true.
> We were very pleased that 1968 is, so far, the only year in which no person was executed.

We have syntactical ambiguity when there is doubt about the antecedent of a pronoun: "The National Mining Company has contracted with the American Mining Company to supply 7,500 tons of its zinc"—but who is selling the zinc to whom? Certain key words like "only" are sometimes placed so as to keep two possible interpretations of a sentence in delicate balance. In recent years (especially around the time of the Pueblo affair in 1969), there has been uninformed discussion of the military "Code of Conduct" that is supposed to govern the behavior of captured military personnel. General S. L. Marshall (retired), one of its original drafters, has had to explain from time to time that when Article V (quoting the Geneva convention of 1949) says that a prisoner is "bound" to give "only rank, name, age, and serial number," it does not mean that he is bound to give no more than this information, but that he is bound to give no less. Perhaps the code is not as free from syntactical ambiguity as its drafters thought—though as General Marshall has noted, the so-called Spartan interpretation (that the captive should not talk at all) is somewhat at odds with the larger context, which pledges the captive not to talk about "things hurtful to the cause of the country or to allies or fellow prisoners."

It is usually not difficult to clear up syntactical ambiguity, once we recognize that it is present: We must make the grammatical relationships determinate and explicit, perhaps changing the order of words, supplying the antecedent of a preposition, giving the verb a different voice, filling in an ellipsis. The result may lack some of the neatness and epigrammatical quality of the original, but it will at least be susceptible of only one interpretation, so that what the reader understands it to mean is just what the writer understands it to mean.

A word or phrase is **semantically ambiguous** in a certain context if there is more than one sense that it can have in that context. A local columnist reports:

> Embarrassed officials of the Acme Roofing Company are concerned about continuing reports that their own roof, despite all their efforts, continues to drip water every time it rains. The word is that they are trying to plug the leak.

Is "the word" that they are trying to stop the literal leak in the roof or the metaphorical leak of embarrassing information? We cannot be sure without a larger context.

> The legislature passed the anti-obscenity act after stormy controversy in the public press. The American Civil Liberties Union was vigorously opposed.

"Opposed" can mean here (1) in opposition to the bill or (2) attacked by others on account of its view. This is one way of exposing the ambiguity; by substituting two synonyms of the ambiguous term, each bearing one of the two senses, we get two new sentences, both unambiguous. The original ambiguity is not removed, for the context still does not enable us to choose decisively between the two senses; but at least we know what the alternatives are.

As a living language develops and changes, semantic ambiguities may appear or disappear. For example, Article II, Section 4, of the United States Constitution says that civil officers of the United States (including the President and Vice President) "shall be removed from office on impeachment for, and conviction of, treason, bribery, or other high crimes and misdemeanors." With a special sense of "misdemeanor," as contrasted with "felony," well-established in present-day statutes and legal practices, this article may be said to have become somewhat ambiguous—and it certainly has given rise to a good deal of puzzled discussion. But probably it was not ambiguous (though it was undoubtedly somewhat vague) when written, for in the eighteenth century "misdemeanor" could cover seriously wrong actions—including a (not necessarily criminal) failure to carry out the duties of the office.

Most cases of ambiguity can be quite readily classified as syntactical or semantical. But we have to leave room for some mixed cases. The best procedure in dealing with ambiguity seems to be to begin by considering the syntax. In some cases, if we rewrite the syntax in two ways, we eliminate all ambiguity and bring out the two meanings clearly. Then we have pure syntactical ambiguity.

> *A:* "Our dog is just like one of the family."
> *B:* "Which one?"

B's reply is a bit stupid, of course, but it does show that *A*'s remark can be understood in two ways:

> *A′:* "There is a member of our family whom our dog is just like."
> *A″:* "Our dog is treated, and deserves to be treated, like any member of the family."

Of course we could think of more drastic ways of rewriting, and they might be still clearer; but they are not necessary. It is true that "like" has different senses, so that some semantical ambiguity is involved, so to speak, in the syntactical ambiguity; but once the latter is cleared up, the former disappears.

In other cases, we do not need to change the syntax at all, but simply substitute two different synonyms for the troublesome word. Then we have pure semantical ambiguity. A labor contract might read:

> Every effort should be made to resolve grievances at an early stage through informal discussions with the lowest-level officials who can resolve the issue.

If the contract were carelessly written, and "grievance" not defined, a serious ambiguity might result: Are all complaints classified as grievances, or only those that allude to the terms and conditions of the labor agreement under which the employees are working? We have, then:

> (1) Every effort should be made to resolve *complaints of objectionable treatment by the company* . . .
>
> (2) Every effort should be made to resolve *complaints that the company has violated the labor agreement* . . .

There still remain some cases where the syntax needs to be juggled, and yet when its problems are straightened out, some semantic ambiguity remains. These are the mixed cases. If we hear about Mr. Jones, "the elusive bug expert," we can sort out the syntactical readings easily enough:

> (1) the expert on elusive bugs.
>
> (2) the elusive expert on bugs.

But "bugs," for all we can tell, may still mean either "insects" or "electronic eavesdropping devices" (especially in the first phrase), so the semantical ambiguity remains. This example has to be somewhat artificial, in order to be brief; but mixed ambiguity occurs more subtly in longer passages.

Crude as it is, this example, like some of the preceding ones, raises an important question. Often, we can discern two possible readings, but we can also perceive that, in such context as we are given, one is a good deal more far-fetched than the other. It is hard to think of circumstances under which we might be talking about bug experts, where it would not be perfectly obvious that one of these senses is much more appropriate and sensible than the other. We can speak of *degrees of prominence* of such alternative meanings. And we can note, first, that when one of the alternatives is not at all prominent, but has to be reached for and nudged into the limelight, the ambiguity is not likely to be very troublesome; and, second, that the recessive sense may still be worth noting, because later in the discourse, when the context changes, it may become more of a live option, at least enough to mislead a reader who is not on his guard.

One who speaks or writes an ambiguous sentence has in effect failed to say what he wanted to say (even if he thinks he has succeeded), because he has not narrowed down the options to the point where his sentence means just what it was supposed to mean. The danger is, first, that he will think he has said exactly what he wished to say, and hence is unprepared to be misunderstood; but, second, that someone else may seize upon the other possible meaning, without realizing that it is not the only one, and take the speaker or writer to be saying something very different indeed from what he had in mind. When both are good at spotting ambiguities, in their own words or those of others, and recognize the present ambiguity before it is too late, there may still be a chance of restoring communication, if the context can be expanded by further interchange. If the ambiguous author is no longer accessible, however, we can only note that the ambiguity is there and hence the message remains indeterminate. We cannot agree or disagree, because nothing definite has been said.

A check-up quiz

Which of the following headlines are syntactically ambiguous? Which are semantically ambiguous?

1. U. S. BICENTENNIAL TO BE CELEBRATED WITHOUT FANFARE
2. REVOLTING POLICE TAKE OVER BOLIVIA
3. CHARM EXPERT ADVISES COOKING PARTY GUESTS

4. LINCOLN TUNNEL IS UNDER WATER
5. RADIOACTIVITY PERIL TO EGGS, HENS REPORTED
6. THREE MASKED MEN STEAL $100,000 ON WAY TO BANK
7. MOTHER SLAIN WITH AX BEFORE 2 CHILDREN
8. NUCLEAR-DUG HOLE WEIGHED
9. POLICE ORDERED TO STOP DRINKING AFTER MIDNIGHT
10. VENTO HATED SLAYING VICTIM, JURORS TOLD
11. WOMAN FIGHTS OFF MAN WITH KNIFE
12. DILWORTH TOURS SOCIETY HILL TO CHECK ITS GROWTH
13. RATS IN LABORATORY ARE FOUND TO SMELL
14. JOHNSON URGES WORLD DRIVE ON EDUCATION
15. MARINE CORPS RESERVE STAMPS OUT TUESDAY
16. DR. KANDLE DECLARES NEW JERSEY MUST PUT $450 MILLION INTO SEWERS
17. FREE PONY RIDES THREATENED HERE
18. 3 FIREHOUSES TO BE CLOSED FOR EFFICIENCY
19. MOTOR VEHICLES IN STATE HIT 2,487,770 LAST YEAR
20. GERMAINE GREER LOSES APPEAL

§ 11. Equivocation

When a word shifts its meaning within a particular discourse the shift may be quite harmless, if it is plainly marked and the reader is alert; but when that discourse happens to be an argument, the shift may be disastrous from a logical point of view. We would have no quarrel with someone who reasoned in this way:

All cats are animals.
Fluff is a healthy cat.
———
Fluff is a healthy animal.

But what about the following deductive argument, which is exactly the same, except for one small word?

All cats are animals.
Fluff is a large cat.
———————————
Fluff is a large animal.

This won't do at all.

The trouble with the second argument is easy to spot, though not so easy to describe precisely. The adjective "healthy" divides the class of cats more or less cleanly (there are of course degrees of health) into two subclasses, and it also divides the class of animals into two subclasses, in such a way that the healthy cats all belong in the class of healthy animals. But the adjective "large" behaves in a more complicated way, since it reflects an implicit comparison. A large cat is a cat that is large for a cat; a large elephant is an elephant that is large for an elephant. So the actual size that is meant by "large" depends on the noun it is attached to, that is, the class in question. Not even the largest cat is among the largest animals. In short, "large" shifts its sense in the course of this argument, and in such a way that the conclusion cannot validly be drawn.

But isn't the second argument a syllogism? No, it is not a syllogism; it has too many terms. It is time we gave a more exact meaning to this term "term," which we made use of in Chapter 2. A *term* is not just a word or phrase, but a word or phrase *taken in a certain sense.* "Joint" is the same word, whether it is used in discussing lamb or marijuana, but since it has two senses (among others), we count it as two distinct terms, one for each of its distinguishable senses. A word that is ambiguous in a certain context is not strictly a term, for it does not yet have a definite and determinate sense at all, but hovers between two senses until one of them is fixed by a fuller context. "Sentence" and "statement" are best used in a parallel way: A statement is a sentence with a certain set of truth-conditions. When you say, "I'm hungry," and I say, "I'm hungry," we utter the same sentence, but we are saying different, and indeed logically independent, things. Thus two statements are made, which have different truth-conditions, since they refer to different persons.

Our second argument above, then, involves four classes (besides Fluff): cats, animals, cats over a certain (average?) size, animals over a certain (but different) size. So it is not a syllogistic argument, nor is it valid by any other rules. An argument in the course of which some word or phrase shifts its sense so that the conclusion does not follow commits the **fallacy of equivocation**. And the offending word is the equivocal word. It does not matter whether the shift is intentional or unintentional; a debater might equivocate deliberately, or he might fall into the fallacy inadvertently or unwittingly. It does not matter whether the person addressed in the argument is actually deceived. If there is a shift, and if the shift has a bearing on the logical soundness of the argument, then there is equivocation.

The most pernicious equivocations are those that develop through fairly long discourses, where the shift of sense can be gradual and hence less likely to be noticed. Short summaries of such arguments are often somewhat implausible, because the senses, when sharply juxtaposed, are glaringly different. This is a good reason for summarizing arguments when you want to analyze them carefully and critically.

Another source of trouble is that the equivocal word may not be featured very prominently in the discourse, or may be glided over hastily, so that we neglect to stop and take a close look at it. Consider an argument that has been made in recent years (by Vance Packard, among others) that there is very little "upward mobility" for working Americans, despite the promises of the "American Dream." What is involved in the concept of upward mobility? First, you have to think of society as divided into classes, defined in some social and/or economic terms; and second, you have to think of them as hierarchically ordered, as status classes, so you can say that when *X* is in Class *K*, and *X*'s son or daughter moves into Class *L*, there has been upward (or downward) mobility. Now, how many classes are there? This is a central question for sociologists, and different sociologists divide things up differently, as we might expect. But of course the fewer classes in your social classification-scheme, the less mobility there will be. *X*'s son or daughter might make a great deal more money, change to a very different "life-style" (as they say), and think of himself as having made it; but if we distinguish only two social classes, he may still be in the same one as *X*. On the other hand, if we set up a scheme with ten social classes, then relatively slight changes in income, tastes, way of life, or whatever, will count as movement from one class to another.

It is not my intention to turn this book into a work of sociology, but only to give an example of how equivocation works on a large scale. Mr. Packard's book, *The Status Seekers,* has been criticized on the ground that when he is arguing that the United States of America is a highly status-conscious society, he conceives of that society as divided into several classes; but when he argues that there is very little occupational mobility, he works with very few classes. Perhaps the criticism is not deserved; in any case, the fallacy is an interesting and instructive possibility. For any change in the way one classifies society really is a change in the meaning of "upward mobility," since "upward mobility" means (roughly) "movement from a lower to a higher status class." If an argument slips from one meaning of "upward mobility" to another, and depends on this slip to make its conclusion plausible, then there is equivocation.

Perhaps no more depressing and persistent equivocation has been committed over the years than that involving the term "natural," in discussions of the equality of the sexes and the differentiation of sex roles in society. "Natural" is of course a very rich word, and we need its various meanings, though not all in the same word. It means one thing as opposed to the supernatural (what is not in space and time), another thing as opposed to what is artificial (what is made by human beings), another thing as opposed to the rare or infrequent, another thing as opposed to what is called "unnatural," in the value sense (what is undesirable, like a two-headed calf). There are various sorts of argument that get what plausibility they have from equivocation on "natural." If they were put in a summary fashion, they would not be very plausible:

(1) The average woman is less qualified to perform action *X* than the average man (where *X* may be anything that seems to make this premise true, such as weight-lifting).
(2) *Therefore:* Doing *X* is more natural to men than to women.
(3) *Therefore:* It is unnatural (unsuitable, un-rolelike) for women to do *X*.

The second statement is the pivotal one. If it is to follow the first statement, "natural" must mean just "frequently possible"; but if it is to yield the third statement, "natural" must mean "desirable." "Natural" is thus ambiguous in statement two; it connects in one sense with what precedes it, and in another sense with what follows. The ambiguity facilitates the equivocation.

But this maneuver is too obvious. We need to imagine (since we cannot supply it here) a chapter of one of those anti-feminist books almost at any time during the past hundred years and more, in which it is argued at great length that women are, as a group, at least in modern Western societies, different in some way from men, as a group. Of course nothing follows from this about what *individual* women should or should not do, or may or may not be qualified to do. It is equivocation, drawn out over many pages, and supported with appeals to fear, prejudice, religion, and immemorial custom, that steers the argument to the illegitimate conclusion.

The subject is complex, of course, and again it is not substantive issues but modes of argument that primarily concern us here—although while we are considering arguments, we may as well consider some arguments about things that matter. I cite one other variation on the same theme, again schematically:

All societies known to us distinguish man-roles from woman-roles.
Therefore: To make such a distinction is natural.
Therefore: The sex-roles assigned in our society are natural.
Therefore: It is unnatural (undesirable, unthinkable) that anyone should reject or even question our society's sex-roles.

One kind of equivocation involves two people who are disputing with each other: one makes a statement using a word in one sense, and the other replies in a statement that twists the word into a different sense. Again, the equivocation can be done on purpose or out of carelessness. Sometimes the equivocal reply is a way of pretending to give an argument against the original assertion, without actually doing so. Sometimes it is an attempt to give a relevant argument, but it misfires because of a confusion between different senses of the key word. When that famous television show, *Laugh-In*, finally folded after six years, many people regretted its passing, but some criticized it, saying that it had lost its healthy irreverence. To which Dan Rowan replied "What they don't understand is that there is nothing left to revere in this country, so it's pretty hard to be irreverent." There's not enough of a context to be sure of equivocation here, but one should not put it past Mr. Rowan to have the last laugh. Setting aside the merits of the questions at issue, it seems likely that "irreverent" in the original criticism meant something like "taking lightly what some people actually revere." And it is quite plain that in the response, "irreverent" means something like "taking lightly what ought to be revered." If we leave out the word "irreverent" altogether, and recast the bit of dialogue in synonymous terms, we get:

> *Critic:* *Laugh-In* has lost its healthy custom of taking lightly what some people actually revere.
>
> *Rowan:* Since there is nothing that ought to be revered, *Laugh-In* could not be expected to take lightly what ought to be revered.

The reply is simply beside the point, and this is easy to see once the equivocal word is out of the way. Whether the critic's criticism is true or false, and whether Rowan's reply is true or false, remain open questions; in any case, the statements appear to be logically independent of each other.

For a somewhat more serious example, consider this:

> *A:* What I find so exasperating and unsatisfying about' contemporary visual art is that it is simply not sincere: The painters seem to paint less from what they feel in their hearts and need to express than from a desperate desire to startle and shock, to gain notoriety by starting some new and short-lived movement.
>
> *B:* I disagree. What you overlook is that present-day painters, more than any of their predecessors, paint what they want to paint, and are free to follow their own inclinations and wishes. What could be more sincere than that?

A seems to be saying that the artists are not sincere, meaning by "sincere" something like "given to expressing emotions one really feels." *B* seems to be replying that the artists are sincere, meaning by "sincere" something like "given to painting the way one wants to paint." *B*'s assertion thus is not in any way incompatible with *A*'s, nor is it a reason for not believing *A*'s. Indeed, there is no real dispute between them. They affirm and deny the same sentence:

> *A:* The artists are not sincere.
> *B:* The artists are sincere.

But they do not affirm and deny the same *statement*. Since "sincere" means such different things, the dispute is merely verbal, i.e., one that is not genuine, but seems genuine because of equivocation.

When we discover that a dispute is merely verbal, and explain to ourselves exactly in what way it is verbal, we have not, of course, resolved any of the issues involved. We have merely gotten the dispute back on the track, so that it can proceed to the point. *A*'s statement still remains unchallenged, and if *B*'s first response is logically irrelevant, perhaps he will succeed next time around in giving a real rebuttal. Or perhaps he cannot. In any case, we will at least know whether or not a rebuttal has been given.

A check-up quiz

Which of the following arguments involve equivocation? Point out the equivocal words, and explain their shift in meaning.

1. Surely it is obvious that patriotism—simple affection and regard for one's own land—is good, and should be encouraged. How, then, can people be so lacking in patriotism as to criticize their own country and even denounce its actions abroad, implying that other countries might be right when they disagree with us?

2. Increased trade with Russia and China is bound to be advantageous for all parties concerned; for it will be an advantage to the Russians to buy much-needed wheat and other grains, to the Chinese to buy machines and electronic gear, and to the Americans to buy such raw materials as oil and minerals.

3. The Congressman has been attacked for various shady deals, dubious involvements, lobby-directed votes, but in politics you have to consider honesty in terms of the prevailing standards; and by these standards he is honest (that is, well above the average politician in personal integrity and moral accountability). But, as has been said, "an honest man is the noblest work of God," and that's our Congressman. Since he is honest, he is worthy of our trust; and since he is worthy of our trust, we should get out and vote for him.

4. The President's claim to executive privilege when it comes to the question of allowing his staff members to testify in Congressional investigations is wholly unwarranted. Why should the President, even if he is the Chief Executive, have privileges that ordinary citizens do not have?

5. The world is not better for A. J. Muste's having been in it. If it were, it would be better than it was eighty-two years ago; and it isn't. There doesn't seem to be much good that a man can do, not even if he spends a long life at it. [Milton Mayer in *The Progressive*.]

§ 12. Vagueness

Assertive discourse is chiefly—though by no means solely—used for the communication of ideas. Thinking can only be done by individual persons, but generally speaking the best thinking is likely to be done by individuals who can share some of their thought-processes with others—drawing on other persons' ideas as premises for reasoning or as leads to new hypotheses, and passing on ideas to others who can examine them critically, more impartially, to see whether they hold up in the light of broader experience.

The communication of ideas can be frustrated or prevented in various ways—not least by government censorship. But we are concerned at the moment with significant features of language in which ideas are expressed, and four of these features can be serious hindrances to communication.

First, there is ambiguity, which we have already discussed. When a discourse is ambiguous, it leaves the reader (or listener) unable to choose between alternative possibilities of interpretation. He can wait for, or request, a further message that will provide a context large enough to remove the ambiguity. Sometimes he can say: "If it means this, then it is false, for the following reasons; if it means that, then it may be true, though it hasn't yet been proved." But until the discourse succeeds in meaning one thing, to the exclusion of the other, it is not to be considered seriously.

The second source of trouble is **obscurity**. Some discourses are more difficult to comprehend than others; if the key words are unfamiliar (they may be technical terms of, say, epistemology), or if the syntax, however correct, is highly complex (as in Kant's *Critique of Pure Reason*), we may have to make a considerable effort to grasp what is being said. But obscurity is difficulty that is due to faulty style—to the misleadingness of the syntax or to clashes between implicit meanings of the words. The notions of "misleadingness" and of "implicit meanings" will be made clearer in the following chapter, but a few samples will serve our present purposes. There is of course the language of "Bureaucratese," which is often deplored but still flourishes.

> No further conditional commitments will be issued except pursuant to firm reservations of contract authority issued to developers on or before the close of business last Friday, until further notice from the Secretary. No further fund reservations will be made except in accordance with instructions to follow from the Secretary. Firm commitments may be issued pursuant to outstanding conditional commitments and conditional commitments issued pursuant to reservations of contract authority made before close of business Friday . . . .

This "directive" was sent out from the office of George Romney, Secretary of Housing and Urban Development, to HUD field units, in January, 1973—as part of the Administration's cutback in its housing program. Now, part of the difficulty does lie in technical terms that would be understood by those familiar with the operations of HUD: "conditional commitment," "contract authority," "fund reservation." But the concepts are also choked together in sentences with too many modifying phrases and clauses, and they are introduced in an order that does not clearly reflect the actual order in which the processes would take place in funding new housing.

A delightfully baffling passage comes from a newspaper in New Jersey:

> Charles W. Bogert, borough clerk, announced yesterday that there seemed to be some confusion about the days when the scavenger firm picked up the extra material cleaned out by householders. The confusion is presumably due to an earlier announcement that scavengers would make the cleanup pickup on the last collection day of each month.
>
> That this was not completely accurate was explained by Mr. Bogert, who said that if the last pickup day of the month fell also on the second pickup day of the week, that would be the day for picking up the cleanup material, but if the last collection of the month was made on Monday, Tuesday or Wednesday the cleanup pickup would not be made then but on the previous Thursday, Friday or Saturday. In other words, if the last pickup day of the month was the first pickup day of the week it would not be a special pickup day—and if anyone needs a clearer explanation, perhaps he'd better ask the scavenger on his route.

It is an interesting question what makes this so difficult to read. The answer is quite complicated, but a few points are especially noteworthy. The term "cleanup pickup" is a highly condensed abbreviation for "the collection of objects that householders wish to throw away but are too large or heavy for inclusion in ordinary trash." The explanation of the regulation is, on the other hand, far too wordy and roundabout: The central idea seems to be that there are two trash collections each week (one in the first half, the other in the second half), and that cleanup objects will be taken on the last collection day of the month that falls in the second half of the week. Maybe you can find a way to say it more simply and straightforwardly than that.

The third potentially troublesome feature of discourse might be called **relative indefiniteness**. Any attempt to impart information will, of course, have to leave out something: If you tell me that your brother has joined the police force, you haven't told we what police force, when, why, etc. If I happen to know your brother, I might be interested in knowing more, and my curiosity would so far be left unsatisfied. But these other bits of information are not strictly called for by the original statement. Suppose, however, you told me that your brother has been suspended from the police force, and in total violation of his constitutional rights. Now the questions that come to my mind—what is he accused of? Was he accorded due process? When will the matter be adjudicated?—become relevant questions; that is, their answers would help me make up my mind about the truth or falsity of your judgment of the situation. In that case, I would say that your statement so far is too indefinite, and hence not sufficiently informative.

It is easy enough, in comparing two similar statements, to say which is the more definite one. But we can't make so clear-cut a decision when indefiniteness is excessive. When, in pursuing a course of reasoning, we require certain information, then we feel the lack of it. If we are getting the information, say, from a witness, who tells us that he saw the defendant wearing a coat, we want to know what sort of coat: what fabric, color, style, length, degree of newness, etc. "Jones wore a coat" is more *general* than "Jones wore an old tan topcoat."

Some years ago, a writer in *Punch* (Tom W. Harris) drafted an all-purpose letter to send in reply to those maddening "casual clue" letters (as he called them) that we sometimes get from our friends or from near and dear—letters in which they allude to matters never mentioned previously. I quote parts of it:

> Dear Bill:
>
> Good to hear from you. We have the respirator out of the kitchen, but the horse is still around. What do you do in a case like that?
>
> Not much local news since the murders, except that Mayor Harvey has finally got the water drained. Three feet.
>
> They caught Pete Billings. Would you ever have thought it of him? I still blame those cub scouts.

The toothpick and the diving suit have been found, but the locomotive is still missing. . . .

I'd write more, but it's hard to see down here in the cave. What's new out your way?

Best regards.

Tom

The fourth feature of discourse that can cause difficulties in communication is vagueness, which we must now consider somewhat more extensively.

Many of the words we use to classify the things about us are, or at least purport to be, either-or words: they mark a distinction of *kind.* Something is either an apple or not, either an electric fan or not, either ambiguous or not. Other words are more-or-less words: they mark a distinction of *degree.* Apples are more or less tasty, electric fans are more or less noisy, ambiguous words more or less troublesome. But distinctions of degree can be turned into distinctions of kind by introducing some new rules. For example, consider the noisiness of electric fans. Suppose we select one that is moderately quiet, or seems about average; we may even measure its sound in terms of decibels at, say, six feet. Now we can introduce the word "noisy" in a new sense, not to compare degrees of noisiness, but to separate noisy fans from fans that are not noisy: The noisy ones are those fans that make more noise than our average fan, the quiet fans are those that do not make more noise than our average fan. We have divided fans into two classes, or kinds.

This sort of classification goes on all the time in our language, of course, and it is enormously convenient. For it enables us to speak of large tomatoes, intelligent children, tall buildings, corrupt political machines, etc., etc. Nor need such ways of speaking get us into any difficulties, as long as we bear in mind that they are subject to an important limitation. If the quality we are speaking of can be measured in some way, as noise is measured in decibels, then we can make a fairly sharp division between the classes we wish to separate. But most of the comparative terms we make use of in daily life do not refer to anything measurable, or at any rate, even if the qualities are measurable, we are not measuring them. And even if we *can* make a sharp distinction between, say, buildings that are tall and buildings that are not tall, we ordinarily don't bother. So there is simply no rule in our language for drawing a definite line. How tall must a building be to be a tall building? How large must a tomato be to be a large tomato? How corrupt must a political machine be to be a corrupt political machine? To answer such questions we would have to appeal to a rule of some kind on which there is agreement; but since there is no such rule, the questions have no answers. This is what is meant by saying that these terms, "tall building," "large tomato," etc., are **vague**.

A vague word does mark a distinction. There must first be some things to which it does decisively apply—or at least, some things we can think of which, if they existed, would clearly fall under the word. Take a term like "clean air," or one of the other terms that are so heavily relied on in the various statutes and government commission reports and regulations about air pollution: "reasonable air quality, "substantial effect on air quality," "economically feasible limits on emission of air pollutants." Even if we cannot find any examples of clearly and unmistakably clean air, we can name some: say, the air in Las Vegas, New Mexico, in 1663. Second, there must be some clear-cut examples, real or imaginary, of things to which the term does *not* apply: the air over Northern New Jersey on a hot breezeless day in 1973. Unless a word definitely includes and definitely excludes something, it marks no distinction at all.

But, third, there is also a twilight zone between the definite cases at each extreme: an *area of indecision*, or range of things about which it has not been settled by any rule that the word applies or does not apply to them. A person who is thirty years old is not middle-aged; a person who is sixty years old is definitely middle-aged; but somewhere in between there is a range of ages that we can call "middle age" or not, as we wish, arbitrarily, since the application of the word is not that fixed. Of course, the area of indecision is not sharply marked out; its edges are blurred, too. Sometimes the area of indecision is comparatively small, so we can say that the word is not very vague, or that its vagueness is restricted. Other words have a wide area of indecision, and indeed this may be deliberately sought for particular purposes. The drafters of some air-pollution laws seem to have left things about as vague as possible, so that even factories that emit a great deal of pollution can argue that they have no "substantial effect on air quality," and that any effort to clean things up would not be "economically feasible."

The difference between vagueness and ambiguity is that between two kinds of indecisiveness. An ambiguous statement offers you a choice among interpretations, but doesn't guide you to a correct choice. A vague statement doesn't leave you in doubt as to which quality is in question (cleanliness of air, noisiness, tallness), but only of how much of it is there. The more vague the statement, the less informative it is. When you are told that someone is middle aged, you know he is not ten years old or ninety years old. When you are told by a government official that the air in your city or town is "clean," you do not really know how much in the way of dangerous chemicals might still be hovering about.

How vague we can permit a word to be—or, contrariwise, how precise we must make it—clearly depends on the purposes at hand, and the sort of argument we have in mind. If our purpose is to give as much leeway as possible to the courts, we will be vague. If our purpose is to make certain practices clearly illegal, we will be less vague, if we can. Constitutional law is, of course, a special case: Some of the most essential terms in the Bill of Rights, such as "unreasonable searches and seizures," "due process of law," "cruel and unusual punishment," are, in their original context, quite vague—though sometimes the records of the original debates and other commentaries can help to narrow our interpretation. It has been left largely to the Federal courts to build up a body of principles in terms of which "due process," for example, can be given a good deal of restriction: As the term is now used, a person who is fired from a government job without a hearing or an opportunity to reply to charges against him has definitely been denied due process; and one who has been accorded a series of opportunities to be heard, to confront his accuser, to be impartially judged, and to appeal, has definitely been accorded due process—but, again, the area of indecision is not wholly eliminated.

The sort of problem to which vagueness gives rise is illustrated by the United States Supreme Court's recent (June 1973) decision in five obscenity cases, in the majority opinion written by Chief Justice Burger. For a good many years, the Court had followed the principle enunciated in the *Roth* (1957) case, that what has "the slightest redeeming social importance" (in Justice Brennan's words) is not obscene. Under that principle, an allegedly obscene motion picture, say, could be defended on the ground that it had some aesthetic or other kind of value, that it was not utterly lacking in such value. Justice Burger's opinion revised this criterion, declaring that states may punish the showing, printing, sale, etc., of works "which appeal to the prurient interest in sex, which portray sexual conduct in a patently offensive way and which, taken as a whole, do not have serious literary, artistic, political, or scientific value." The phrase "patently offensive" no doubt has its area of indecision, too, and it also is odd in this context, since how can something offend someone when it appeals to his prurient interest? Offensiveness is relative, too, since what offends one person may not offend another, and the court tried to deal with that problem by allowing different "communities" to set their own standards—though it did not define "community." In any case, relativity is not the same as vagueness, and it is rather the phrase "serious literary, artistic, political, or scientific value" that I wish to call attention to. How much literary value is "serious" literary value? Is it enough if the film is amusing, or well-acted, or well-photographed, or has a complicated plot? The new standard of obscenity is evidently a good deal more vague than the old one, and in an area where one would think the court would want to try to make it less vague, if possible.

When we use a vague term we often find it useful to draw a tentative and provisional line somewhere in the area of indecision, just to keep unnecessary questions from arising. Since there is no general rule, we can draw the line where we like, and indeed we can draw it at different places on different occasions. If the city wants to encourage upkeep and rehabilitation of "old" houses, it can decide to call a house "old" if it was built at least seventy-five years ago. There is no way of avoiding the appearance of arbitrariness in drawing such a line: Why not seventy-four years or seventy-six years? To say the line has a certain arbitrariness is to say that no good reason can be given for drawing it exactly there, rather than a little to the left or right. But this can always be said whenever we are dealing with vague terms to which we are trying to give a more exact meaning, for special purposes. And the important point is that we *can* give a very good reason for treating the oldest houses differently (for example, in terms of taxes), if we want to preserve old residential neighborhoods—and we can give a good reason for drawing the line *somewhere* in the vicinity of seventy-five years. It is a subtle, but serious, fallacy to think that just because we cannot show that seventy-five is a better place to draw the line than seventy-four, we therefore cannot show that seventy-five is a better place to draw the line than, say, fifty (when the house may still be going strong) or one hundred (when it may be too far decayed to be reclaimable).

This sort of fallacious reasoning gives rise to what is known as the **black-or-white-fallacy**: which is an illegitimate appeal to the arbitrariness of drawing certain lines in order to prove that no lines at all can reasonably be drawn. The fallacy has two forms, both taking advantage of the same basic principle.

The first form of reasoning is roughly this:

> A large difference of degree is made up of many small differences of degree.
> *Therefore:* A large difference of degree is not large after all.

That is, differences in shades of gray don't count; everything must be black or white. A university Dean might argue:

> This university has already recognized, I am glad to say, that we cannot sit still while the vast educational inequalities in this country, including this city, are continually perpetuated. We have gone out into the ghetto schools to find students with native ability, despite their extremely poor

> preparation, and admit them to college here under special dispensation. We have set up programs to help them improve their reading and writing and mathematics, and prepare them to enter regular college courses after a year or two—and many of these students are making great progress. But once we begin this course, we must recognize that in all logic, as well as humanity, we should expand the program—otherwise we will not be fair to the many students who don't have such an opportunity. We can't be sure whether an underprivileged student has ability or not, so we had better not consider native ability a necessary condition of admission. But then it is a short step to question the very meaningfulness of the grades they got in elementary and high school. In short, there is no clear ground for exclusion, and the only policy that makes sense is a complete open admissions policy, admitting everyone who wants to come, and trying to help them all succeed.

My purpose is not to deny the educational wisdom of so-called open admission, but to deny that this is a good argument for it. It does not itself give reasons for moving on to each step, broadening admissions, but rather argues that, once some disadvantaged students are admitted, there can be no good reason not to go the whole way. This claim, however, is not true, or at least not proved here. There might well be good reasons for admitting only a relatively limited number of special students, or for admitting only those whose promise has been attested to by earlier teachers, or for drawing lines in some other way.

The second form of black-and-white reasoning moves in the opposite direction: from Go to Stop. Another Dean might be talking:

> Although I of course sympathize with the students picketing the Admissions Office in protest against what they call a "discriminatory" policy of admissions, I cannot condone their disruptive action. They claim that their demands are moderate, and negotiable; but the point is that they *are* demands, and we would be negotiating under compulsion. We must not give the students what they ask for, when they ask for it; that would set a dangerous precedent. Once we gave in on the Admissions policy, they would propose changes in the curriculum and the course schedules, and we would have to negotiate and compromise on that. They might then ask for students to serve on faculty committees and on the Board of Trustees, and we could not consistently deny them this, since we would have in effect conceded their right to make demands. What if they then came to dominate the University, and determine what is taught and who is hired? The ultimate consequence is too horrible to contemplate; the only logical policy is to stop at the beginning, and refuse all demands.

The underlying argument seems to be:

> A large difference of degree is made up of many small differences of degree.

Therefore: The small difference of degree is really a large one after all.

It is simply not true—or not proved here—that if no good reason can be given for moving on to stage 3 from stage 2, therefore no good reason can be given for moving to stage 2 from stage 1. There might be many good reasons for stopping at one point or another. Yet this "slippery slope" argument—that since each step is relatively small, the first step commits you to going the whole way—is often alarming enough to be persuasive. Not that there are no such things as slippery slopes. We might say: don't start sliding down the hill, because once you start, you won't be able to stop. That is a perfectly good argument, but note that it is a *causal* one: It rests upon the assumption that an action will inevitably have effects that will follow whether we like them or not. But that causal argument is quite different from the *logical* one, which is that once we admit that we would be justified in doing *A*, we therefore have somehow implicitly conceded that we would be justified in doing *B*, because *B* is only a little different from *A*. It's true that a person who has smoked fifty cigarettes in one day probably won't do himself a significant amount of further harm by smoking the fifty-first one; but nevertheless, he may have a better reason for stopping at fifty than he has for stopping at seventy-five.

A check-up quiz

Which of the following arguments commit the black-or-white fallacy?

1. Gentlemen, in drawing up plans for our next presidential campaign, there are a few basic strategies to be decided upon. Now, no one, I believe, will regard it as in any way immoral, unethical, or illegal to play a few amusing tricks on the opposing party: for example, we could have someone put our bumper stickers on their campaign cars, or have someone infiltrate their campaign staff and pass out obviously phony press releases. But if this is conceded, it would be hardly more of an interference with the other party to spread a few well-chosen rumors that the candidate has broken his leg, or to call up some of the towns he is to visit and say that his visit has been cancelled. A bit more amusing, perhaps, and really not significantly different from the moral or legal point of view, would be to do a little harmless phone-tapping, just to keep track of what they may be up to—and, if the campaign gets tight, perhaps to make up a few letters purporting to be evidence that their candidate once made money by writing pornographic novels, and is the father of several illegitimate children. These may be "dirty tricks," but they are not different in kind from any other tricks.

2. "Oh what a tangled web we weave / When first we practice to deceive!" Like the poet says. When I started out as a DJ, I played the recordings I thought were good, and if agents of the record companies came around afterward and gave me presents, I was pleased. Then they began pleading with me to play some other records more often, just to give them a fair chance—appealing to my better nature. And it seems only natural that they would want to make it possible for me to live in a little better life-style by slipping me extra funds now and then. Finally, one day, they told me to feature a recording that was a real clinker, and I didn't want to. So they said (a) this was worth money to me, and (b) they had bank records of deposits in my name, and they would hate to have to tell the D.A. about them. Well, you see how it is. One thing leads to another. That's how I got so deep into the payola business.

3. The courts have long held that teachers and others are allowed to make what is called "fair use" of copyrighted material—that is, for example, to Xerox a few copies of a poem, if they are using it in teaching, and not making money out of it, and only giving it minimal distribution. But where do you draw the line? First thing you know, it will be O.K. to Xerox a whole chapter of a textbook and hand out copies to the students; then two or three chapters, so that they don't even need to buy the book, and the author and publisher can't make money from it. If a couple of copies can be made, why not a dozen or a score or a hundred? And if the teacher asks the students to make a "voluntary contribution," to help him defray the cost of the Xeroxing, who is going to check up to make sure that he doesn't slip a little of it into his own pocket? Practically everything becomes "fair use," if we allow it at all; and it is therefore clear that we must not allow it at all. When the publisher says on the verso of the title page, "no part of this work may be reproduced in any form without permission from the publisher," this must be allowed to mean exactly what it says, and all violators must be prosecuted.

4. The courts have wrestled continuously with the slippery concept of "state action," and the application of the Bill of Rights and the Fourteenth Amendment to particular cases. How much does the state have to be involved in an action in order for the Bill of Rights to apply? It is often held, for example, that a municipal swimming pool cannot practice racial discrimination by refusing to admit black swimmers, because it is owned and operated by an agency of government (in fact an agency created and legalized by state statute), but that a private swim club may do whatever it likes. Now the Supreme Court, in a case involving a lodge of the Loyal Order of Moose in Pennsylvania (June, 1972) has ruled that just because the club has a liquor license which is granted by the state, that does not mean the state is sufficiently involved in it so that the club's refusal to serve Negroes is unconstitutional. But surely the Court is misreading the Constitution. A bar that is owned and operated by the state may not discriminate; but if it is licensed by the

state, the state is making its existence and functioning possible, and is therefore deeply involved. Moreover, even if a group of private citizens starts a swim club, the land on which it exists is taxed by the city or county; its buildings are protected by police and fire department, and its water is inspected and approved by the health department. Surely these are forms of state action, too. In fact, there can be no *purely* private organization, which is wholly independent of the state, and therefore the constitution, properly understood, prohibits *any* organization from discriminating in *any* way.

5. If courts are allowed to penetrate the President's constitutional privacy and independence by demanding from him any evidence he may have about criminal matters that are before the court, the whole fabric of the separation of powers among the three branches of government (legislative, executive, and judicial) must crumble. For the next court may claim the right to see the President's papers having to do only with suspected crimes or possible crimes being investigated by a Congressional committee. The next court will claim this as a precedent for making the President routinely turn over his records and memoranda of discussions and consultations among officials within the executive branch, and everything done by that branch will be under the open scrutiny and influence of the judiciary and the Congress.

OUTLINE-SUMMARY: chapter four

Seven distinguishable features of language can interfere with clear and cogent thinking. They may be placed under three heads:

A. Variability of meaning. A word that has one sense in certain contexts and a different sense in other contexts is said to have (1) *variable meaning* ("the key to the house"; "the key to the cipher"). A special case of variable meaning is (2) the fallacy of *equivocation,* which occurs when a word changes its sense in the course of an argument in such a way that the conclusion does not follow ("Jewels are hard; she is a jewel; therefore, she is hard").

B. Complexity of meaning. When a word has several distinguishable senses in the same context, all of which are relevant to the context, then it is said to have (3) *multiple meaning* (in "It is the East, and Juliet is the sun," the word "sun" means something that brings light, something that brings promise of a new life, something indescribably wonderful, and more). When the subtler senses of a word, or the complex syntax in which it appears, work to make the meaning difficult to disentangle, then the passage is said to be (4) *obscure* ("Dissemination of this directive is restricted to personnel directly concerned with the implementation thereof").

C. Indecisiveness of meaning. One term is more definite than another if the application of that term conveys more information (to know that something is a small bluebottle fly is to know more than that it is an insect). A term may be (5) too *indefinite* for some purposes. A word is (6) *ambiguous* in a certain context if it may have either (but not both) of two (or more) meanings in that context. *Semantical ambiguity* is uncertainty about which sense the word has (in "the Bible prohibits swearing," "swearing" can mean *taking an oath* or *speaking impiously or irreverently). Syntactical ambiguity* is uncertainty about how the sentence elements are grammatically related ("the love of God" may be God's love of man or man's love of God). A word is (7) *vague* if it refers to a characteristic that objects can possess in some degree or quantity, and there is an area of indecision, that is, a range within which there is no rule that the word must either apply or not apply ("the immediate context of a word" is vague, in that whether it includes part of a sentence, or the adjoining sentences, or the adjoining paragraphs, is left open).

Comparative words (especially vague ones) and others defined in terms of them can be used to commit the *black-or-white fallacy,* which consists either (a) in illegitimately minimizing a large difference in degree, or (b) in exaggerating a small difference in degree, by appealing to the fact that any difference in degree is made of minimal differences ("A miss is as good as a mile, because if you miss by one inch, that's hardly any worse than missing by an inch and a quarter," and so forth).

Exercise 17

Examine the italicized words in the following pairs of sentences. Are the senses the same or different? If they are different, show the difference by substituting synonymous words or phrases.

1. (a) There is no beer in his refrigerator, because he doesn't *care for* it.
   (b) His flowers and shrubbery are dying, because he doesn't *care for* them.

2. (a) She *comes* to Dr. Pangloss *for* her arthritis.
   (b) She *comes* to the drug store *for* her prescription.

3. (a) The archaelolgist *found* an ancient cup.
   (b) The jury *found* the defendant guilty.

4. (a) Jones *wrote* a book.
   (b) Jones *wrote* his name on the check.

5. (a) You'll have to *draw* your own conclusion.
   (b) If you can't describe the thief, perhaps you can *draw* a picture of him.

6. (a) My *love* is like a red, red rose.
   (b) My *love* will last forever.

7. (a) The Governor created a *scandal* by divorcing his wife and marrying his secretary.
   (b) The Governor created a *scandal* by accepting large payments from the state highway contractors.

8. (a) In a sound argument, the reasons *support* the conclusion.
   (b) Our organization is raising funds to *support* the struggle of the Catholics in Northern Ireland.

9. (a) The discovery of the initialed memorandum showed that the Secretary of Defense's denial of knowledge about the action was a *lie*.
   (b) From time to time, it may be necessary for public officials to tell a *lie* in the national interest.

10. (a) He *doesn't think much about* his uncle.
    (b) He *doesn't think much of* his uncle.

Exercise 18

In each of the following passages, rewrite any ambiguous part in two different ways to bring out the nature of the ambiguity, semantical or syntactical.

1. Mr. Niarchos, who is 5 feet 7 inches tall and has graying black hair, is believed to be the largest shipowner in the world.
2. Reagan ran unsuccessfully for the Republican presidential nomination in 1968 and close political friends are urging him to do so again in 1976.
3. Earlier, Miss Taylor had burst into tears after one of the guests, who flew to Budapest from all over the world, insulted her.
4. Nobody but Marylanders know this little woman with bright brown eyes—and comparatively few of those.
5. What have you to offer? Ten years experience buying and selling and managing girls. Also some factory work. Write Box 1198, Post-Telegram.
6. Joining in the appeal to the planning board were a spokesman for the New York Chapter of the American Institute of Architects, which feels the office building proposed for the site might be built over the opera house, conductor Laszlo Halasz and a half dozen other speakers.
7. Ottawa.—An investigation has been ordered into the rash of sinkings of steel tugboats of Canadian registry by Paul Hellyer, transport minister.

8. First came one of those infuriating 2½-hour delays on the ground while a mechanic replaced a faulty electrical relay, a standard item on any jet transport.

9. THE LUXURY apartment of your dreams, 3½-4½ rooms, in the heart of Zameret Park (Rehov Weizmann). No neighbors, lifts, hot water, central heating, gas, telephone, installations and parking.

10. The Forest Home Sewing Circle will meet at 3 p.m. Thursday with Mrs. Charlotte Strong, Trumansburg Rd. The program will be in charge of Mrs. Marjorie Kellogg and Mrs. Lily Ann Newbury. Each member is to bring food for a bake sale and the recipe of the food. Members are asked to note the change in the hostess.

11. The trunk on a Dart is actually bigger than the one on many full-sized cars. And a family of five fits inside nicely.

12. LAW L9177. Seminar in types of criminals in New York City. Professor Radzinowicz. 2 pts.

    On the basis of empirical studies and other sources, reports are presented and legislative solutions proposed on a variety of categories of offenses and offenders in the City of New York, such as robbing and mugging; violence and property offenses by addicts; pornography as a business; chronic drunkards; police assailants; violent sexual offenders; embezzlers. Specialists in various fields are invited to participate. [Catalogue of a school of law.]

Exercise 19

Analyze the equivocation in the following arguments. Explain the senses involved and show how they shift in the course of the argument.

1. The basic principle of preventive detention is simple: someone who is preparing to commit a crime (such as a man who is going around a parking lot trying car doors), is apprehended, and held until he can be searched and fingerprinted and investigated, so that he can be kept from performing the criminal act. That is why I simply cannot understand the outcry against City Council's new preventive detention ordinance, which allows the police to take into custody anyone suspected of harboring criminal intentions.

2. Fast emerging as one of the most serious problems in present-day America is that of how to cope with the vast increase in leisure time—by which is meant time spent in activities not required for, or designed for, economic support of oneself or one's dependents. This problem is already much greater than most social thinkers realize. They can see that the number of hours in typical work-weeks is decreasing, and so more

and more forms of play and recreation have to be made available to fill up the longer evenings and weekends. But they overlook the extent to which the occupational activities of many people—especially successful business men, artists, teachers, and others—are inherently rewarding and satisfying, and thus, strictly speaking, are also leisure-time activities.

3. Despite all the attacks by knee-jerk liberals on the Administration's policy of appointing only strict constructionists to the United States Supreme Court, the fact remains that strict constructionism—that is, faithful adherence to the text of the Constitution and to the intention of its original framers—is the only defensible principle of Constitutional interpretation; anything else is simply rewriting the Constitution to satisfy the wishes of some special pressure group that imagines itself to be unfairly treated. There is far too much permissiveness today, and strictness is exactly what we need more of. The rights of the criminal are cherished above the rights of the victim, the demands of the minority over the needs of the majority, the license of the individual over the preservation of order in the state. That is why the Administration seeks to fill the Court with judges who will take a strict and narrow view of the individual's claims, when the individual complains that the Federal government or a state government has infringed upon his liberties—for that is the strict constructionism that the country must have if it is to survive.

4. As the very etymology of the word "pornographic" tells us, pornography is concern with the flesh; it is enough to read (if you can bring yourself to read) the description of sexual activities in such works as the novels of Jacqueline Susann and Henry Miller, to realize that these works can only be called pornographic, if the word is used strictly. Recent investigations have shown us more about pornography and have given a better and fuller understanding of what it really means. A pornographic novel by definition is one that tends to deprave or corrupt the reader through its explicit and overt descriptions of sexual activity. Note those weighty words "deprave" and "corrupt"! It is evident that we must make every effort to keep the admittedly depraving and corrupting works of Susann and Miller out of the hands of the public.

5. James Rowland Lowe Jr.'s claim in his letter (July 8) that witnesses before the Ervin Committee are being subjected to punishment ("scars imposed by the hearings") is simply based on equivocation. The Constitution forbids legal punishment without trial and due process, but not those natural consequences of investigation which Mr. Lowe is pleased to call "punishment." If Mr. Lowe were right then the Constitution would forbid the natural inconveniences which are attendant upon coming to trial, and, in consequence, no trials or Congressional investigations would be constitutional. Mr. Lowe has the right to use the word "punishment" as he pleases, but any argument based on equivocation is just invalid. [Letter to the *New York Times,* from Kenneth Stern, July 15, 1973.]

Exercise 20

In the following passages, *B* and *C* are replying to *A*'s assertion. If one or both of them uses one of *A*'s words or phrases in a different sense, rewrite the reply so that the speaker no longer equivocates.

I

A: The Administration permits enormous inflation, an increase in crime and drugs, perversion of the electoral process, and bribery by big corporations. It simply is not a responsible administration.

B: It has done its best to clean up the ills of society, which cannot be done over night; and it is working on the problems of inflation and improving the electoral process. I believe it is behaving responsibly.

C: How can you say that? Certainly an administration that was elected legally and by a heavy majority is responsible to the 200 million Americans whom it represents.

II

A: We are fortunate that there are still principled and high-minded men who uphold and defend the conservative ideology that has been our tradition and made free enterprise a cornerstone of our republic.

B: As a conservative, I must take issue with you. Conservatives have no ideology; they are opposed to ideology, unlike liberals and radicals with their abstract intellectual schemes for reforming society and their ruthlessness toward people and tradition.

C: It does no harm to have a few dodos about, so long as we don't take them too seriously. When our biggest industries (e.g., Lockheed) are constantly coming to the Federal government for huge sums of money to keep them from going out of business, it is ridiculous to talk about free enterprise.

III

A: Pendleton has finally become what he aspired to be all his life, a short-order cook in a diner. He has succeeded in fulfilling his dreams, and he is a success at last.

B: Pendleton's work does not rank very high in most people's estimation; it is not one of the status jobs. It is absurd to call him a success.

C: Pendleton is not really a success, even if he thinks so. With a take-home pay of $79.50 a week, he cannot be regarded as a complete failure, but he has not become a genuinely successful man.

IV

A: Agatha Christie may be one of the champion detective-story writers over the years, in terms of total output, but from a serious literary point of view, she has to be classified as a hack writer, for her works lack any pretense to literary excellence.

B: How can you call Agatha Christie a hack writer? She produces varied and ingenious plots, and can be lively and amusing—and these are certainly literary merits.

C: I agree with you that Agatha Christie is a hack writer, precisely in that she has followed tested commercial formulas to achieve financial success. The unevenness of her output is irrelevant.

V

A: Individualism versus collectivism—that is always the central problem for political man. Whether to embrace the philosophy that society consists of individual persons, and the apparatus of state is simply an instrument they use to develop themselves as individuals, or the philosophy that the state is more than a means, but an end in itself—that is the question. America has chosen individualism. That has made America great.

B: I don't defend collectivism, but rather community. It is individualism that has pitted man against man, with its doctrine that each can stand by himself independently of others, and its resulting encouragement of that insane competitiveness that has racked our social fabric and produced so much misery.

C: Individualism is dead; it should be buried and replaced by a better, a more humane philosophy. The essence of individualism was suggested in President Kennedy's words, "Don't ask what your country can do for you." This attitude that I, my individual self, am the most important thing, and I have a right to expect the state to serve me, is what leads to millions living on welfare, without working, at the expense of others.

chapter five

SOME RESOURCES OF LANGUAGE

To manage well the verbal texture of an argument—so that it moves with, rather than against, the grain of the argument—we have to be aware, not only of the ways in which meanings can go astray, but of the ways in which they can give the argument unusual richness, subtlety, and force. Some of the greatest challenges to the writer or the reader are offered by the language in which he does his thinking, and especially by some of the most admirable features of that language: its capacity to build complicated structures of ideas and to convey delicate relationships among them.

The basic distinction we must now explore is that between two levels of meaning in a discourse: what the discourse says *explicitly* (its plain or main sense, such as a brief paraphrase might report) and what it says *implicitly* (what it hints, insinuates, conveys indirectly or guardedly). These are different levels, because the second meaning rests on the first: We can sometimes make an explicit statement with very little, perhaps even with no, implicit meaning; but in order to hint at something (say, that the hour is getting late), we have to say something explicit (such as that tomorrow is another day, or that we must all get together again some time). Reading a news story hastily, you can get the gist of it; but if you miss the implicit meanings, you may lack information that could be very important in trying to form a rational opinion about a pressing social problem. Writing a letter hastily, you may easily get across the main point you have in mind; yet if you pay no attention to the other meanings implicit in what you are saying, you may discover later that you have said something you didn't "mean" at all, and in fact rather regret:

> Dear Susan:
> Please excuse haste. Sorry I can't get to your party Saturday night. I have something important to do.
> Yrs,
> Harry

Tactlessness, whether conscious or unconscious, very often comes from just this sort of failure to see what is going on at the second level of meaning. Harry may have been unaware that he was sending two messages, but probably Susan got both of them: the explicit one that Harry was rejecting her invitation, and the implicit one that Harry attached little or no importance to her party.

§ 13. Connotation and Metaphor

It is no part of the purpose of this book to give an account of meaning in general, to explain what is involved when a word or a sentence means something. Such an inquiry would take us far afield into technical problems of philosophy and linguistics. Yet I can't avoid making extensive use of the word "to mean," and I think that by using it carefully, and by offering some initial clarifications, I can use it safely for present purposes.

The first clarification is a restriction. We use the word "to mean" in several widely different ways. Here we are concerned only with *linguistic meaning*, that is, with meanings of words (not, for example, with such usages as "When the bell rings, that *means* the lecture is over"). Second, a word's having a meaning should probably be kept distinct from another feature of (some) words, that is, their capacity to serve as names, or labels.

When we think of names, we think most readily of *proper names*, or singular terms, which refer to individual things, whether persons, groups, places, objects, or events:

Gerard Manley Hopkins
Watergate
the Rio Grande
the Pentagon Papers
the massacre at My Lai

True, two distinct things might be given the same proper name—two buildings might be called "Watergate"—but still "Watergate" is a proper name, for in each case it is assigned, by some naming procedure, to one and only one thing: It is just not sufficient to pick out that object from all others, unless we enlarge it ("the Watergate in Washington, D.C.").

Besides proper names, there are common names, or general terms:

poet
building
river
document
massacre

We speak of *a* poet, *a* document, of this or that building. These terms refer not just to a single thing, but to all the members in some class of things (if the class has any members: "ghost" refers to no thing, since the class of ghosts is empty). The term "poet" *applies* to each and every poet; for convenience, let us say that it *comprehends* such persons as G. M. Hopkins, W. B. Yeats, Robert Lowell, Theodore Roethke, etc. Note that the class of poets is not confined to living poets; the **comprehension** of the term "poet" (i.e., the class of all the things it refers to) includes past, present, and future poets.

In a broad sense, we could consider comprehending a kind of meaning; in ordinary speech, we might loosely say that "building" means (among other things) the Taj Mahal and the White House. But it is probably clearer to contrast comprehension and meaning. For, more strictly, meaning is not a relationship of words to things but of words to the *properties* of things. Take the class of rivers: What are, so to speak, the conditions for admission to this class? The word "river" is governed, more or less strictly, by a set of language rules. First, nothing can be correctly called a river unless it is a stream of water; a pond or lake is water standing still, and that's ruled out. (You may object: What's wrong with saying that a bureaucracy is drowning in a river of paper? But this example supports my statement, for it is a metaphor and a metaphor—as we shall shortly see—involves a misapplication of a term.) Second, to be a river, a stream must be a natural stream; water running through a pipe doesn't count. Third, the stream has to be of a certain size—and here is a respect in which the word is vague. One dictionary says a river must be "larger than a brook or creek," but doesn't tell us how large a brook or creek is. It does tell us that a stream that would be called a creek in Pennsylvania might be called a river in New Hampshire, so that in this respect there are regional variations in the rules for applying the word "river." It also tells us implicitly, by its silence, that there are no rules in any region that fix exactly the point at which a brook or creek becomes a river—there is an area of indecision.

Still, vague rules are rules, if they mark any distinctions at all; and no one will question the fact that the Rio Grande is definitely a river, while a three-foot-wide stream running through a cow pasture in Connecticut is not. The rules of application, then, for a given term, tell us (more or less precisely) what it applies to and what it doesn't apply to; these rules are framed in terms of certain **necessary properties** which something has to have in order to qualify. These necessary properties I shall call the **designation** of the term; putting it the other way round, the term **designates** these properties. "River" designates the properties of (1) *being a stream of water*, (2) *being natural*, and (3) *being of substantial size* (not less than twenty feet wide, perhaps). If we want to make the third property more precise, we will have to set up different designations for different parts of the country—but even then we can't be wholly precise, or we would be falsifying the facts about the way "river" is used.

In many contexts, the full meaning of a word is more than its designation. When something is called a "river," for example, other properties may implicitly be attributed to it: It is something that teems with life (or would, if it were not polluted); that moves (except for tidewater) always in the same direction, inexorably toward the sea; that serves as an artery of communication and commerce, bringing distant people together; that also differentiates people by marking a boundary between states or countries or language groups (like the Rio Grande). How does this second mode of meaning come about? Much needs to be said to answer this question well, but here we must be content with a somewhat schematic and simplified account.

When the members of some class of things are comprehended by a general term, there are always certain necessary properties of the class: the conditions of applying the term. There is also a set of nonnecessary properties that are associated with the necessary ones. These **attendant properties** are of several sorts, which we can put together. (1) There are properties that most rivers have, so that when we think of a river it is easy to think of these properties (for example, that some kind of craft can travel on it). (2) There are properties that rivers are generally *believed* to have. Even if most rivers become polluted, so that nothing could live in them, if it were widely thought that rivers harbor life, *life-givingness* and *life-fosteringness* would be attendant properties of rivers, in my sense of the term. (Experts tell us that the lion is a less active predator than the hyena, or than a lioness, and that it cares little for its cubs, but so far the lion's proverbial reputation for kingliness remains undented.) (3) There are properties that some of the best, or most outstanding, or most characteristic, or most famous, rivers have, and that are hence often mentioned in speaking about rivers: for example, that they mark important political, cultural, or linguistic boundaries.

The attendant properties of a term's comprehension are a potential repertoire of implicit meaning: they need only be converted into connotations. And the principal method of conversion is metaphor.

A metaphorical description (phrase or sentence) consists of two parts: there is the term that is used *literally* to refer to the thing or things being described; and there is the term that is used *metaphorically* (the metaphorical term). Though metaphors are often phrases ("the winding down of the war," "the cover-up of Watergate"), it is convenient to take statements as primary ("The war was winding down," "Watergate was covered up"), since statements display the nature of metaphor more plainly, and what we say about them can always be transferred to phrases.

What is a **metaphorical statement**, then? It is a statement that has two essential features. First, it is *literally absurd*: Considering only the designations (that is, literal meanings) of the terms involved, it evidently cannot be true, for it involves either a logical contradiction or a physical impossibility or a patent falsehood—at least in its context. A child's wind-up toy can literally wind down—that is, it can have the properties designated by "winding down." But a war is not kept going by a hidden coil spring that gradually loses its tension; it is kept going by human decisions and actions. To speak of a "river of paper" is to form a contradictory concept, since rivers are, by definition, what papers, by definition, are not: that is, streams of water. But not all literal absurdities are metaphors. For, second, a metaphorical statement is *nonliterally intelligible*: Since it appears to be seriously asserted by someone who must be aware of its literal absurdity, we are led to rummage among the attendant properties of the things comprehended by the predicate-term, selecting those that can be applied without absurdity to the subject of the statement. "The war was winding down" is understood by this procedure: The statement attributes to the war all those attendant properties of things that are (literally) winding down, except those properties that make no sense when applied to wars and those properties that are ruled out by the larger context. For example, something that is winding down does so just by being unhindered; it goes from a state of tension to a state of comparative relaxation; it is capable of being wound up again at a later date. These three properties, among others, can also be applied to wars—whether truly or falsely—and to say "The war in Vietnam was winding down" is to apply them to a particular war. Metaphorical statements are not always (metaphorically) true, of course—perhaps the Vietnam war was not winding down but merely being altered in some way—but they are intelligible, that is, we can make sense of them, and often quite important sense.

Any interesting metaphor illustrates both the two great values and the two great dangers in metaphorical statements. Consider, for example, a remark by Senator Fulbright when the scope of the Nixon Administration's Watergate scandals began to be made public in early 1973: "Watergate is the bursting of the boil of Presidential power." As always in this book, we must refrain from getting into the substantive issue: whether the President had too much or too little power, as compared with Congress. Our questions are: What does this metaphor mean? And what is good or bad about it from a logical point of view?

On the good side, there are two points to notice. First, metaphors are compact—they are able to condense a number of statements into one, and present them in a single bundle. That is what makes them interesting and illuminating. To say that Presidential power has become a boil is to say that it is a kind of Constitutional infection, that it is troublesome and painful, that it has kept increasing in size until it has to come to a breaking-point, that when it has been properly treated, the process of government will become more normal and healthy, etc. Some of these meanings of the metaphor are quite obvious, others perhaps more gently hinted at and beneath the surface. A metaphor often gives the impression of a deep well, whose bottom one cannot see; no matter how much meaning you draw from it, you have the feeling that if you go back to it later, and think on it further, you will find other meanings you had overlooked.

Besides the great potential richness of meaning in metaphor there is also its creativity. Metaphors give us new meanings, enlarge the capacity of our language to express subtle differences and name qualities of the world for which we may hitherto have had no words. Hence a well-chosen metaphor is likely to catch on, and stay with us, becoming part of the language, since it shows us how to say something we recognize to be worth saying. As it is used again and again, and becomes familiar, we may find ourselves paying attention to only part of its meaning, and using it as a quick label for things; then the metaphor takes on the air of a cliché (not just because it is repeated, but because it comes to have a more restricted sense), and finally one of its metaphorical senses may become standardized. Then we have a dead metaphor, which is no metaphor at all: "the eye of a needle, "a head of cabbage."

The two main dangers of metaphorical talk are on the other side of the same coin. First, because of its very complexity, its multiplicity of meaning, a metaphor is hard to control—to keep from saying things you don't want to say, along with the things you do want to say. Clark Kerr is reported to have remarked—though he may have been misquoted—that "the aim of a university is not to make ideas safe for students, but to make students safe for ideas." I take it that "safe" is a metaphor here, since it does not mean protection against physical harm—though one value of this example is that it shows how a metaphor can be comparatively unobtrusive. Part of what is implicitly meant by "make students safe for ideas" might be readily agreed to, as when we think of ideas (metaphorically) as powerful and potentially dangerous. like the things firemen and bomb squads are specially trained to handle. But the metaphor also seems to say that college education exists to insulate students, somehow, or indoctrinate them so fully that they cannot be injured or shaken up by the new ideas that they may come across. The speaker no doubt did not mean this, but his words may have meant it. I say "may have," because everything depends on the context: The way to rule out the unwanted parts of the metaphorical meaning is to make sure that the context disallows them. Adding a strong defense of the freedom of ideas and of debate in the university would help to trim the metaphor and point it, so to speak, in the right direction. If you can manage the context, you can manage the metaphor. But if that doesn't work, you may have to abandon the metaphor, however picturesque and quotable it may be, and go back to straightforward literal language.

But it is not only meanings that sometimes tend to run away with us in metaphor; it is thinking itself. A metaphor can be extremely helpful to thought, when it suggests an analogy that opens up new lines of inquiry; but if the image is strong and colorful, it can fasten itself upon us and control our thinking too rigidly. This fault has been charged against the famous metaphor—not in the Constitution itself, but from a private letter written by Thomas Jefferson in 1802—about the "wall of separation between church and state." The First Amendment, of course, simply says that "Congress shall make no law respecting an establisment of religion or prohibiting the free exercise thereof . . ."—and the Fourteenth Amendment is now understood to extend this prohibition to the state legislatures as well. We can think in abstract, literal terms of the implications of this rule: that the government (Federal or state) may not interfere with religious practices (though there are recognized limits when it comes to criminal acts), and that the government may not contribute to the support of religious institutions. So the courts have said. But what is conjured up when we picture this situation as a "wall of separation"? A wall is opaque and impermeable; it marks areas off decisively and definitively; it is more solid and enduring than, say, a fence;

the parties on both sides might not even be aware of each others' existence; etc. If we follow what is hinted at in this metaphor, we may end up by going much farther than we wish, or than we can justify on Constitutional grounds. Is the government permitted to buy schoolbooks for religious schools? to transport children to religious schools? to subsidize hospitals run by religious groups? to underwrite mortgages for retirement homes built by religious groups? to let the fire department put out fires in churches? All these are difficult questions, requiring much careful thought; the danger is that we might let picture-thinking take the place of logical thinking, and come to a conclusion just because the metaphor seems to call for it.

The consequences of trying to carry through a coherent process of thought largely in metaphorical terms show up at their most absurd in those passages that *The New Yorker* likes to quote under its heading of "Block that Metaphor!" Mixed metaphors are a perfect expression of garbled thought. From a University student newspaper:

> But, no doubt, it is one of the inevitable occupational diseases of teaching, subordination of individual conviction for the goal of open-mindedness—so very open that it is an undigested mass of incongruities crowned with information that systematically beats around the bush.

Except for the absence of "information," which may be supplied by the context from which this passage is excerpted, one might think that the writer is trying to show in his very style the danger he warns against. Certainly there are many curious metaphorical incongruities here to reflect on. Here is another example:

> Like a man trying to look two ways at once, the distilled spirits trade is likely to meet itself coming back—at least on the questions of taxes and inventories. In its own inimitable fashion, the trade has snagged itself squarely on the horns of a dilemma, through a seemingly normal attitude of not looking where it traveled until it got there, and now, sadly shaken, stands in need of some sane, solid thinking, to cut through the miasma of fear and doubt which stalks it like a self-perpetuating monster.

The need for "sane, solid thinking" remains so far unfulfilled: and anyone who starts out to deal with the problems of the distilled spirits trade by getting hung up on this mixture of metaphors (and similes) already has two strikes against him (to compound the confusion further).

In a metaphorical statement (or phrase), the characteristics actually meant by the metaphorical term are its connotations in that context. As a word continues to be used metaphorically in various contexts, more and more of its attendant properties become connotations in one context or another. So at any given time, we can speak of the term's **connotations** as such, consisting of all those attendant properties that the term has been used to mean (but not designate), in one context or another up to that time. At any given time, then, a word may have three sets of properties connected with it: (1) those designated by the term, (2) those that belong to its connotation, and (3) those other attendant properties that have not yet become part of its connotation, but may be added as new metaphorical uses for the word are found. In a living language, though there is some stability in these classes of properties, there are also significant shifts from time to time. Three processes are especially important in these changes of meaning: (1) the metaphorical process, by which attendant properties are constantly being converted into connotations; (2) the standardizing process, by which connotations become so frequently activated that they turn into new standard senses, or designations (dead metaphor); (3) social (including technological) change, by which certain designations become obsolete (as certain objects or practices become outmoded), and linger on as connotations. Thus "garble" originally meant "to sort out," in general; and later to select those parts of a discourse that you are attacking so as to prove your point. Thus it came to connote, and later to designate, misrepresenting and confusing things. So we see how in a few hundred years, "garble" reversed its designation, from sorting out to mixing up, through the connotations it developed. A similar reversal happened to the word "person," which is now so important in our ways of speaking. In the King James version of the Bible (1611) it is said several times that "God is no respecter of persons," which is puzzling today. But "person" then had the same sense as its Latin root, "*persona*," the name for the actor's masks worn in classical tragedy, and hence the character the actor assumes, what he pretends to be. The point was that God does not pay attention to the way people look, or pretend to be—their face value—but to what they really are. Through a series of shifts, the word for the outward appearance came to be the word for the inner reality, and today we contrast a person (or his true self) with his mask (or the selves he presents to others in playing the roles of daily life.)

Even when words are not used metaphorically, we have to be sensitive to their connotations, or they may get in the way of straight thinking. Any word that occupies a key position in a discourse—that plays an important role in its reasoning—carries with it a range of connotations that can make it informative or misleading. They emerge when we contrast the word with its near-synonyms, whose designations may be closely similar or, more usually, subtly different but overlapping. The advertising copywriter must be skillful at manipulating these marginal meanings; and to preserve ourselves (by resisting new forms of environmental pollution and new perils in packaged foods), we may have to be just as skillful at detecting and unmasking them. In New York State (perhaps everywhere), horse racing is called the "horse racing industry." There may be difficulties with the available alternatives, but "industry" connotes a kind of productivity that some find hard to associate with horse racing—although the oft-repeated slogan of one (genuine) industry, "Progress is our most important product," may have succeeded in so confusing the public that this incongruity goes unnoticed. The term "compact car" is credited to George Romney and is often cited as a triumph: Whereas "small car" is said to have various undesirable connotations (especially after the Detroit emphasis on hugeness), "compact car" conveys the idea that you have lost nothing, really, only got it all together in a smaller space at a thrifty price. One more example: Though unleaded gasoline will be a necessity not too far off, and each oil company is under Federal orders to market one unleaded fuel by July 1, 1974, Shell has put lead temporarily back into its no-lead gasoline, and called it "Super Regular"—an apparent attempt to combine all the connotations one could wish for.

The political uses of connotation should also be noted, however briefly. Some of them will be given fuller attention in the following section, where we shall consider propaganda in general. In recent years, perhaps the principal political use has been to make light of serious and consequential matters, to play down errors and evils in the hope that they will be overlooked or ignored. We have seen this in a whole string of euphemisms that the United States public has been treated to by its leaders—to the point where it seems that the government must employ experts whose full-time job it is to devise such ways of calling a spade anything else but a spade. We have had "racially impacted areas" as a substitute for "racially segregated areas"—connoting the properties of being more a misfortune than the result of anyone's deliberate decision, and of being rather minor and unalarming. We have had "routine, limited-duration, reinforced, protective reaction air strikes" and "limited air interdiction," to describe heavy bombing. We have had "incursion" as a cheerful name for invasion. And, on the domestic front, we have heard a planned double break-in at Democratic party headquarters, with photographing of documents and planting of bugging devices, described as "the Watergate caper," "the Watergate incident," "the Watergate affair," and (by the President's press secretary Ronald Ziegler), "a third-rate burglary attempt." Certainly in all these cases, there can be a legitimate dispute about which of the (very) roughly equivalent terms is the most exact description for the event in question. But there can be no dispute about the fact that the choice of "air strike" rather than "bombing," or "caper" rather than "crime," minimizes unpleasant features by connoting others.

A check-up quiz

Compare the alternative words inserted parenthetically in the following sentences, and point out in each case two respects in which their connotations differ.

1. In trying to help the poverty-stricken and culturally undernourished in our city, we must follow a policy of (outgoing initiative, aggressive outreach),
2. We noticed the (aroma, smell) of his pipe.
3. Naturally, just as we were about to call the police, she (walked, traipsed) in.
4. (Artificial gardens, fake plants) are becoming more popular.
5. There is something (childlike, childish) about him.
6. He soon became active in the (political organization, political machine).
7. The (speech, address) was well received.
8. The book which he (wrote, authored) was published last year.
9. Few of the volunteers were (chosen, selected) for the mission.
10. "Her appearance is masculine but not mannish." [E. M. Forster, *Abinger Harvest*]

§ 14. Suggestion and Slanting

To assert a statement is to manifest belief in it; and the primary use of assertions is to inform others (or yourself at a later date, if you are keeping a diary) of your beliefs. Another use, of course, is to misinform others about your beliefs, as in a lie, where the ostensible or purported belief is not the real one. Beliefs are interconnected in many subtle ways, logical and illogical, and living languages are able to take advantage of this fact to increase the flexibility and the compendiousness of discourse. Thus when you assert a statement, you may show not only that you believe that statement (if you do) but that you believe other statements, too—statements that you don't make explicit, but never the less quite clearly convey.

Perhaps the simplest way to do this is to stress some part of what you are saying, in order to call attention to what you are *not* saying. Someone remarks of a motion picture director: "Oh, his *first* film was really good"; and the emphasis on "first" has the effect of withholding the judgment from the later films, and thus showing that the speaker probably believes they were *not* really good. Perhaps I am reading too much into the sentence; but in some circumstances, at least, this reading would be justified. In this remark, then, we can distinguish two levels of sentence-meaning, parallel to the two levels of word-meaning discussed in the previous section: it is stated that the director's first film was really good; it is suggested that the director's later films were not really good. What is **suggested** by a sentence, in a certain context, is a belief that the speaker or writer manifests, but does not explicitly state. He may not even be aware of what he is suggesting. But if he chooses a certain form of words, the suggestion will be there.

Suggestion is determined by certain linguistic conventions that depend on there being alternative ways of making the same statement or an equivalent, or nearly equivalent, one. To stress the word "first," rather than just say the whole sentence in an even tone, is to claim special significance for that word. To say "Sally is taller than Sue," rather than "Sue is shorter than Sally," is to make Sue's size a standard, and to suggest that Sally is unusually tall, rather than that Sue is unusually short.

Suggestion occurs in many other ways. Just to introduce an adjectival or adverbial modifier may, in some cases, suggest that you are assuming a distinction: To speak of "undesirably unhealthy children" is to classify implicitly, and we wonder immediately whom you would put into the category of *desirably* unhealthy children. A great deal of suggestion depends on such implicit contrast. For example, a Gallup poll in August, 1971, found that a great majority of labor union members supported President Nixon's economic policies. Perhaps the finding was true, but the evidence left something to be desired. For the question they were asked was this: "Do you support President Nixon's plan for providing jobs and halting inflation or don't you?" Since no alternative plan was mentioned, the question suggested that it was this or nothing; and who is against providing jobs and halting inflation? The more sophisticated pollees no doubt set the suggestion aside and answered the explicit question, but perhaps many were misled.

Much suggestion comes by way of presupposition; the remark is straightforward enough, by itself, and yet it would lack point unless something else were true; and that something else is what is suggested. The Senate debated a bill to raise the ceiling for Federal spending, and there was much discussion of one provision of the bill, requiring the President to report to Congress whenever he impounds (that is, refuses to spend) funds authorized by Congress. Some senators wanted to keep this provision, because they were angry at the President's insistence that he had a right to impound funds whenever he chose to; other senators objected that to insert this provision would be implicitly to concede the President's right to impound funds. Some years ago a federal judge dismissed a suit in which the parents of a kindergarten pupil objected that the pupils were required to recite a verse which was actually a prayer, in violation of the First Amendment. The verse went:

> We thank you for the flowers so sweet.
> We thank you for the food we eat.
> We thank you for the birds that sing.
> We thank you for everything.

The judge said, "Its religious connotation, if any, was completely incidental to implanting gratitude in the children for the things about them, irrespective of who placed them there." But to thank *X* for creating "everything" is to suggest that *X* is a Supreme Being of some kind; and surely this verse does implicitly make a religious commitment. At the opposite extreme, I remember reading about a "Witchmobile," or mobile anti-witchcraft unit, which made a tour of many cities in 1972: It was designed to warn people against becoming "involved in the occult," as its sponsor, Morris Cerullo, said. But Mr. Cerullo's interest in these problems had begun in the Far East, where he had spent some time combatting evil spirits and demon powers, and the underlying assumption of the Witchmobile seems to have been, not that people would be led into superstition, but that there actually are witches who ought to be scrupulously avoided.

Much suggestion depends on the juxtaposition of statements, claiming a connection between them that the reader (or listener) is asked to supply himself. Generally there is no difficulty in this: When the novelist writes, "Jack told a joke. Jerry laughed," he does not need to add pedantically, (1) that Jack's joking caused Jerry to laugh, and (2) that Jerry laughed at Jack's joke. The problems with this sort of suggestion come when we try to jam too many disparate facts together in a sentence or short paragraph, and the juxtaposition generates unsuspected, even ridiculous, suggestions.

> The Rev. Beitler had a very busy day this past Sunday, beginning with an early-morning meeting with the Youth Group, continuing with the regular service, at which his eloquent attack on "The New Permissiveness" was well received and much complimented, and including both a wed-

> ding and reception in the afternoon, and a meeting of the church Board of Trustees in the evening, at which funds were voted for repairing the church roof, but the trustees refused the Rev. Beitler permission to take a leave of absence next year.

This makes it sound as though the sermon had been rather *too* effective.

Some of the most difficult problems in controlling suggestion come up when we have a series of items to relate to each other, in a sentence or paragraph. There are three principles in our language that are at work here, not always in cooperation with each other. First, when items are given a parallel syntactical position, it is suggested that they are of the same sort, at least in relevant respects; and if they turn out not to be of the same sort, then there is a confusion.

> To Sharon Francis, beautification is not just a pansy or two in the front yard of a slum dwelling. It involves air and water pollution, good design, and freeways that don't carve up cities.

The phrase, "air and water pollution," has to be taken elliptically ("It involves *doing away with* air and water pollution"); but that suggests that good design and non-carving freeways are equally objectionable. Second, when three items are referred to in a sentence, it is suggested that the third one is the most important. If it really is the most important, the sentence rings—"I came, I saw, I conquered!" (and here the rising order of importance is paralleled by the chronological order). If non-carving freeways strike you as a bit less important than unpolluted air and water, then the passage about Sharon Francis will be a letdown at the end. Third, if a list of several items is presented, it is suggested that those at or near the top are more important than those later on—which is why, if you want to avoid this suggestion, you have to say explicitly that the items are in no special order, or perhaps put them in alphabetical order.

In June, 1966, Pope Paul spoke at a Eucharistic Congress in Pisa, and asked the audience of a hundred thousand to "imitate the faith of Galileo, Dante, and Michelangelo." Since Galileo was born in 1564, the year Michelangelo died, the three names are not in chronological order, and Pope Paul may have meant to emphasize Galileo by putting him first (though the suggestion actually works the other way). The important point, however, is that by putting in Galileo at all, in parallel with the others, he in effect rehabilitated Galileo, ending a long period since the time when Galileo was accused of heresy and required by the Inquisition under threat of torture and death to recant his scientific theories. On November 30, 1968, *The New York Times* reported on the construction site for a new jetport in the Everglades, 40 miles from Miami:

> Populated now by deer, alligators, wild turkeys, and a tribe of Indians who annually perform a rite known as the Green Corn Dance, the tract could someday accommodate a super jetport twice the size of Kennedy International in New York and still have a one-mile buffer on every side to minimize intrusions on the lives of any eventual residents.

A more horribly instructive example of suggestion could hardly be found. First, note that by putting the Indians in a list with deer, alligators, and wild turkeys, the writer suggests that they belong in the same category as these subhuman species. This impression is reinforced by the allusion to the "Green Corn Dance," which, when dragged in in this way (since it is irrelevant to the rest of the story), can only suggest that this kind of silly superstitious activity sums up their lives. And the impression is driven home sharply at the end when we get to the need to "minimize intrusions on the lives of any *eventual* residents"—the Indians, of course, can hardly be counted as real residents (I guess because they don't have mortgages).

The critical reader or listener has to be constantly alert to the suggestions in discourses that come his way. The danger in what is said implicitly is that we may be led to accept it unthinkingly, or at least fail to challenge it at the right time, because we are not fully aware of it. Sometimes we may have to state explicitly what we find suggested in a discourse, just to make sure that we are clear about what it is. A speaker can be challenged; we can ask him whether he actually believes what his words implicitly say and can defend that belief. A writer can't be questioned so readily; but sometimes we can tell, from a close reading of the whole context, whether or not the writer would wish to stand by what he seems to have suggested. It may be that something is clearly suggested in one paragraph, but the general tenor of the article or book runs the other way, and we ought not to hold his suggestion against the author. It is still a stylistic fault, of course; but it may not be a mistaken belief.

The problem for the writer, or speaker, is one of control. Suggestions are vital to ordinary language; they enable us to save many words, and they can give a discourse wit, subtlety, penetration—but they can also get out of hand. We must approach our own writings the same way we approach others'—reading them over, searching for unwanted suggestions that we may have missed. Sometimes a slight rephrasing, the addition of a word or two, a switch to another syntactical construction, will eliminate the suggestion. Sometimes it is hard to eliminate in that way, and the best we can do is put in a warning ("I do not mean to suggest that . . ."); this is not elegant, but it is honest, and it may be prudent. We will seldom have to go so far as the lawyers do, when they have to be most careful, but it doesn't hurt to be able to do the kind of suggestion-controlling that is amusingly described by Edward B. Packard, Jr., in an essay in the *Columbia University Forum* (Spring 1967):

> A lawyer who said, "My client feels you made a mistake," would be derelict in that he may have implied that no one else has that feeling and, worse, that there was only one mistake. The assertion would be more lawyerlike (a favorite word among lawyers) if put: "My client, among others, feels that you made a mistake, among others." It would be an error to put an "among others" after "you," because that might imply that others too, made mistakes, opening the door to a defense that those other mistakes were the legally significant ones, if any. The proper retort is, "Your client, if any, is wrong, and my client's mistake, if any, caused no damage, if any occurred." Once the lawyers have thus made their positions clear, the chances of a lengthy lawsuit are excellent.

Note that Packard uses "implied" for "suggested," as many do; though "implied" properly connotes what is implicit, rather than explicit, I think it is best reserved for logical connections, such as those we discussed in Chapter 2.

Taking a discourse as a whole, we can think of its meanings as comprising two layers, or levels. Its *explicit* meaning consists in what it states (or commands, or asks, or exclaims, if it contains nondeclarative sentences), taking into account only the standard designations of its words. Its *implicit* meaning consists in (1) what it suggests about its subject (the objects or events described on the first level), and (2) what it says about its subject by virtue of the connotations of its words. Now when a discourse is true on the first level but false on the second level, and carries the suggestion that because it is true on the first level it is also true on the second level, that discourse is **slanted**. Since it contains some truth, it invites our belief, but under cover of that truth it slips in suggestions and connotations that may (if we are not on guard) lead us to believe other things that are in fact false. We hesitate to call such a discourse "false," so we would usually say that it is "misleading." False advertising is advertising that claims the price is $3.98, when it is really $4.98; misleading advertising says the object sells for "ONLY $4.98," which gives the right figure but falsely suggests that the price is unusually low.

The distinction between outright misstatement and what might be called "misrepresentation" is brought out by the manager of the United Press International audio network, Frank Sciortino, in a discussion of how to doctor a tape-recording of a conversation—which can be done so as to be practically undetectable even with a spectrograph. Eliminating the word "not" from a sentence and thus transforming it into its contradictory is certainly a change on the first level. Moving a sentence from one context to another so that it purports to be an answer to a quite different question is a second-level change—though it may be just as damaging and morally objectionable. "The easiest editing of tape is to leave out words or entire passages and thus eliminate certain information. More sophisticated editing can compress or extend portions of conversation without altering the pitch, change inflections or even change the apparent emotional frame of mind of a speaker—to make him sound hesitant or confident or even evasive. Pauses can be eliminated or added, 'Uh's' or stutters can be added or subtracted."

Even if we suspect that a tape has been tampered with, there is no way of recovering the truth, unless we can lay our hands on the original. And the same predicament is presented by a slanted news story. If we were at the scene of the accident ourselves, we may be able to tell where the account has been slanted—though it would be wrong to be dogmatic about this, since even eyewitnesses can be mistaken. If the language is highly colored, and has a jazzed-up dishonest ring to it, we have reason to be suspicious of its second-level truth, even if we don't know what the truth is. When we can compare two news reports (of the same event) that are slanted in different directions, we may be able to make a tentative reconstruction of at least part of the truth. In the end, what has to count most heavily is our confidence in the source: that the reporter or the periodical can be trusted at least to aim at objectivity (i.e., nonslantedness).

A slanted discourse builds up a general impression of its subject: it invites us to share a point of view. A news profile, or a biography, of a certain statesman or political figure may present him sympathetically, or admiringly, or contemptuously, or in a way that makes him appear ludicrous, stupid, pitiful, or absurd. Maybe he *is* stupid, and if you say so plainly you're not slanting; it is only slanting if he is not really stupid, or not as stupid as he is made out to be, and the impression of stupidity is created by suggestion and connotation. We could distinguish various techniques of slanting, all depending on these two resources of language; perhaps the distinction most useful to keep in mind is that between two kinds of slanting technique (which, remember, can be used deliberately or unknowingly). These two kinds of technique are illustrated by the discussion of tape-doctoring. Slanting by *selection* is choosing certain facts and omitting others that are known and pertinent to the matter at hand. Slanting by *distortion* is arranging the facts selected so as to suggest relationships that do not really hold.

It is not easy to spot cases of selection, unless you have some special knowledge of the subject; the newspaper editorial doesn't tell you what it has left out. But sometimes you can think of questions that haven't been answered, and that you would want answered before you would be prepared to accept the discourse as true (or substantially or approximately true) on both levels. And sometimes, if you search, you will find that someone else—an editorial writer in another newspaper, or the spokesman for an ecological or consumer group—has given an answer, and pointed out the essential but missing data. The Administration announces that the middle class is the group that benefits most from what are commonly called "tax loopholes." In 1972, persons in the $7,000 to $10,000 (adjusted gross) income groups realized a total savings of $310 million in mortgage interest deductions, while persons in the over-$100,000 bracket saved only $55 million. Conclusion: if you're in the middle class, support tax loopholes. But a Ralph Nader tax reform group replies that there are about 12 million individuals and families in the first (middle income) group, and about 91,000 in the second (upper income) group—so the average individual savings amounted to $24.00 in the first group, and $602.00 in the second group. Which persons are really benefiting more?

Sometimes it is debatable whether slanting has occurred. The chairman of the city housing authority, Mr. Golar, boasts that the crime rate in public housing projects in New York City is only one-third that of the rest of the city (11.2 per 1,000 persons, as against 33.2), and with eight percent of the city's population, the public housing projects have less than two percent of the murders. Sounds good. But the City Council president, Mr. Garelick, says the comparison is unfair: The relevant, indeed crucial, fact omitted is that housing projects have no banks to rob, no stores to burglarize, no gas stations to hold up. Criminal opportunities are comparatively limited. Perhaps public housing project crime rates should be compared with private housing crime rates—which might give quite different results. Often the most difficult and basic issue is precisely over what is, and what is not, relevant to the question—and this issue can only be resolved, in the end, by a good deal of inductive and deductive reasoning. *Time* reported on a new American history textbook for public schools, *Land of the Free*, which aimed to give a true picture of the role of minorities, especially black people, in American history, but which was running into opposition in California for being "un-American." This book, in other words, aimed to correct the slanting (by omission) of earlier books. Yet *Time* called it a "blooper" that "the text, for example, relates the pioneering civil rights leadership of W. E. B. DuBois, fails to note that he became a Communist in later life." Was this slanting? You could argue that, since DuBois's pioneering work in several areas was done before he joined the Communist Party, this fact is quite irrelevant to it, and was properly omitted.

There are more clear-cut cases. A booklet put out by General Motors, "What is Air Pollution? A Story of Air Pollution and Cars," for free use in elementary schools, does seem a little one-sided in its selection of facts when it fails to mention that air pollution can have adverse effects on health, that it can damage buildings, destroy recreational areas, and cause lung ailments. (Its cartoon depictions of various pollutants as little pixies that annoy, but run away fast, are a form of visual slanting.) And American histories, especially of the age of Jackson and Van Buren, do seem to be slanted (even if they win Pulitzer Prizes), when they make no mention at all of the Trail of Tears, the forced removal of more than 125,000 Indians from the Southeast, in defiance of the United States Supreme Court, causing enormous hardship and suffering, and thousands of deaths. No doubt every historical work is selective, but the silent treatment of various groups, and most especially of American Indians, has been a conspicuous example of slanting by selection.

Slanting by distortion is also difficult to detect without background knowledge; but again we can be cautious and skeptical. Any set of facts can be arranged in various ways, by juxtapositions and syntactical constructions; and each arrangement claims a connection of some kind. If you have independent reason to believe that the connection exists, there is no problem; if not, you may have to withhold judgment until you can check further—especially when you are dealing with the advertising copywriters. A well-known gasoline used to advertise that its gas was "made with platinum." True, in a sense; platinum was used as a catalyst in raising the octane to the required level. But a catalyst is used to promote a chemical reaction without itself entering into it. And the suggestion is that the gas has platinum in it, which would show how valuable it is, and how cheap at the price. A not-so-well-known toothpaste used to claim that "only Brisk toothpaste gives you the same fluoride dentists use. . . . The same tooth-decay fighter proved for ten years in drinking water." The suggestion is that because there was considerable evidence that the use of fluoride in drinking water does diminish tooth decay, there was also considerable evidence that brushing teeth with fluoride will do the same—and this suggestion was false.

The most extreme examples of slanting, especially (but not exclusively) by distortion, can be found in everyday sexist writings. These are so easy to find, and so nauseating, that it is tempting to omit examples. But I cannot. When the New York State Court of Appeals ruled that a woman could not be denied the opportunity to become a baseball umpire merely on the ground of sex, the *Daily News* headlined the story:

GAL UMP WINS THE DECISION
COURT PUTS HOUSEWIFE AT HOME PLATE

and went on:

> The Court of Appeals ruled yesterday that a woman's place can be behind the plate rather than at home. The final score was Mrs. Bernice Gera, 5, Professional Baseball, 2, as the petite Jackson Heights housewife won her bid to become baseball's first woman umpire.

This paragraph alone provides a fairly extensive lesson in slanting, from its general impression (that Ms. Gera was not to be taken seriously) to the details of suggestion (e.g., that her struggle was only a game to her, not a serious ambition) and connotation (e.g., "petite," "housewife")—including more than the hint of a pun on "home plate." Much the same kind of slanting can be done with less heavy-handedness. Here is the beginning of a *New York Times* story about a woman who had already run twice for public office:

> Sitting in a German restaurant sipping a gin martini with two olives, Linda Jenness looked more like a suburban housewife having lunch in town than the candidate of the Socialist Workers party campaigning for President. The 30-year old blonde secretary from Atlanta was wearing a handsome pants suit, and her freckled face beamed with goodwill as she outlined her goal—a Socialist government for the United States within her lifetime.

Freckled faces may be in the style of souped-up human-interest journalism, and a good deal of anti-woman slanting in newspapers, magazines, and television, goes unnoticed (though it still indoctrinates) because we are so used to it. A good way of bringing out the slant is explained by Pamela Howard, author of the article in (*MORE*) from which these examples have been lifted: Try rewriting the passage and applying it to a male political candidate. It would still be a put-down, but the allusions to hair, clothes, age, and the "suburban housewife" would not work nearly as well.

In these examples we see how slanting can generalize, and make the individual into a representative of a group: It is not only the particular woman trying to become a baseball umpire, or working to achieve socialism, who is implicitly said to be stepping out of her true social role, revealing her incompetence and making herself ridiculous, but women in general. To become sensitive to this kind of slanting we must bring our own relevant experiences and convictions to what we read. But even if we are puzzled about what to believe—about whether, say, it is proper for a woman to be a baseball umpire—so that, strictly speaking, we do not know whether the implicit meanings here are really false, still we will be hopelessly muddled if we do not at least recognize the implicit meanings for what they are. There are many problems here, and people disagree, but one thing is sure: we shall not be able to solve these problems, and resolve these disagreements, if we cannot learn to think about the women's movement in clearer and sharper terms than these.

A check-up quiz

What is suggested by each of the following headlines?

1. COLLEGE GRADS HIRED IN
   CITY TEACHER SHORTAGE
2. VOLUNTEERS AID
   CHILD-ABUSERS
3. MISSING CHILDREN
   FOUND AT HOME
4. UNION LEADERS CONSULT RANK
   AND FILE ON PENSION PLAN
5. PRESIDENT CLAIMS PRICE FREEZE
   SUCCESS; ENDS FREEZE NEXT WEEK
6. MAN JUMPS OFF BRIDGE;
   WAS TO TESTIFY TOMORROW
7. MAYOR RELUCTANT TO RAISE CITY TAXES;
   WOULD VIOLATE MOST POPULAR CAMPAIGN PROMISE
8. SMUT CASE GOES TO TRIAL;
   JURY PICKED IN RECORD TIME
9. BEEF SHORTAGE SEVERE;
   HARD ON HOUSEHOLD PETS

10: CONCERT POORLY ATTENDED;
   MENDELSSOHN VIOLIN CONCERTO
   PERFORMED BY GORSKI

§ 15. Emotive Language

Although in this book we are concerned with words primarily as they are used to frame assertions and arguments, we must not lose sight of the fact that words can be used for other purposes as well. For often when we use words we are doing two or more things at the same time, and sometimes these purposes get in each other's way.

An important feature of words is their emotive aspect, or their connection with emotions and feelings that enter into the situations in which they are used. Words are emotive in two ways. First, they have **emotive tone**: This is their capacity, when used in certain contexts, to reveal the emotions or feelings or attitudes of the speaker. The strongest examples are, of course, racial and other group epithets. Those American soldiers who were stationed for a time in Vietnam and who felt hate and contempt for Vietnamese, called them by the now-famous names, "gook," "dink," "slope," "zip" (this last derived from "zero intelligence potential"). Once acquired, emotive tone is a property of the words, and is present when anyone uses them, even if he happens to be unaware of their emotive tone and does not in fact feel the emotion that the words display.

Second, words have **emotive force**: This is their capacity, when used in certain contexts, to arouse emotions or feelings in those who read or hear them. Group epithets have this capacity, too, though "fag," for example, will of course tend to arouse different feelings in different audiences: contempt in one, anger and indignation in another. The words "massive," "compulsory," "wholesale," when conjoined with "bussing" by the practiced demagogue, and the phrases "exacerbated racial frictions" and "heightened racial tensions," as applied to further efforts to desegregate the public schools, still have their dependable emotive force for large numbers of voters.

In speaking of emotive force, we must keep it distinct from the simple arousal of emotion in general. If someone says he put arsenic in the soup you have just finished eating, he may succeed in evoking an an emotional response. But that response is caused by your belief that his statement is true, and it reflects a reasonable concern about your health. Emotive force is something more direct and immediate that works independently of belief, so that the emotions are in excess of what is reasonably called for by the situation. When environmentalists some years ago criticized the pollution in the Houston ship channel, caused by indiscriminate factory effluences, a public official told a reporter, "'Arsenic' is a scare word." If little or no arsenic was involved, but the word was thrown around, then its emotive force was being exploited; if, however, the environmentalists were alarming people by uttering a simple truth that dangerous quantities of arsenic were being dumped into the water, they were not relying upon emotive force at all.

We describe the emotion aroused by a term as having a certain quality: fear, hope, affection, pity. We also describe it as having a certain direction along an axis of approval/disapproval. A *laudatory term* evokes a positive or favorable feeling toward the things within its comprehension: "treasure," "bargain," "masterpiece," "the Constitution of the United States." A *derogatory term* evokes a negative or unfavorable feeling: "dirt," "crook," "pollution," "sky-jacking." In between there are more or less *neutral terms,* which seldom, if ever, evoke a definite emotion: "ecological niche," "alpha-wave," "negotiable instruments," "syllogism." Neutrality is nothing to be dogmatic about, though: Unless a term is a technical term from science or industry, used only in special contexts, it may take on emotive force sooner or later, especially if it comes to be used in discussions of social problems that are themselves matters of passionate dispute. One would think that "Gross National Product (GNP)," "Federal highway system," "housing project," "space program," and other such familiar and handy terms would be neutral enough, and no doubt they are often used neutrally; yet in the course of public debate and disagreement, they have taken on marked emotive force in certain quarters, among those who feel quite strongly about the problems.

The variability of emotive force can hardly be overstressed. One of the difficult tasks of a writer or speaker who resorts to emotive language is to be sensitive to the responses that may be expected from the audience he addresses—as well as to be aware of the way others will probably react. Perhaps certain words have nearly the same emotive force for nearly everyone who speaks the language, at least in a particular year. "Freedom," for example—who is against it? Well, there are those who have complained bitterly about what they call the "permissiveness" (bad word!) of present-day American society, and sometimes contrasted freedom unfavorably with the kind of order and tradition they would like to have prevail. Perhaps they have not yet made "freedom" a pejorative term, but it is less positive for them than for others. "Toleration" used to be positive for many, but it has become negative for some, since the critiques of what is (oddly) called "repressive toleration." Recent attacks by the counterculture gurus on science, intellect, and "objective knowledge" (so much less desirable to them than "subjective knowledge") have given these terms some negative emotive force in certain circles.

The emotive force of a term, whether positive or negative, depends in large part upon its meaning. Two terms may have the same, or nearly the same, comprehension—that is, apply to the same things—and if they differ in emotive force, that may be because of the difference in what they designate. Perhaps the very same countries that were once called "backward," later "undeveloped," are now called "emerging." If United Nations officials decide to choose one of these words rather than another, it is because they designate different properties; and some of these properties are thought to be more desirable, hence more suitable for public emphasis, than others. Two terms may have the same, or nearly the same, designation, and their difference in emotive force may depend upon a difference in connotation. I suppose that "bugging" has pretty much the same designation as "covertly overhearing conversations by electronic means"; but it has come to connote undesirable qualities that are not part of the meaning of its paraphrase: for example, a nefarious purpose, disreputable personnel, little regard for others' privacy.

We need emotive words—that is, words with marked emotive force or emotive tone—for many purposes, not least to give honest and accurate expression to our strong feelings when the occasion calls for that. But when we are trying to conduct an argument, or carry on a reasonable dispute with someone over a difficult issue, emotive language can cause trouble. Since it carries implicit judgments of approbation or disparagement, it may beg the question at issue, and give us the illusion that we have proved what we only fervently believe. It may throw the argument off the track by arousing irrelevant feelings of distress or annoyance. It may make it hard for us to grasp subtle logical relationships, because we are blinded by rage or too scared to distinguish between the real and the imagined peril.

Suppose a discussion begins this way:

> *A:* It does not make me proud of my country to think of the way we have hired thousands of Korean and Thai and other mercenaries to fight for us in Southeast Asia. It's cowardly and it's like the Hessian mercenaries the British brought against us in the Revolution.

We can imagine various responses; here we are interested in those that are influenced by the rather emotive word "mercenaries" that *A* has introduced. One continuation shows the extent to which *A*'s own thinking has been affected by this word:

> *B:* Come, now. A mercenary is one who gets paid for performing military service for some government besides his own—otherwise the proposed volunteer American army that is supposed to replace the draft would consist of mercenaries! The Korean and Thai soldiers were carrying out orders of their own government which simply wished to support us in holding back the advance of Communism in Asia. Surely you admit this important distinction.

> *A:* We hired people to fight for us; I call them mercenaries, in plain words.

The "plain word" is not so plain, after all; and perhaps it is partly because of *A*'s enjoyment of the emotive significance of "mercenary" that he is unable to grasp, or too impatient to attend to, the relevant distinction that *B* proposes. Evidently this discussion is not going to get very far if important complications are brushed aside. *A* wants to express his dislike of the United States subsidy for foreign troops; the emotive word suits him fine. *B* does *not* want to express dislike of the subsidy—at least, not until he is convinced that it was wrong. If *B* gives in and uses the word "mercenary," he will be in effect expressing a negative attitude he does not really have; if *A* insists on this word, therefore, they are at an impasse.

Another continuation shows how the emotive word might affect *B*'s thinking, if he were less wary:

> *B:* That's a nasty thing to say about our great allies in the war against Communism. Comparing them to Hessians, and calling them "mercenaries," as though those brave soldiers were only interested in money, and did not care who they fought for, so long as they got paid! The fact is, they had something no Hessians had: a faith in democracy and an abhorrence of totalitarian Marxism. Of course Korea and Thailand are poor and need financial help—unlike Australia and New Zealand, which also contributed troops to the war in Vietnam. That's what the war was all about, after all: giving the free nations of Southeast Asia the opportunity to develop their own governments under freedom and achieve economic advance with free enterprise. Of course we had to pitch in and help them.

Note what has happened. The word "mercenary" has worked so strongly on *B* that he lashes back with equal ardor, losing sight of the original statement which he started out to refute, and ending up by defending a proposition (namely, that the United States military action in Vietnam was justified) that *A* never denied. The discussion has been derailed by emotive force.

We see here two ways in which strong feelings can affect thinking and lead to fallacious argument.

In the first place, feelings can narrow attention, limiting the range of important data that are taken into account, the number of possible hypotheses that ought to be considered, the number of distinctions that need to be made for clear thinking. When feelings are aroused in a dispute in such a way as to lead a disputant to leave out relevant ideas or facts, we shall call this the **fallacy of oversimplification**. *A*'s rejoinder above is an example. The oversimplifier, or capsule-thinker, may take advantage of other fallacies that we have noted—the black-or-white fallacy or the argument from analogy. He often says that the point can be put in a nutshell, or boils down to a short formula. When you are trying to make him see that criticizing certain policies of the government is not being disloyal to the country, he just says, "Love it or leave it!" When you point out that before we make up our minds whether some alleged criminal who is being tried in the public press rather than in court is really as guilty as he seems, we would have to have a good deal more information, he only says he's tired of listening to "bleeding hearts."

In the second place, feelings can shift attention. When we feel rather similarly about two things that are really distinct, we may jump from one to the other, even though facts that have a bearing on one may have no bearing at all upon the other. Thus one party in a dispute—like *B* in his second reply, above—slips away from the point at issue to other points that are not at issue, dragging in remarks that only confuse the course of the argument. When feelings are aroused in a dispute in such a way as to lead a disputant to bring into the discussion ideas or facts that are not relevant to the question at issue, we shall call this the **fallacy of distraction.** The grasshopper thinker is recognizable by the exasperating and confusing way in which he turns from one point to another, even though the connection is slight. When you are trying to convince him that the city should raise taxes to keep the schools and subways running, he says his father instilled in him early a deep distrust of taxes, and that anyway the schools don't teach reading properly and the subways are dirty. When you give him reasons to support your contention that Picasso was the greatest painter of the twentieth century, he replies that when his little sister paints, she too puts the eyes anywhere on the face; that Picasso had too many mistresses; and that, after all, what can you expect from a dedicated member of the international communist conspiracy?

Both of these fallacies (here very broadly defined) are much facilitated by emotive language—and they can be guarded against to some extent by careful control over emotive language. Contextual control is one kind: fairly high-powered emotive words can sometimes be packed in a context that absorbs and reduces their heat. The emotive significance is played down by cues to a more complex and flexible attitude, and indirectly the emotive force is also reduced.

> Those Korean and Thai mercenaries of the United States—if I may use this convenient term without wishing to suggest that they were in any way bad people or lacked noble motives—do raise, I think, important policy questions that ought to be pondered by future United States governments.

The calm tone and thoughtful air, and the explicit rejection of any conscious effort to express or arouse negative feelings, do a good deal to damp the fire. It may be that if *A*, in the dialogue above, had been able to talk this way, *B* would never have been so upset; and maybe *A* himself would have been capable of straighter thinking. But there is always a danger, as long as the word remains; its emotive force and tone are damped down, but not extinguished, and at some later point, if *B* is incautious enough to allow *A* to continue using the term, *A* may (wittingly or unwittingly) take advantage of its latent emotive force to make *B* feel, illegitimately, that the use of such mercenaries was a kind of exploitation, a morally wrong thing to do.

The second, more drastic, treatment of emotive language is to dispense with it when it gets in the way and turn to comparatively neutral substitutes. If *A* becomes aware that he is relying a little too much on the emotive force of "mercenary" to make his speech effective, or that his discussion with *B* is getting hung up on *B*'s unwillingness to conduct it in these terms, he may decide to withdraw the word and substitute something less abrasive. He could say:

> *A:* Well, forget the word "mercenary." Let's just call them "troops subsidized by the United States." You can hardly object to that term, since it seems like an accurate description. Now, my point, if you recall, is that we should not have subsidized those troops during the war in Vietnam.

This could help to get the discussion back on the track.

But it is not only the emotive force of single words that can lead to oversimplification or distraction; often more complicated maneuvers are used to arouse emotions in a questionable fashion in order to obtain unearned assent. As the argument moves along, other matters are introduced, not because of their logical relevance, but because of their emotional appeal—in the expectation that the emotions they arouse will make it easier for the receiver (the reader or listener) to overlook flaws in the argument: an equivocation or a syllogistic fallacy or a hasty generalization. These *emotional appeals*—deliberate attempts to arouse emotions as a way of effecting oversimplification or distraction—are as various as are emotions themselves. Moreover, they work best when combined in subtle ways and developed carefully through a long discourse. But it will be well to give brief examples of some of the major types.

Among the most effective is alarm, or the *appeal to fear*. Of course, there are times when we should be alarmed, because we have good reason to be; there is nothing illegitimate about telling someone that inflation will continue, and that his worst fears of higher prices will almost certainly be realized—if that's what the evidence indicates. But the emotional appeal to fear is something else; the possibility of some undesirable or frightening eventuality is held up, without adequate evidence, to alarm the reader or listener and shake him up.

> I don't want to be pessimistic, and I don't have any inside information or anything. But just think what would happen if the trash-collectors went on strike: the garbage piling up, the stench, the germs, the diseases, the deaths! How can you even think of giving them the right to strike?

Of course, ghastly things *could* result from a trash-collectors' strike: but this writer hasn't really given any arguments to show they will happen, nor has he shown that the evil effects outweigh the serious limitations on economic freedom that are created by statutes prohibiting certain groups of employees to strike. All he does is throw a scare.

The *appeal to hate* is perhaps even more widely employed. Of all emotions none is more likely than rage to render someone wholly unfit for rational thought. And it seems that this is the easiest emotion of all to arouse in many people who are frustrated and oppressed by their circumstances and by the social system under which they live.

> If you don't think that the welfare system in this country is a rotten mess that needs complete overhauling, you listen to that great recording by Johnny Cash about the typical families on relief sitting around drinking booze before their color television sets, or driving around in Cadillacs, while you—you, the hard-working, thrifty, honest Middle American—do the work and pay the taxes to make this possible.

A song, even a popular one, is of course not really evidence (unless you consider it evidence of the singer's attitudes), and the picture given here of the "typical" family on welfare does not have the slightest resemblance to the situation revealed by existing (and overwhelming) evidence. Still, by talking this way, and by singing the song, you can make people mad just thinking about "welfare chiselers"; and once you put them in this frame of mind, they may be prone to accept any "solution" you propose, however impractical, futile, or cruel.

The *appeal to pity* can have the same power to induce acceptance of plans and projects that would not stand up at all under calm, cool, critical examination. Of course, one could argue that pity is a somewhat more appropriate emotion than hate to feel toward people who can find no escape from a life of extreme poverty and deprivation (though maybe is is not as enjoyable an emotion to feel). But welfare reform proposals that are adopted hastily in a mood of strong sympathy may also turn out to be impractical and futile—though probably not so cruel. Pity can also be used to get inaction. In 1972 there was a widely-printed advertisement by the Foulke Fur Company, which was designed to counter the frequent protests against the killing of Alaskan seals to make fancy fur coats. According to this advertisement, the clubbing of seals was really "one of the great conservation stories of our history," a mere exercise in wildlife management, because "Biologists believe a healthier colony is a controlled colony." Not a dry eye in the house, what with the "increased disease, starvation and fatal injuries" to which unkilled young seals would be exposed. It sounded as if the little seals were practically lying down begging to be clubbed to death so that they wouldn't starve from overpopulation. In this case, pity for the seals was not misplaced—as *Environmental Action* (April 15, 1972) showed in its analysis of the facts omitted by this advertisement—but not exactly for the reasons given.

The *appeal to respect* takes advantage of the audience's already existing acknowledgment of someone as an authority, whose opinion or judgment carries weight. When the authority does indeed know whereof he speaks, when his expertise is precisely in the field under discussion, there is, of course, no fallacy: If we are disputing about business cycles, we can properly call on an economist (though when we find other economists strongly disagreeing, we may run into a problem trying to decide among the authorities). When we cite an authority in some other, unrelated, field, we make an illegitimate appeal to authority: Just because the economist is an expert on business cycles does not mean that his judgment carries any special weight when it comes to questions about the contemporary novel, the ethics of genetic engineering, the theology of Martin Buber, or the desirability of building a bridge across Long Island Sound. Everyone knows this, of course; yet people continue, from time to time, to try to persuade others to accept, say, statements about the safety of cigarette smoking on the expert testimony of air line pilots.

The *appeal to pride*, or flattery, is most used by political speakers who know that by making the audience bask in a warm glow of self-congratulation and smugness, they can weaken its critical defenses. Many a rather outrageous thesis has been set forth by a speaker and warmly applauded by an audience already carefully softened up by such phrases as that in the example above: "you, the hard-working, thrifty, honest Middle American." If this is the image you have of yourself, or the way you like to think of yourself, you can only admire the perceptiveness and insight of a speaker who recognizes you for the fine person you are; and such a speaker, of course, will give you reasonable statements and support them by sound arguments, even if you don't clearly see how the conclusions are supposed to follow.

There is one more kind of emotional appeal that is very common: its best name is the *ad hominem* argument. In a dispute, there is some question at issue, some statement about which the parties disagree. Evidently it is one thing to talk about the question at issue (*ad rem*), and another thing to talk about the people who are disputing (*ad hominem*). To switch from one topic to the other is a form of distraction. But it may be quite effective if it succeeds in undermining confidence in what the speaker *says* by saying something negative about what he *is*.

Certainly the Foulke Company's defense of killing seals to provide luxury

> pelts to the favored few raises important questions, which must be carefully considered. But don't forget that this is an advertisement; it is presented by a company that is in the business (having a very handy monopoly contract with the United States Department of Commerce) of selling fur for a profit. That has to be their primary concern. How then can we believe anything they say?

Certainly, in considering all aspects of this dispute between the fur company and the wildlife conservationists, it is well to be aware of special interests and the danger of special pleading. But this paragraph essentially argues:

> The fur company's statements are motivated by a desire for profit.
> *Therefore:* The fur company's statements are false.

This is an obvious *non-sequitur* (it simply doesn't follow); yet the error may sometimes be hard to see when it is embedded in lively and emotional prose. Many things may be true of a writer or speaker—that he is a felon, a racist, a public relations man, or the President's press secretary—and they may legitimately put you on guard. But nevertheless his statements have to be considered on their own merits, in the light of the evidence for or against them. When we lose sight of this point, we fall victim to the *ad hominem* arguer.

A check-up quiz

In each of the following pairs, one term is laudatory, one derogatory. For each pair, find a term (which may consist of several words) that has a closely similar designation but is fairly neutral.

1. trusting . . . gullible
2. resolute . . . fanatical
3. public servant . . . person on the government payroll
4. innocent victim . . . dupe
5. associates . . . accomplices
6. philanthropic reformer . . . do-gooder
7. exercizing firm and decisive leadership . . . being dictatorial
8. keeping one's eye on the ball . . . having tunnel vision
9. cautious in deciding . . . indecisive
10. ambitious . . . on the make

OUTLINE-SUMMARY: chapter five

A common name, or general term, *comprehends* a class of individuals (as "college" comprehends Mt. Holyoke College, Grinnell College, San Jose State College, etc.); it *designates* a set of properties which are necessary conditions for belonging to its comprehension (since an institution cannot correctly be called a "college" unless it teaches something, the property *teaching* is part of the designation of "college").

The *attendant properties* of the comprehension of a term are properties that all or most of the objects in its comprehension have, or are widely believed or frequently said to have (as dangerous, sneakiness, and so forth, are associated with copperheads). A *metaphorical statement* ("This man is a copperhead") states an absurdity in the literal sense, and hence must be false on the level of designation; to interpret it, we look for attendant properties of the predicate-class that can be attributed without absurdity to members of the subject-class (as a man *can* be dangerous, and so forth). The *connotations* of a term are those attendant properties that have been made a part of the meaning of the term by the metaphorical use of that term in previous contexts.

Besides what it states, a statement may also *suggest* that certain things are true, by showing that they are probably believed by the speaker ("I won't go if *he* drives" suggests—but does not state—that I *will* go if someone else drives). A *slanted discourse* is true as far as the designations of its terms go, but false in respect to what they connote, or is true in what it states but false in what it suggests, and it claims to be true on the level of connotation or suggestion *because* it is true on the level of designation or statement. Whether composed deliberately or unwittingly, it is misleading. The techniques of slanting can be classified as *selection* (giving a one-sided impression by leaving out an important part of the picture) and *distortion* (giving the wrong impression by juxtaposing things in a suggestive way).

The *emotive tone* of a term is its capacity to reveal the emotions of one who utters it. The *emotive force* of a term is its capacity to arouse emotions. This force may be either positive ("immense scholarship" is laudatory) or negative ("academic pedantry" is derogatory) or neutral ("displaying considerable learning and use of scholarly methods"). Since the emotive force of a term is largely dependent on its meaning (both its designation and its connotation), when we substitute a neutral term for an emotive term (that is, one with marked emotive force), it is never an exact synonym, but it may be sufficiently close in relevant respects to replace it in a particular discussion, where it will be less likely to interfere with the reasoning. Emotions get in the way of a dispute by *oversimplifying* the issue, that is, leading the disputants to leave relevant facts out of account, or by *distracting* them from the point, that is, leading them to bring in irrelevant facts. Certain *emotive appeals* are common: to fear, pity, hate, pride (flattery); reliance on illegitimate authority; the *ad hominem* argument.

Exercise 21

In each of the following pairs of statements, either the same word is used metaphorically in two different contexts or similar metaphors are used in the same context. In each case, point out some differences of meaning between the two metaphorical uses.

1. (a) The Administration was trying to *cover up* the scandal.
   (b) The Administration was trying to *keep the lid on* the scandal.
2. (a) The candidate appealed to the *silent majority*.
   (b) In most administrations, the Vice President is more or less a *silent* partner.
3. (a) If the neo-isolationists had their way, the United States would *retreat* from its responsibilities abroad.
   (b) The rational foreign policy for the United States is to *untie* some of its entanglements abroad.
4. (a) The cities are being *strangled* by the superhighways.
   (b) The cities are *choked* by their traffic.
5. (a) "The very *glue* of our ship of state seems about *to become unstuck*." [Justice Harry A. Blackmun on the effects of Watergate.]
   (b) The ship of state is about *to founder on a rock*.
6. (a) "Let others *wallow* in Watergate, we are going to do our job." [President Nixon.]
   (b) Others may *flounder about* in the Watergate mess; we shall do our job.
7. (a) Most of television is a *wasteland*.
   (b) Most of television is *Kool-Aid*.

Exercise 22

State explicitly what is suggested by each of the following.

1. Ophthalmologists have concluded that there is no reason to believe that the *eyes* are permanently damaged by watching television.
2. At Le Pavillon, one of the oldest French restaurants in Philadelphia, Chef George Jolly has established a reputation for the finest cuisine without unnecessarily exorbitant prices.
3. Richard M. Nixon told a cheering breakfast audience today, "Never in history has the United States been in more trouble in more places."
4. In his book on the S.D.S., Kirkpatrick Sale gives the organization credit for alerting students to "automation, poverty, disarmament, and the bankruptcy of the Cold War."

5. He looked at the hard eyes under the little beaky nose and decided that Husker was at least a man, and probably not a fool.

6. THE BETHEL INN. The "Gem of New England Inns" offers you our own 9-hole course, heated pool, tennis, private beach club, cocktail room, delightful dining and beautifully redecorated rooms. We still do all the things the right way—from June 1 to October 10.

7. Solita Alconcel, wife of the Philippine consul general in Hawaii, returned from an 18-day visit to her homeland yesterday with glowing reports of the advantages of martial law. "The rich can now go out without fear of being shot or molested," she said.

8. Shortly after the liner left Cobh, Ireland, her last port of call, Albert Ittner, boatswain's mate, became ill, and the ship was reduced to half speed while Dr. Cletus B. Walker, surgeon, performed an emergency appendix operation. Within a few hours five stowaways were discovered.

9. [Senator Roman L. Hruska, of Nebraska, replying to charges that President Nixon's nominee for the United States Supreme Court, Judge G. Harrold Carswell, was at best a mediocre judge.] Even if he were mediocre, there are a lot of mediocre judges and people and lawyers, and they are entitled to a little representation, aren't they? We can't have all Brandeises, Frankfurters, and Cardozos.

10. I agree with Eric Fromm's profound observation, in a recent *New York Times Magazine* article, that man's "vital interests" are "life, food, access to females, etc."

11. The House, by a vote of 118 to 69, approved yesterday an amendment to outlaw premarital and extramarital sex in Pennsylvania. A final House vote is expected next week on the bill, which makes malicious mischief in caves a misdemeanor.

12. [Mayor Richard Daley of Chicago] Gentlemen, get the thing straight once and for all—the policeman isn't there to create disorder, the policeman is there to preserve disorder.

13. [From an essay by Lewis F. Powell, who later became a Justice of the United States Supreme Court.] Rather than "repressive criminal justice," our system subordinates the safety of society to the rights of persons accused of crime. The need is for greater protection—not of criminals but of law-abiding citizens.

14. My position has been completely misunderstood. I am wholly opposed to the indiscriminate use of chemicals, germs, etc., in warfare.

15. [John J. Wilson, attorney for H. R. Haldeman and John D. Erlichman at the Senate Watergate hearings, when reporters questioned him about his having referred to Senator Daniel K. Inouye of Hawaii as

"that little Jap."] That's just the way I speak. I consider it a descrip- of the man—I wouldn't mind being called a little American.

Exercise 23

The arrest of five men in the headquarters of the Democratic Party, at the Watergate building complex on June 17, 1972, led in time to an extraordinary sequence of revelations. The Senate Select Committee on Presidential Campaign Activities held hearings through the summer of 1973. Here are parts of two newsmagazine reports of one of the most dramatic weeks of those hearings—five days of testimony by John W. Dean III. Since these reports are abbreviated here, the impression they give may not be completely faithful to the whole context, but you are to consider only what is given here. Read them carefully, and compare them with respect to the following questions:

1. How do they differ in the general impression they give (a) of John Dean and (b) of President Nixon?
2. What statements are included in one of the reports, but not in the other, and how does the inclusion or omission of these statements affect the general impression?
3. How does the order in which statements are introduced differ from one report to another, and how do these differences in arrangement contribute to the difference in general impression?
4. Find pairs of approximately synonymous terms from the reports. How does the difference in meaning (designation or connotation) contribute to the difference in general impression?

I

. . . Now the grave charges against the President had passed a point of no return. Carried with chilling reality into millions of American homes and spread massively on the official record of a solemn Senate inquiry, the torrential testimony of John W. Dean III fell short of proof in a court of law. But the impact was devastating. As President, Richard Nixon was grievously, if not mortally wounded.

Nixon was a continent away at San Clemente, going about the business of the presidency. He reached a historic compromise with Congress on halting the Cambodia bombing by Aug. 15 *(see page 14)*. He prepared to celebrate the nation's 197th Independence Day, a Fourth of July dimmed by deeply troubling questions (in the words of the Declaration) about the "just powers" of the present Government and by increasing doubts about the "consent of the governed." Though not present in the packed hearing room, Nixon was personally and directly confronted by the crouched figure of his youthful accuser, until lately his faithful counsel.

Leaning into the microphone, Dean, 34, spoke in a lifeless monotone that would long be remembered by TV audiences. There were just enough unexpected angles and lines in his face, including a slightly crooked grin, to rescue it from mediocrity. Thanks to a pair of glasses, he looked more owlish than his earlier, boyish pictures had suggested. With impressive poise and a masterly memory, Dean spun his detailed web of evidence. He readily admitted his own illegal and improper acts. But he emerged unshaken from five full days of recital and cross-examination, with his basic story challenged but intact.

Clearly, without some kind of direct and detailed Nixon reply, the committee—and the country—would have difficulty believing that the President was not an active and fully aware participant in the Watergate cover-up, as Dean charged. In fact, how and when the President would reply became a decisive factor in his hopes for political survival. Chairman Sam Ervin and other committee members had already begun to ask for his appearance.

With dozens of dates, snatches of dialogue and some documents, Dean had similarly implicated Nixon's most intimate former aides, John Ehrlichman and H. R. Haldeman, in multiple actions in the Watergate cover-up. Less vigorously but still deeply, Dean had also drawn into that circle of conspirators a man he much admires, former Attorney General John Mitchell.

Focusing Blame. While Nixon's deputy press secretary quickly revealed that the President had no intention of submitting himself to senatorial questioning, a White House counter-strategy seemed to be emerging. It was to blame Dean and Mitchell for the Watergate wiretapping and its concealment. Ehrlichman and Haldeman will likely take the blame for shielding the clandestine activities of the White House team of agents—"the plumbers"—but plead that these were separate from Watergate and necessary in the interest of national security.

The focusing of blame on Mitchell triggered speculation that he might become angry enough to lash back at the entire White House. But his attorney said last week that Mitchell will not implicate the President when he becomes the next Ervin committee witness, as scheduled. Although Mitchell talked almost daily with Nixon last year even after quitting the President's re-election committee, he has told investigators that nothing the two men discussed would indicate that Nixon knew about the wiretapping in advance or the concealment later or who had been involved. Mitchell will apparently deny, as he has all along, that he ever approved the political espionage plans.

The White House strategy showed in a harsh assault contained in a memo from one of Dean's White House successors, Special Presidential Counsel Fred J. Buzhardt, and a list of 39 White House-inspired questions. Read by Senator Daniel Inouye, they failed to rattle the accuser. Contradicting point after point in quick response, Dean easily handled the attack.

Indeed, the effort backfired, which is perhaps why the White House quickly disavowed Lawyer Buzhardt's friendly personal contribution to the proceedings. It failed by straining credulity in portraying the slender, subservient Dean, a born follower, as the "mastermind" in the Watergate cover-up, with former Attorney General John Mitchell as "his patron." It contended, in effect, that this cunning pair participated in planning the political espionage at Democratic National Headquarters and then, to conceal that fact, they hindered the investigation by the FBI, compromised the CIA, ordered evidence shredded, and arranged for payoffs and offers of Executive clemency to the arrested burglars to ensure their silence. Creating a constitutional crisis almost alone, the Buzhardt statement in effect charged, Dean and Mitchell kept the truth of all that concealed for some nine months from such shrewd White House officials as H. R. Haldeman, John Ehrlichman, Charles W. Colson —and the President.

While White House records and future witnesses before Senator Sam Ervin's Watergate committee may yet impugn Dean's story in a convincing way, it emerged from last week's test by fire as more credible than either Buzhardt's conspiracy theory or the President's less accusatory brief of last May 22. Instead of depicting a duped President and innocent top-level aides. Dean's damning version held that the lawless efforts to conceal the political implications of Watergate were an automatic and widespread White House response intended to protect the President's re-election prospects—and Nixon as a self-interested participant. Dean admitted his own role, but said that, rather than being what Buzhardt termed "the principal actor," he took orders, often reluctantly, from his domineering superiors, Haldeman and Ehrlichman. Claiming relatively little influence in shaping policy at the White House, Dean insisted that "my title was the best part of the job."

More specifically, Dean contended that the Watergate wiretapping operation was known in the White House by Chief of Staff Haldeman before the June 17 arrests—and since Haldeman regularly reported fully to the President, Dean "assumed" Nixon could have known. He said that he did not know firsthand, however, whether Nixon did, in fact, have such advance knowledge.

But, as early as Sept. 15, Dean charged, the President clearly indicated his awareness that a cover-up was under way. Then and later, Dean claimed, the President talked directly to him about Executive clemency and hush money for the wiretappers, as well as about ways to prevent the potential damage of Justice Department investigations, Democratic Party civil suits and congressional hearings.

If Dean's claims are true—and his supporting details as well as some of his circumstantial documents were impressive—that would make Nixon's May 22 denials outright lies or at least render the presidential statements once again "inoperative." At that time Nixon said flatly that he had known nothing about offers of clemency or of any efforts to provide the defendants with funds and that he had taken no part in any efforts to cover up Watergate.

Dean's direct charges against the President still lacked corroboration. Dean's motives remained suspect, since he obviously hoped to avoid a long prison term for his admitted illegal acts. Yet even if those facts leave many unconvinced of Nixon's complicity in Watergate, Dean's dismaying description of the climate of fear existing within the Nixon White House is almost as alarming as the affair that it spawned. With little regard for the law and under repeated proddings by the President himself, Dean contended, the Nixon staff used or contemplated using almost any available tactic to undermine political opponents, punish press critics, subdue antiwar protesters and gather political intelligence, including lists of "enemies" *(see story page 19)*.

Dean insisted that in this fortress of fear he served "as a restraining influence against many wild and crazy schemes." Periodic surveillance of Senator Edward Kennedy was surreptitiously ordered, even when he was on a trip to India, but it turned up nothing of interest to the White House. However, when a round-the-clock tailing of Kennedy was demanded by Haldeman, Dean got the project canceled on the sound theory that the tracker might be mistaken for someone posing a threat to Kennedy's life.

Although a Colson associate later claimed that it was only a joke, Dean took seriously Colson's suggestion that Washington's Brookings Institution be fire-bombed and raided to get some politically sensitive papers. In fact, Dean grabbed a military jet to California in order to persuade Ehrlichman to order Colson to forget the idea. Dean said he simply filed away many suggestions that he considered extreme and responded to them only if there were persistent pressures from his superiors.

It was Nixon's personal outrage at being exposed to demonstrators that seemed most dramatically to set the pre-Watergate White House mood. Dean told of Nixon's spotting "a lone man with a large ten-foot sign stretched out in front of Lafayette Park" within sight of his window. Soon a White House aide was rushing to round up "thugs" to take care of the protestor. Dean intervened, got police to persuade the man to move. A man who broke police lines during Nixon's Inauguration but was knocked down by Secret Service agents well short of Nixon's car so angered the President that Dean was repeatedly badgered for not getting the man prosecuted. An investigation was launched, but Dean found that the trespasser had had no intention of harming the President. Dean could only explain helplessly that crossing a police barricade was too trifling a violation for officials to pursue.

However trivial each of such incidents seemed in isolation, together they formed an ominous pattern that made Watergate comprehensible to Dean. What he called "an insatiable appetite for political intelligence" stemmed directly from Nixon, as Dean told it in his matter-of-fact manner. The President was convinced that antiwar Senators had links with U.S. radicals, who had foreign ties, and he continually demanded evidence of this. Intelligence agencies repeatedly said is was not necessarily so. "We never found a scintilla of evidence . . . this was explained to Mr. Haldeman, but the President believed that the opposite was, in fact, true." He demanded better intelligence.

Lawyer-like, Dean resisted most attempts by the committee to draw him into discussing personalities or making value judgments. He conceded that the Watergate break-in was "the first act in a great American tragedy" and said he found it "very difficult" to testify about what others, including "men I greatly admire and respect," had done. He found it easier to admit that he had obstructed justice and helped another man commit perjury in the affair. Yet Dean's story did, indeed, indict others.

II

For Richard Nixon, it was a week such as few Presidents in history have had to endure.

For five days—from June 25 through June 29—much of the nation watched on television while a witness swore under oath before Senate investigators that the President not only knew about the White House cover-up of the Watergate affair but actually participated in that cover-up himself.

The witness was John W. Dean III, who was the White House legal counsel for three years until fired by Mr. Nixon on April 30.

More troubles ahead? Unless the Dean story is effectively refuted, many in both parties suggest it could raise serious questions about the future of the Nixon Administration.

Already, a move toward impeaching the President has begun in the House of Representatives. A resolution calling for the House to be provided all Watergate information has won sponsorship of 17 House members.

The embattled President has run into growing trouble with his legislative program in Congress. The trouble shows up among Republicans as well as among Democrats.

One Republican strategist in the House puts it this way:

"Recent votes—on Cambodia and welfare appropriations—reflect desertions from the party leadership. A lot of Republicans are thinking in terms of every man for himself."

The story of President Nixon's role in the Watergate affair is still far from finished, however.

Witnesses who were even closer to the President than Mr. Dean are still to be heard from.

One of those witnesses—former White House chief of staff H. R. Haldeman—predicts that "when the truth is completely known" it will clear President Nixon, and Mr. Haldeman as well.

Even before Mr. Dean had finished his long testimony, the White House —although not the President himself— began to fight back. It presented the Senate investigating committee a statement challenging the Dean version of events.

The White House statement charged that Mr. Dean himself "was the principal actor in the Watergate cover-up" and that "he had a great interest in covering up for himself." Also, it suggested, Mr. Dean "must have immediately realized that his patron, Mitchell, would also be involved.

This was the first statement from the White House that implicated former Attorney General John N. Mitchell in the Watergate case.

It was also the first White House reaction to the Dean charges.

A spokesman said the statement, prepared by presidential counsel J. Fred Buzhardt, was "not reviewed" by Mr. Nixon and "does not represent a White House position," but was prepared only as a base for cross-examination of Mr. Dean. It was read into the committee record by Senator Daniel K. Inouye (Dem.), of Hawaii, with the comment that "the President is entitled to his day in court."

As for Mr. Nixon, he stood by his denial of May 22, the core of which appears on this page.

The White House rejected suggestions by committee members that the President should testify. But aides indicated he might speak out at a news conference after the major witnesses have told their stories.

The main story that the President will be called upon to answer came from the lips of John Dean.

In the beginning—. Mr. Dean freely admitted his own participation in the cover-up. And he testified to being present at two meetings where plans for the Watergate bugging were discussed. But he said he thought those plans had been rejected. And he insisted:

"I do believe I was a restraining influence at the White House. There were many wild and crazy schemes, some of which I have not testified to."

As principals in the Watergate cover-up, Mr. Dean named such close Nixon associates as Mr. Mitchell, who was Mr. Nixon's former law partner and campaign director, as well as Attorney General, and two men who once were the top White House aides —H. R. Haldeman and John D. Ehrlichman.

All these had been mentioned in earlier testimony. Mr. Dean was the first witness to claim first-hand knowlege about the role of Mr. Nixon himself.

Mr Dean, in effect, called Mr. Nixon a liar. When asked if he believed the President was telling the truth in his denials of Watergate involvement, Mr. Dean answered: "No, sir."

In his prepared statement of 245 typewritten pages, which took him an entire day on the witness stand to read, Mr. Dean told of a meeting with Mr. Nixon on Sept. 15, 1972—almost three months after the June 17 break-in and bugging of the Democratic Party headquarters in Washington's Watergate complex.

At that meeting, Mr. Dean testified, "the President told me that Bob [Mr. Haldeman] had kept him posted on my handling of the Watergate case" and "told me I had done a good job." He related that "the President was pleased that the case had stopped with Liddy." G. Gordon Liddy, named by several witnesses as the author of the bugging plan, was among seven men convicted as participants or conspirators in the raid. Then Mr. Dean added:

"I left the meeting with the impression that the President was well aware of what had been going on regarding the success of keeping the White House out of the Watergate scandal."

Scrutinizing the testimony. This statement by Mr. Dean became a major target of senatorial cross-examination. Under questioning by Senator Edward J. Gurney (Rep.), of Florida, Mr. Dean conceded that he had not discussed "any aspects" of the Watergate cover-up at that meeting with President Nixon, and he had only assumed that the President had been filled in by his top aide, Mr. Haldeman. Declared Senator Gurney:

"Your whole thesis, in saying the President of the United States knew about Watergate on September 15 is purely an impression. There isn't a single shred of evidence that came out of this meeting that he knew anything about it."

Replied Mr. Dean: "Senator, I don't have a thesis—I'm reporting the facts as I have been able to recall them truthfully to this committee."

Asked by committee counsel if he had any doubts after September 15 "about the President's involvement in the cover-up," Mr. Dean said, "No, I did not."

When reminded that it was his word against that of the President—who has categorically denied any knowledge of the cover-up—Mr. Dean said he was willing to take a lie-detector test. . . .

Exercise 24

Analyze the emotive appeals in the following passages, and show how they are used for oversimplification or distraction.

1. The whole trouble with the country today is that the Supreme Court, until the past few years, was simply violating a series of natural laws. You can't change a natural law, because it's rooted in nature; but if you try to change it, you will end up doing mischief. One is the law known as "preemption," formulated by that great poet Colley Cibber, "Possession is eleven points in the law." This law is attacked when the Court rules that the American white race should surrender the position it has possessed historically. Another is the old adage that every man's

home is his castle—which is being flaunted every time local sovereignty and states rights are undermined. Another is that of President John Adams: "There are inequalities which God and Nature have planted and which no human legislature can ever eradicate"—which is a sufficient answer to all attempts to do away with race prejudice, poverty, etc.

2. American education is a system devised by political oligarchs and their "educator" hirelings to cope with the awkward situation posed by the mistake of throwing open the schools to all. How can you keep the mass of ordinary people ignorant and politically manageable, given that you are not allowed to keep them out of school? This was the problem set for American educators; and the solution was not to teach anything important to anybody. Even the students are now rebelling, because they are so bored and they see more clearly how they are being duped by a system that pretends to teach them but mainly babysits to keep them off the streets. The only solution is to give up compulsory universal education, put the ineducable ones back to work, and revamp the whole system so that it really gives the few elite students what they need to learn if they are to run this republic well.

3. We representatives of the packaged-food industry do not, of course, object in principle to what is called "truth-in-packaging." But for Congress to pass a new bill under this title is to suggest that all packaging in the past has lied to the consumer or deceived him or misrepresented the amount of food the package contains. Sure, I know that a steady stream of housewives trooped before Senator Hart's committee telling about alleged malpractices in packaging baby foods, cereals, cookies, candy, detergents, cake mixes, etc. No doubt it taxed their brains to do the calculations necessary to realize that sometimes a pound package is bound to contain only 14½ ounces, and that the bigger package does not always contain the most, and that rice that costs 29¢ for 14 ounces is more expensive than one that costs 12¢ for 5 ounces. The point is that the industry is being hurt by all this bad publicity; as our trade paper *Packaging* has said, "If we don't smother all this talk about how the consumer is being deceived and cheated, our whole economy will emerge sell-shocked."

4. Nothing seems more obvious to people—even those who profess to be true Christians—than that when there is a natural disaster, a flood or drought or tornado, etc., the government should step in and help the victims. They call that "charity." But this is a serious error, and a dangerous one. The concept of charity is inescapably individual; only persons can be charitable in a Christian sense, for only they can give away something that belongs to them. Governments can only take from some and give to others—which is a form of robbery under another name. When a disaster strikes, we must count on the good will of private individuals to rally around and organize help. That is acting virtuously. We must not compel help through taxation, and there is no virtue in

giving when you have no choice. It leads inevitably to the welfare state, to the proliferation of wasteful bureaucracies, to Stalin's collectivization of the farms for the people's "own good," no matter how many had to be killed to do it.

5. Although the popular image of capitalism is getting better all the time, as it shows more and more (in Germany and Japan, as well as in the United States) how capable it is of providing the good life, we have no reason for complacency. Opinion polls show that each year more people believe that there should be a limit on the profits of corporations. But this is really a limit on human ingenuity and creativity, a limit on man's greatest potentiality. Dynamic industry cannot operate with the straightjacket of a profit ceiling. What is wanted is more freedom to free the inherent powers of capitalism. What made America great was not the fear of growth, of progress, of greater and greater challenge. Remember what a famous Attorney General used to say, "When the going gets tough, the tough get going." That is the heart of the matter.

6. Believe it or not, the greatest danger to America in recent decades has come from those who have benefitted most from it, and who have, ironically enough, in their best hours, given it the most power. I am referring to the scientists of America. Sure, they were helpful in developing the big bombs, radar, rockets, and the rest. Fine. But the scientific mind is essentially a fixing mind, it is organized to look at technical problems and solve them. It does not, it cannot, understand the practical problems of the real world of politics and international relations. So we have physicists telling us that we should ban the bomb, limit testing, stop piling up our atomic inventory, etc. Maybe they have a built-in death-wish; maybe they are just too wrapt up in atoms to understand people; maybe they are all soft on left-wing ideas about peace and brotherly love. Anyway, they will be the death of us unless we follow this sage advice: *keep the experts on tap, not on top!*

7. As usual, any serious attempt to keep children from being brainwashed by their textbooks is scurrilously attacked by the Know-it-alls. Two widely used junior and senior high school history textbooks have recently been purified here in Virginia, so that they will represent the Virginia point of view, not that of some other state. We are constantly urged to make our school textbooks dwell on the so-called horrors of slavery, the slave trade, slave ships, etc.—in other words, to give a completely one-sided view. But I am glad to see at last that a balanced view has been restored. One of these valuable texts, for example, points out that "The slave did not have to work as hard as the average free laborer, since he did not have to worry about losing his job. In fact, the slave enjoyed what we might call comprehensive social security from cradle to grave. Life among the Negroes of Virginia in slavery times was generally happy. The Negroes went about in a cheerful manner making a living for themselves and for those for whom they worked."

8. [Letter from a mail-order firm]
Dear Friend:

We've never met in person, but I feel like I already know something about you. (See if I'm not right.) You're a person who recognizes and appreciates quality. You take pride in owning fine possessions. And when you buy something, you demand performance and value for your money.

How do I know all that? Not from gazing into a crystal ball! Simply because the kind of purchases you have made in the past show that you are a discriminating buyer.

Now let me ask you this: Don't you wish you could depend on genuine quality and craftsmanship in *everything* you bought? Well, that's a pretty tall order. You know how much shoddy merchandise is being put out these days . . . stuff you wouldn't have in your own house, and would be downright ashamed to *give* anyone. Because you realize that every gift is a reflection of your own taste.

I'm in a luckier position than most. As a professional shopper, I do my buying *worldwide*. One week might find me in Japan, the next in Holland or Italy. That way I can check out *firsthand* what the world's finest craftsmen, designers and manufacturers are producing. I can ferret out the best values—and, if need be, do a little good old-fashioned Yankee haggling! . . .

9. I feel that it is about time someone stood up for the taxpayer, and exposed these do-gooders, the "New Jersey Society for Abolition of Capital Punishment," who have taken upon themselves to cry out for the murderers, but hardly ever give a word of sympathy to the victims, or their families, who do not consider the cost to the taxpayer, or the time of responsible officials, to listen to their pleas of mercy, but ignore hearing the pleas of the victims, as they were dying, begging for mercy from these animals, who now themselves want mercy.

Knowing of my stand for seven years as a Legislator, of opposing the abolition of capital punishment, I have received many letters and phone calls requesting me to make a public statement of condemnation of this group, and to ask the Bar Association to also speak out, before the public lose faith in lawyers because of a few who have sought to cast reflection on their profession. [Letter to the Philadelphia *Bulletin*, August 8, 1960, from Assemblyman Francis J. Werner, Camden, N.J.]

10. A professional car-thief speaks: "I do a lot more for this country than most people realize. First, I create jobs. I hire men to steal cars, repaint them, fix them up, forge new papers, drive them out of state, find customers. This takes a lot of talent that might otherwise go to waste. And it's good for the economy. Second, I help working people to get what they could otherwise never afford. Say a guy is dying to own a Cadillac, but he hasn't the income; I can get him a nice one, and save him maybe $2,000. Now he's happy. So is the guy whose car we stole; he gets a brand new Cadillac from the insurance company, minus the

scratches and dents we had to take out. The Cadillac company is happy, too, because they sell another Cadillac. Naturally, the insurance company is not happy, but it's so big that nobody cares *personally*. They're protected. I'm sending two kids to college, and keeping my wife happy with clothes. So what's wrong with what I'm doing?"

Exercise 25

Study the following dialogue, and comment on the ways in which emotive language or emotive appeals interfere with the logical orderliness of the dispute.

GUN-CONTROL LAWS?

X: Another family murdered with mail-order guns that any vicious hoodlum seems to be able to buy! When are we finally going to have some legislation to register guns and keep them from being sold to criminals?

Y: There's no need to get hysterical and start screaming for anti-gun laws just because of a murder or two. Murders will happen, after all, if not with guns then with pitchforks or neckties. Let's be calm and keep our perspective on this thing. It's not guns that kill; it's people. Do you want to eliminate people?

X: The point is that many deaths occur because guns are handy when somebody is angry, and because guns are easy to get hold of (even if you have a long criminal record). Last year around 25,000 people died in this country from bullets fired by accident or with murderous or suicidal intent. Reasonable regulation of firearms would certainly lower this figure. Statistics are cold, but think of the young policeman lying dead in the street with a bullet in his back—the presidential candidate struck down by the mail-order assassin—the gas-station owner robbed of his money . . .

Y: But think of the sportsman, with his favorite guns, the real he-man and woodsman, embodying the best of the American spirit of rugged independence and self-reliance, going forth into the wild woods to hunt. You're proposing to take his gun away from him.

X: I'm not proposing to take his gun away from him—though I don't think it takes much of a he-man to go around shooting defenseless deer. My idea would be that if he has no criminal record and uses his gun only for sport, not for robbery and murder, then he can keep it; but it should be registered, in case it is stolen and falls into less dependable hands.

Y: But what about the Communist menace? The day may come, you know—oh, I know you'll scoff at this, but I'm deadly serious—when all those yippies and hippies and leftist Democrats and their radical subversive Weatherman followers get together, lay their hands on a lot of bombs and guns, and start to overthrow the government. Then a man's home has to be defended, like those pioneers of yore when the Indians came to scalp them and their families. Everyone should have a gun to protect himself against those who have guns.

X: But you're undermining your own argument. If we had adequate firearms regulation, genuine subversives would have to register their weapons, like everyone else, or be subject to criminal prosecution.

Y: Hah! You think they'd register their guns?—those guys won't even sign loyalty oaths! You think you can work out the proper laws and regulations, and all that. But basically the situation is this: If guns are outlawed, only outlaws will have guns.

X: Of course we don't want to outlaw guns completely, but there are far too many lying around already, and a lot of the ones being used to wound and kill have been stolen from the homes of people who bought them to "protect" themselves. And if they are not stolen, the kids get them out of the closet to play with them, and next thing you know, another child dies playing with his father's loaded gun.

Y: So you are attacking the home! I thought it would come to that—first they want to take away guns, then they are telling people what they can and cannot do in their own homes! Let me remind you that the Constitution, the very Bill of Rights that all these civil liberties types are constantly haranguing us about, provides that the "right of the people to keep and bear arms shall not be infringed." There it is in black and white—a constitutional right. I say it's an infringement if you tell me I can't buy a gun, or if you make me register it, so that when the government decides to take the guns away, they will know exactly who has them and where to find them.

X: That passage in the Bill of Rights refers to the need for a "well-regulated militia," and the meaning is not that any individual person has unlimited freedom to amass his own secret arsenal of dangerous weapons, but only that the government is forbidden to round up and confiscate firearms from people wholesale. You have to recall the conditions that prevailed at the time this Amendment was adopted; the situation is very different today. We are not expecting Indian raids or foreign soldiers to land in rowboats on Long Island; it is no protection in modern warfare that every house have a well-oiled rifle in it.

Y: Well, I suppose I'm not smart enough to understand all these subtle sophisticated constitutional distinctions; I try to get to the heart of the matter, without a lot of hair-splitting. Do you realize that the licensing of guns would tend to discourage hunting, and that would mean that the millions of dollars paid for hunting licenses would not be available to spend on state parks, picnic areas, forest conservation, and the like? All of us benefit from these.

X: Of course we benefit, but is that the only way the money could be raised? If we really want parks, surely we can pay for them. . . . But I don't want to get off on a discussion of how to pay for parks. The central issue is guns. Do *you* realize that there are over 90 million guns in private hands in the United States, with a million and a half manufactured or imported every year? That guns are used in 65 per cent of all homicides, 63 per cent of all robberies, in this country? That there are 135 handguns for every 1,000 persons in this country, as compared with 30 per 1,000 in Canada, 10 per 1,000 in Israel, and 5 per 1,000 in Great Britain? So each year 10,000 are murdered by guns in this country, 176 in Canada, 30 in Great Britain. Don't you see that guns have become an obsession, a psychotic need, a constant invitation to violence? Is it any wonder that children grow up thinking the gun is the solution to everything, and learn to get an obscene thrill from Bonnie and Clyde killing! I don't know what we're coming to; I can only foresee increasing numbers of gun deaths, to the point where nobody is safe anywhere.

Y: I'm tired of this kind of defeatist talk; it smacks of un-Americanism. The people who are demanding gun controls now are the same voices we have long heard in every fuzzy civil liberties effort to protect criminals and hamstring the police and courts. These days three freaky suburban housewives with a mimeograph machine and a grant from some foundation can get more attention than 5,000 hard-working, taxpaying ordinary citizens. When will we learn to stop listening to this nutty and discredited liberal talk? Gun control would put a sign on every home: "There are no firearms inside; burglars need have no fear of getting shot." Is that the best way of combatting crime?

X: Well, for one thing, it might encourage them to leave their guns at home, if they have any. O.K., they might rob the house, but at least nobody would get killed in the process—and when I say "nobody," I mean nobody, because, much as I hate burglars, I can't forget that they, too, are human beings, with perhaps wives and mothers, lured into a life of crime by circumstances that may have been beyond their control; so they may not be beyond the hope of rehabilitation, if we can get to them in time and steer them into lawful ways of life.

Y: Lawful ways of life! There beats the bleeding heart! If you are so concerned with the criminal, why don't you work on him? Gun control, as Senator Frank Church has said, is like trying to cure measles by forbidding spots. Go after the criminals, not the guns.

X: Some analogy! It stands to reason that if a criminal has no gun, he can't shoot anyone. Surely that's clear enough, even for a fanatical gunslinger like you. I don't care for guns, and I don't hate guns, so my argument has some objectivity; but you are already a convinced firearms collector and hunter, so I don't think we can set much store by what you say.

Y: I resent your insinuations. I hope the day won't come when we sportsmen of America, in order to defend our constitutional rights, have to stand, like the embattled farmers of Lexington, and defend our right to possess arms by force.

X: That's the kind of argument that I expect from you. I remember reading an editorial in *The American Rifleman,* the organ of the National Rifle Association. It was entitled "Goodbye to the Y"; it reported a movement to withhold support from the YWCA for coming out in favor of gun control to end the senseless killing; and it suggested that "others may follow suit"— a clear invitation to economic pressure of the crassest sort, a low blow indeed!—and a very unchivalrous one, coming from the gunslingers' chief organization.

Y: I don't have anything against the YWCA, which I love, and which my sister belonged to once. But, after all, what can you expect from a bunch of Nervous Nellie women, many of them unmarried, who know nothing about the real world, in which a man has to assert himself or fall behind, has to compete with others who are trying to get ahead of him, who may have his victories and defeats, but can never feel wholly down or lose pride in himself so long as he knows he has a gun that speaks with power and authority when he presses the trigger.

chapter six

DEFINITION AND THE CONTROL OF MEANING

We have looked at some of the powers of language: its capacity to make delicate distinctions, develop complex logical trains of thought, move us to feeling and to action. We have seen the price of power: the burden imposed on the conscientious writer and cautious reader to keep language reasonably clear and exact, and to guard against equivocation and nonsense. We have seen the penalties of power: the danger of falling into confusion of meaning and thought, the possible breakdown of communication and reasoning. We have found remedies, too, as we went along; but there is more to be said about them.

Breakdowns of communication are of two sorts: misunderstanding and failure to understand. The former is much the more troublesome, since both parties may go on believing for some time that they understand each other, when in fact they are talking about different things or making quite different assumptions. Each sort of breakdown requires help, and help of substantially the same sort—namely, a fuller explanation of what is being said, that is, the *elucidation* of its meaning.

Perhaps the simplest kind of communication failure is that which occurs when *A* uses a word whose meaning is simply unknown to *B*. If the character on one of those television medical sagas says that "mediate ausculation of the patient produced no results," someone may have to explain to the viewer that "mediate ausculation" is listening, with the help of a stethoscope, to sounds produced by tapping. To supply such information about the technical sense of the term is to restore communication by bridging a gap: It is to exercise special control over the term in order to insure that it be taken in the right way. In this case the control is easy, since the doctors understand each other, and the layman does not require a technical elucidation. To use the language of the law, or of diplomacy, or of epistemology (that is, the philosophical study of the nature of knowledge), may require very careful meaning-control, if the experts themselves are not to baffle each other or unwittingly mislead each other. In everyday life we seldom need to meet such high standards, but we have all had experiences of being seriously inconvenienced, deeply disturbed, even made miserable, by a breakdown of communication. We must treat language with respect, for to use it at all (like driving a car) is to take on a considerable responsibility.

§ 16. Defining Your Terms

There are various ways of elucidating meaning when the occasion calls for it. When we can, we often give examples. Someone who doesn't know the meaning of a word will surely get some help, and may get a great deal, if we can either produce an example for him to inspect or at least cite an example and give him instructions for finding and confronting it. Say he has never heard of gerbils. If one of the children, or a neighbor's child, has one of these creatures as a household pet, we can show him one. If not, we can advise him to take a trip to the rodent quarters of the nearest well-equipped zoo. Or say he does not know what people mean when they speak of "acid rock" or of "pop art." The best thing to do, at least for a start, would be to play him some examples of acid rock or show him some examples of pop art. But if no examples are handy, perhaps we can name a record to buy or a pop artist whose works he should look at.

A single example may not take elucidation of meaning far; it may leave many questions open. Whatever example of pop art happens to be offered, it will have some features that are not necessarily present in all works of pop art; if we show him an Andy Warhol tomato-soup can or a Claes Oldenburg "soft sculpture," he may think all pop art is related to groceries or that all pop art is three-dimensional. One way of correcting these misapprehensions is to choose our example with great care so that it is a good example of its kind: what is sometimes called a *paradigm case*. In this sense, a good example of pop art may not be one of the best works of pop art, but it will be typical, it will feature the salient properties of pop art.

A paradigm gerbil, in the same way, would not be abnormally small, sickly, with a rare color of fur, but characteristic of its species. A second way of keeping the example from being misleading is to give a number, and a variety, of examples. Suppose we give samples of the work of several pop artists, say Oldenburg, Warhol, Robert Rauschenberg, Roy Lichtenstein, James Rosenquist. One who is puzzled about the meaning of "pop art" might, by trying to see what these works have in common, come at least to some vague grasp of the meaning of the term (which is, after all, a rather vague term anyway).

But examples by themselves, no matter how good or how many, will often be insufficient for elucidation of meaning. This is obviously true for terms that have empty comprehensions, since no example exists: I very much doubt that there are any such things as warlocks, but the word has a definite meaning in the theory and practice of witchcraft. It is even true of the examples we have considered. Unless the person we are speaking to is a zoologist (who will know what a gerbil is, anyway, and therefore needs no elucidation), we will probably have to supplement the example with commentary: "Notice that he differs from other small rodents by having a short, broad head like a chipmunk; so he looks cuter and pleasanter than a mouse or a rat." Certainly when it comes to an artistic movement like pop art, the examples are extremely confusing, in their variety and playfulness, to anyone but an art critic—and even the art critics have spent a great many pages without wholly agreeing on a meaning for the term they nevertheless find so useful and, somehow, apt.

Verbal elucidation of meaning—the elucidation of one word with the help of other words—takes various forms. We may need to say something about the *usage* of a word: that "Ned" is a common nickname for "Edward"; that "massacre" is applied to collective homicides, but not to individual ones; that "supercalifragilisticexpialidocious" (from *Mary Poppins)* is a nonsense-word used by children to exemplify extreme word-length. Sometimes it is helpful to say something about the origin of a word (including its etymology, if it has one): that "sandwich" comes from the Earl of Sandwich, who is said to have invented the sandwich; that "psychosomatic" comes from two Greek words meaning "mind" and "body." Etymology does not, of course, determine meaning, and it is an error to speak of the etymological (or original) sense of a word as its "literal meaning"; but etymology is sometimes illuminating.

The most important kind of verbal elucidation, however, is the definition. You will recall that the properties designated by a term (in a given type of context) are those properties that anything must have in order for the term to be correctly applied to them (in a context of that type). When two terms have the same designations in a certain range of contexts, they are synonymous in those contexts. A **definition** is a rule of synonymy; it can be thought of as having the following form:

> "Hatchetman" *to have the same designation as* "insider who does dirty work for a political figure";

or:

> "Hatchetman" *having the same designation as* "insider . . ." (etc.).

A colon serves as abbreviation:

> "Hatchetman" : "insider who does dirty work for a political figure."

There are several points to notice about this definition, which comes from William Safire (it is offered as a paradigm, but requires a bit of commentary). First, it consists of two parts: the term whose meaning is being elucidated, because someone may be in ignorance or doubt about it (this is the **term to be defined**), and the term that is presented as synonymous with the first term, and is assumed to be more familiar or more explicit (this is the **defining term**). The definition is not a statement about these two terms, but gives a rule about their relationship. Second, both terms are put inside quotation marks; this is because the definition is not, strictly speaking, about hatchetmen, but about the word "hatchetman." If we say "Hatchetmen are indispensable in politics" (because somebody has to run the "department of dirty tricks"), or "Hatchetmen are despicable" (because if nobody ran the department, the political process would be a good deal more fair), we are making statements about hatchetmen. But if we say

> "Hatchetman" has ten letters,

or

> "Chutzpa" is a Yiddish word for unmitigated effrontery,

we are talking about words, and so the words are in quotation marks, as in our definition. Dictionaries do not use quotation marks because they find it neater to use another convention: putting the word to be defined in boldface type.

Third, a definition not only elucidates the term to be defined (if you understand the defining term); it is also a rule of substitution. For if the two terms are synonymous for some type of context, then they may be substituted for each other in any context of that type. If it is true that

> Mr. X is Senator Y's *hatchetman,*

then it is true that

> Mr. X is Senator Y's *insider who does his dirty work.*

Note that in making the substitution here, I have changed the defining term a little, to keep it from being redundant (since we can assume that Senator Y is a political figure). The change I have made is not substantive, and does not affect the designation of the term. A simple definition, such as

> "Warlock" : "male witch,"

allows exact substitution: If Senator Y is a warlock, then he is a male witch, and vice versa.

What makes substitution possible at all, however, is that the term to be defined and the defining term are the same part of speech. And this is an essential feature of an acceptable definition. To elucidate the word "gratitude," for example, it won't do to say:

> Well, gratitude is when a person has a positive feeling toward another on account of having received some benefit from him.

This is rather wordy, anyway; but let us try it in our standard form:

> "Gratitude" : "when a person has a positive feeling toward a benefactor."

This may be too terse to be perfectly exact, but we can use it provisionally. Suppose it is true that

> Senator Y felt *gratitude.*

If we try the substitution we get:

> Senator Y felt *when a person has a positive feeling toward a benefactor*

—which makes no grammatical sense. If we rewrite the definition as

> "Gratitude" : "positive feeling toward a benefactor,"

the substitution is smooth.

The substitutability principle also rules out various colorful ways of speaking that are sometimes called "definitions," but are not really so. A wit (Victor Navasky) defines:

> "Uptight" : "someone who doesn't tell you that which you already believe to be true."

This throws a sharp light on the way many people use the term "uptight," but it shouldn't strictly be considered a definition; it is not intended to allow substitutions. Picturesque metaphorical "definitions" are also sometimes illuminating (at least, if you don't know a great deal about the subject), but they make their point through connotations, not designations, and metaphorical connotations are far too sensitive to contextual change to survive substitutions. Moreover, when you are elucidating connotative meaning, as in explicating a poem, you are doing something quite different from defining. So

"Religion" : "opiate of the masses"

is not a definition.

When you frame a definition, the best way to insure that the defining term will be syntactically parallel to the term to be defined is to begin by thinking carefully of the *category* to which the comprehension of the terms to be defined belongs. What very general sort of thing is gratitude, or a warlock, or religion, or uptightness? Is it an object, a class of objects, an event, a property, a relationship, a process, a state, or condition? Categories are the extremely broad and basic classes in which we place things. Before we can hope to frame a satisfactory definition of "gratitude," we must decide upon a category for it. Gratitude seems to be a condition, more specifically a person's state of mind—so our defining term must also refer to a state of mind, or the definition has gone astray. Sometimes we see that there is more than one way of categorizing the term to be defined. Suppose it is "constitution." In one sense it is an object, a written document; in a more important sense it is a set of rules originally agreed upon, and later added to and modified by political processes conforming to those rules. Questions about categories can take us into deep philosophical problems when we try to define fundamental terms like "rights," "society," "history."

If a term is radically ambiguous, in that (when taken in different senses) it can comprehend objects belonging to different categories, or if the sense that we are interested in is limited to certain verbal contexts, it may be convenient to give a *contextual definition.* In a contextual definition, we do not try to find a defining term that is synonymous with the term to be defined, considered by itself; we define the term in a certain sort of context. This is particularly helpful with adjectives. How shall we define "anthropomorphic"? Well, what sort of thing are we thinking of applying this adjective to? We can speak of anthropomorphic deities, or of anthropomorphic conceptions of deity; and perhaps it would be as well to keep them distinct.

"Anthropomorphic deity" : "deity described as possessing human form or attributes."

"Anthropomorphic conception of deity" : "conception of deity as possessing human form or attributes."

Perhaps this fussiness seems excessive to you, but it may often be of the greatest importance to know whether we are defining a kind of deity or a kind of conception of deity; gods are not thoughts, after all. Some dictionaries ride roughshod over this sort of distinction with definitions like this:

> **Witch.** *n.* person possessing, or believed to possess, magical powers derived from a compact with Satan.

But this is an important distinction. If a witch is someone *actually* possessing such powers, then there are no witches, though some people believe there are. If a witch is a person *believed* to possess such powers, then there are indeed witches (we must include in the comprehension of the term, remember, things past and future as well as present), even if the beliefs are mistaken.

There is a special kind of contextual definition that is available, and should be resorted to, on occasion: the *relational definition.* Consider the term "noise," which is often defined as "unwanted sound." For some purposes we can be content with this definition, but disputes may arise about whether the sound of the motorcycle next door is, or is not, noise, and a more careful elucidation may be called for. We can define:

> "Noise" : "sound that somebody doesn't want"

—which may be useful in certain arguments. The trouble is that it covers too much ground, and nearly any sound can be noise by this definition. For other purposes, in other arguments, we might find this alternative useful:

> "Noise" : "sound that is unwanted by most (a majority of) people."

But then it may be difficult to discover whether a particular sound is indeed noise; perhaps no one has taken a poll. In that case we can fall back on a relativistic definition, i.e., a definition in which the term is defined not by itself but in relation to some person or situation:

> "Noise to *X*" : "sound that is unwanted by *X*."

On this definition, "noise" becomes relative; what is noise to you may not be noise to me, and vice versa. We can no longer speak of noise *per se*, but only noise to such-and-such a person (or group of persons), and this is a limitation; but at least we will be in a good position to prove what we say when we claim that something is noise (to so-and-so).

A rule of synonymy is like any other rule: it can be obeyed or disobeyed. It may be adopted by a great number of people, and become a general practice; or it may be employed temporarily for a special practice, in a particular book or statute or labor contract. Moreover, there are two ways in which a rule may be introduced into a discourse. A while back the newspapers informed baseball fans that the rulers of the American League had decided to allow the lineup to include a "designated hitter," to bat for the pitcher, without the pitcher's having to leave the game: These newspapers were reporting the adoption of a new rule. But when the American League voted to introduce the rule, it was not reporting, but *making*, the rule. In the same way, we can introduce a definition in order to describe a rule of synonymy that is actually being followed by some group of people: then we have a **definition report**. Or we can introduce a definition in order to establish a new rule we plan to follow ourselves or would like others to follow: then we have a **definition proposal**.

A dictionary is supposed to give definition reports: When it gives a definition of "paronomasia," it is telling us how this word is actually used by those speakers of English who happen to know what it means. The dictionary also often indicates the range of contexts in which a word is used, or is used in a certain sense: "rhetoric," "philosophy," "numismatics," "shipbuilding."

> "Paronomasia" (in rhetoric) *has the same designation as* "play on words."

Or, introducing the equal-sign for convenient abbreviation:

> "Paronomasia" (in rhetoric) = "play on words."

This is a statement, and a true one. If, on the other hand, we were to write

> "Paronomasia" (in logic) = "shift of meaning in the course of an argument in such a way as to invalidate it,"

this statement would be false. The term is never used, and (I am quite sure) has never been used, in this sense by logicians.

The parenthetical insertion indicates the *scope* of a definition. Since "paronomasia" is used only as a rhetorical term (a technical synonym for "pun"), it is not really necessary to indicate the scope for which it is here defined. But many a word with variable meaning has quite different applications in different types of discourse, and when a definition report is given, the scope should be specified.

> "To stall" (in automobile discourses) = "to stop the engine of a car, or let it stop, unintentionally."
>
> "To stall" (in airplane discourses) = "to lose sufficient relative air speed for an airplane to sustain controlled flight."

Apparently there are people who would like to take up flying, but are frightened off when they hear about the occasional stalls, and think that this means the airplane engine conks out.

Although it would be false to report that "paronomasia" is actually defined as a shift of meaning, it would not be false (nor would it be true) to *define* "paronomasia" in this way, if it were convenient. I could stipulate:

> "Paronomasia" (in *Thinking Straight) shall have the same designation as* "shift of meaning in the course of an argument in such a way as to invalidate it."

Or, to put it another way as a more explicit optative:

> *Let* "paronomasia" (in *Thinking Straight) have the same designation as* "shift of meaning in the course of an argument in such a way as to invalidate it."

This would be a definition proposal, and it will be convenient to use a varient of the equal-sign $\approx$ to mark such definitions. I have not always been completely scrupulous in this book about letting you know when my definitions are in accordance with established usage among logicians (as when I defined "syllogism" and "vague"), and when they were introduced for this book, without regard to others who may have used them in the same way (as when I defined "equivocation" and "slanting"). But if you look back, you will see that I have given hints, however unobtrusive, in the idioms I used: To say "A syllogism is . . ." is to claim conformity with a generally-observed rule; to say "We shall call . . ." is to offer a proposal, whether or not others will go along. If I did not include the maverick definition proposal about "paronomasia" it is at least partly because we already have a good word for the same idea: namely, "equivocation." We certainly do not require to learn two technical terms with the very same designation, and to use both of them would only introduce further confusion, by constantly suggesting that there is some mysterious distinction between their meanings.

It may be well worth emphasizing that even after we have framed a satisfactory definition, of whichever sort, examples may still be highly serviceable—which is why so many examples are given in this book. We may understand the sense of the term provided by the definition, and yet welcome help in applying the term to particular instances—especially when we find it hard to imagine or envision the kind of instances that are relevant. Thus a *Dictionary of United States Military Terms for Joint Usage* defines:

> "Accidental attack" : "unintended attack which occurs without deliberate national design as a direct result of a random event, such as a mechanical failure, a simple human error, or an unauthorized action by a subordinate."

Here the term "random event," which plays an essential role in the definition, is actually being used in a rather odd new sense, so that the examples of random events (mechanical failures, human errors, unauthorized actions) are very helpful, even indispensable, in enabling us to understand what the definer has in mind, even though the examples are not strictly a part of the definition.

A check-up quiz

Which of the following sentences are definition reports? Which are definition proposals?

1. "Berm" means the shoulder of a road.
2. A liberal is a radical with three children.
3. "Fido" is a dog's name.
4. Any old broken-down ugly building that some antique-architecture freak takes a liking to is called a "national monument."
5. When I speak of "hard-edge abstractionist paintings" here, I refer to nonrepresentational paintings featuring clear geometric designs in which areas are marked by contrasting hues and separated by straight lines."
6. I now understand "overreaction" : it's thinking that where there's smoke, there's cancer.
7. A manticore is a beast with a horned human head, a lion's body, and a scorpion's tail.
8. In this Act, "Federal highway" shall mean a highway of which the Federal government has paid at least 90% of the cost.
9. As I understand it, "surf" just means a lot of big waves.
10. "Detective" means someone like Mannix, Cannon, Ironside, and the like.

§ 17. Testing a Definition Report

Though few of us are lexicographers, whose profession is the making of dictionaries, many of us, from time to time, find ourselves in situations where a definition report is called for. The word we want to use—the most accurate we can think of—may be new to some of those with whom we wish to communicate. Even if it is fairly familiar, we may not be sure they will understand its precise meaning without help. And even if *one* of its various meanings is perfectly well understood, we may have to call attention to another sense in which we wish to use it, to fix that sense in the minds of all concerned, at least for the duration of the discussion.

A definition report is supposed to capture one of the standard senses of a word, as that word is used by some group of people during some period of time. It may turn out to be true or false. And so before we offer it, or accept it from others, we may need to test its truth. First we must be clear about its scope: that we are talking about the way the word is used in England or among Mormons or street-gang members or ufologists (experts on UFOs).

> "Flap" (among ufologists) = "concentration of sightings of extraterrestrial vehicles in a small area within a short period."

The scope indicator makes clear that we are not trying (and failing) to define the word in its colloquial use, veterinary use, or application to garments.

In a complete and exact definition of a term, the defining term and the term to be defined designate the same properties. And therefore they have the same comprehension: Anything that is a warlock is both a witch and male, and anything that is both a witch and male is a warlock. The converse, of course, is not true: Two terms with the same comprehension need not have the same designation. It is a fact, for example, that *all* the books, and *only* the books, published by Prentice-Hall carry the name "Prentice-Hall" on their title pages; here is identity of comprehension. Yet "book published by Prentice-Hall" and "book whose title page contains the name 'Prentice-Hall'" are by no means synonymous. Thus to compare the comprehensions of two terms gives us only a negative check on the correctness of a definition; yet that check can be useful.

We can let a circle of circles represent the comprehension of the term to be defined, and a circle of crosses represent the comprehension of the defining term:

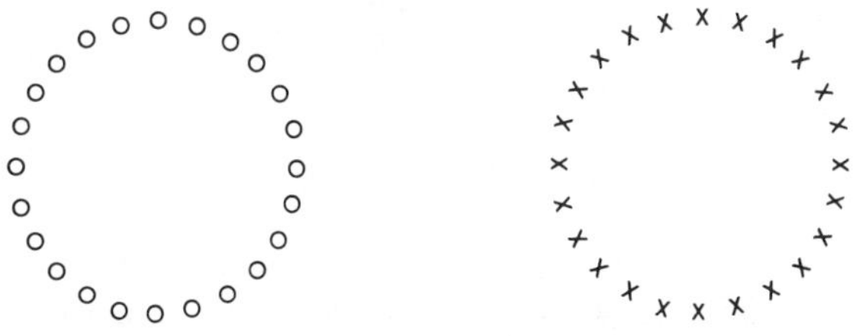

warlock male witch

In a correct definition, the two circles coincide:

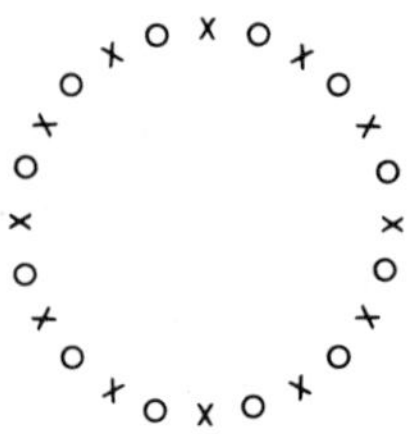

"warlock" = "male witch"

There are evidently two ways in which a definition report can go astray. (1) If the comprehension of the defining term includes some things that are not in the comprehension of the term to be defined, then the definition is too *broad.*

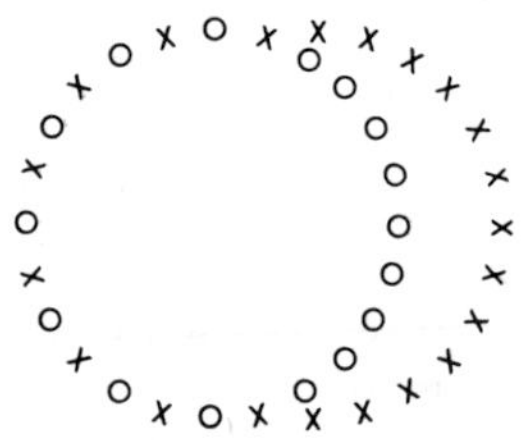

"warlock" ≠ "witch"

Since female witches are not warlocks, the witch-area bulges out beyond the warlock-area. (2) If the comprehension of the defining term leaves out some things that are in the comprehension of the term to be defined, then the definition is too *narrow.*

"warlock" ≠ "militant male witch"

Since nonmilitant male witches are nevertheless warlocks, the crosses fall short of the circles. A definition, of course, can be both too broad and too narrow:

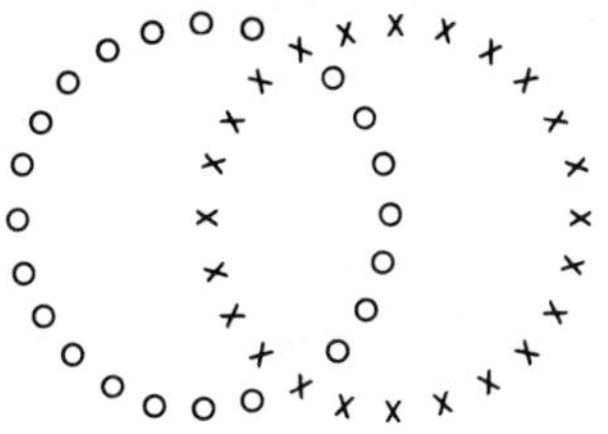

"warlock" ≠ "militant witch"

To define "warlock" as "militant witch" would improperly include female militant witches *and* improperly exclude male nonmilitant witches.

Suppose the occasion arose for framing a definition report for the term "ball-point pen." A very casual beginning might be made in this way:

> "Ball-point pen" (in stationery-store parlance) = "instrument for writing in ink."

Right away we would think of examples of instruments for writing with ink that are not ball-point pens; the definition is evidently far too broad. I don't suppose we should include fingers, which *can* write with ink if properly dipped, but are not really "instruments" and, even if in some extended sense we allow them to be called "instruments," are not "instruments *for* writing," that is, not designed primarily for this purpose. But there are quill pens, fountain pens, felt-tipped pens, etc. To rule out the quill pens we would want to narrow the definition by including a reference to a chamber containing ink (so that the pen does not have to be dipped). To rule out ordinary fountain pens and felt-tipped pens, we would have to say something about the mechanism.

> "Ball-point pen" = "instrument for writing, consisting of a narrow cylinder that contains a reservoir of ink and applies ink to a surface by means of a rotating ball in a socket."

In this way we have succeeded in narrowing down the definition, by adding further properties to the defining term, so that it marks out a smaller comprehension—one that we hope will coincide with the comprehension of the term to be defined. We have gone far enough; the question arises whether we have gone too far. Have we put in too many restrictions and conditions? Suppose someone made a narrow cylinder containing ink and capable of applying ink in the manner specified—but did not intend it to be an instrument for writing. Would he nevertheless have made a ball-point pen? Is the phrase "instrument for writing" properly included in the defining term? This question is not easy to answer, probably because ordinary usage is not that settled; we may not be sure what we would want to say in the case imagined. We could say, "Why, you have accidently made a ball-point pen!" Then being designed for writing is not part of the definition of "ball-point pen"—though it remains an important fact about ball-point pens that they are usually made for this purpose.

The definition reporter can go no further than actual usage does; when we have listed those properties that we find to be necessary conditions for applying the word (those conditions without which an object cannot properly be called a "ball-point pen," or whatever), we have gone as far as we can toward framing a definition. And this information may be very helpful in elucidating meaning, even if it does not tell the whole story about the word's use. Another part of the story can be added in another way. When someone asks for a definition, or is in need of it, part of what he requires is help in distinguishing one sort of thing from another. Say he is learning English, and wants a clear account of the word "chair." Now we can list a number of properties that are used in deciding whether or not to call something a chair (and this problem is not merely academic, when strange new forms of modern furniture keep turning up in department stores). Such properties, which are indicators, or marks, of something's belonging to a certain class, are called *criteria.*

Among the properties we might look for in an object in deciding whether to call it a "chair" are:

having a (roughly) horizontal surface
having a back
having four legs
having room for not more than one average-size person
capable of keeping the occupant in a sitting position, off the floor.

Anything that satisfies all these criteria of chairness is surely a chair; but many of them are obviously not necessary properties of chairs: an object with six legs, or no legs, can still be a chair if it satisfies enough of the other conditions. Some of the properties do seem to be necessary—a chair must have something that *can* be sat on, for example. It must give at least some support for the back. It is at least designed for single occupancy. If we put all the necessary conditions together, we may be able to frame a correct definition. But sometimes there are too few conditions to rule out obvious non-chairs (or whatever); and in that case the best we can do by way of elucidation is present the most useful criteria, noting carefully that none of them is a necessary property. Even dictionaries often give us such information, especially when discussing species of animals, whose feeding habits, nocturnal prowling, typical litter-size, and habitat are not necessary properties, but do help us form a composite mental picture of a sort of paradigm case. Such information could enable us to tell two species apart.

In many important matters we must make do with lists of criteria, rather than strict definitions. Despite all the discussion of drug addiction, there seems to be no exact agreed-upon sense of "addicting drug" that could be embodied in a definition report. But there are very useful criteria: An addicting drug is one that most users continue to take even though they want to stop, decide to stop, try to stop, and may actually stop for days, weeks, months, or even years. It is a drug which people will commit serious crimes and undergo great humiliation to obtain, and which most users continue to use despite threats of long-term imprisonment, and return to immediately after imprisonment. It is a drug to which most users return after treatment designed to end the addiction, no matter what currently existing form the treatment takes. These criteria do not, of course, give us an explanation or understanding of drug addiction or its causes—that is not the function of a definition—but they do enable a psychologist to determine who is addicted and who is not. If he wants a sharper concept of addiction, one that draws more definite lines, he will have to abandon reporting and propose his own definition for the purpose he has in mind.

A check-up quiz

Determine whether the following definitions are too broad or too narrow or both or neither.

1. "Acre" (in the United States and England) = "160 square rods."
2. "Pie" = "pastry with crust and filling."
3. "Stapler" = "hand-operated machine which fastens things by staples."
4. "Race" (in sports) = "contest to determine which of two contestants can travel a certain distance in the least time."
5. "Paperweight" = "object used to hold down papers."
6. "Zip code" = "number representing one of the areas into which the U.S. Postal Service divides addresses."
7. "Fan" = "instrument for moving air."
8. "Cut" (*noun*; medical) = "narrow opening in skin that allows blood to emerge."
9. "Fiction" = "what is not a fact."
10. "Teacher" = "one whose occupation is teaching."

§ 18. The Use and Abuse of Definitions

When a definition is offered in the course of an argument, it is nearly always something more than a report. Even if the purpose is mainly to select one of the existing senses and insure that this is the one kept in mind, the sense singled out is likely to be articulated more clearly and fully just by being expressed in other words, especially if the other words break the concept down into its subconcepts.

> When I insist that Congress, according to the plain words of the United States Constitution has the sole power to declare war, I don't mean by "declare war" just "announce that a war is going on," as some defenders of Presidential power seem to interpret the term; that would make the meaning so trivial as to take away from Congress any effective voice in the matter. By "declare war" I mean (and I think the Constitution means) "place the nation at war" or "bring into existence a state of war."

Even if this is a correct interpretation of the phrase in Article I, Section 8, Paragraph 11, of the Constitution, it might well make the meaning of that phrase more sharp to many of us.

A definition proposal, since it introduces a new usage, cannot rely on present language-habits at all, and may even have to go out of its way to counter them. It may take advantage of an existing sense, but give it a new precision for a special purpose. The Wilderness Society, for example, defines a "wilderness" as "an area where the earth and its community of life are untrammeled by man, where man himself is a visitor who does not remain"—a somewhat poetic defining term, yet marking an important distinction, which may not be far from ordinary usage, but does not attempt to coincide with it either. A definition proposal may give a plainly new and technical sense to a familiar word—as in a labor agreement:

> "Complaint" = "allegation by a member of the collective bargaining unit that the employer has treated him unfairly, illegally, or improperly."
> "Grievance" = "complaint that there has been a breach, misinterpretation, or incorrect application of the terms of this Agreement."
> "Grievant = "one who presents a grievance."

And, as we see from the third example, a definition proposal may even introduce a new term into the language (though "grievant" is now commonly used in labor contracts).

Though a definition proposal is neither true nor false, and therefore cannot be tested, it is by no means immune to criticism, for it may be extremely consequential. It embodies a decision to adopt certain meanings for certain terms, and the relations between those meanings and other meanings already established may make a great deal of difference in practice—especially in law and politics. When a fifty-foot reinforced concrete cross was erected in a city part in Eugene, Oregon, a few years ago, the question of its proper classification became the occasion of some controversy. Some said it was a religious symbol, and therefore unconstitutional on public land, since it amounted to the state's favoring and supporting a particular religious view. Others said it was not a religious symbol at all, but a war memorial (indeed, a majority voted in a referendum that this was the case), and hence perfectly legal under a state statute authorizing war memorials in public parks. How shall we define "religious symbol" and "war memorial"? That is a question for the courts, and evidently something hangs on it.

Even more hangs on the definition of "amnesty"—namely the lives and fortunes of many young men who chose exile from the United States rather than take part in a war to which they had profound moral objection. What is "amnesty"? Some have sternly opposed granting amnesty on the grounds that the expatriates must pay the "penalty" for their "crimes" and "errors" and cannot be "forgiven"; their definition of "amnesty" makes it include pardoning the individual or condoning his violation of the law. Others define "amnesty"—more in keeping with its traditional sense—as deliberate forgetting or overlooking an offense, for the purpose of healing social wounds or putting to rest old social strife. Many people would grant amnesty in the second, but not in the first, sense.

There are several troubles we must guard against in making definition proposals (and sometimes definition reports).

To begin with, we should note that definitions are not isolated pieces of language. When we define "*X*" in terms of "*Y*", we may be taking it for granted that "*Y*" is sufficiently understood in that context or by the audience we have in mind. If it is not, we may have to supply a further definition of "*Y*." Thus in an extended discourse we may have a set of definitions, in which some build upon others—as in the small set from a labor agreement given above. The meaning of "grievant" is explained with the help of the terms "presents" and "grievance"; and "grievance" is explained with the help of "complaint" and other terms. If the set is set forth in a logical order, the meaning will build from the simpler to the more complex. The set as a whole contains a number of terms, which can be divided into two groups. There are the terms that are defined ("complaint," "grievance," "grievant"); and there are the terms that are left undefined—at least in that set. These are the *basic* terms ("allegation," "collective bargaining unit," "employer," "breach," etc.), and it is assumed that their meanings can be presupposed on the present occasion (though some of them may give rise to stormy disputes about their interpretation; and when the contract is renegotiated, they may have to be defined explicitly). When a writer is not clear in his own mind which of his terms are to be basic (in that context) and which defined, he can easily fall into definitional circularity.

Circularity can occur in a single definition, but the futility of such a definition is quite easy to notice.

> "Friend" : "one who treats you as a friend."

Obviously, if anyone does not know the meaning (or your proposed meaning) of the word "friend," this definition will not enlighten him, for he won't understand the defining term. A **circular definition** is a definition in which the whole of the term to be defined appears in the defining term. We have to be careful about applying this definition of "circular definition." Note, first, that it is not itself circular; for although the word "definition" appears on both sides, the term "circular definition" does not appear *as a whole* in the defining term. Some definitions may appear circular, may even verge on circularity, because they don't take us far:

> "To hypnotize" : "to put in a hypnotic state."

No doubt such a definition is unlikely to be of much use to anyone, since if he doesn't understand the meaning of the verb, he probably doesn't understand the meaning of the adjective. Yet by itself it is not circular; the possibility is left open that this cautious one-step-at-a-time definer, if pressed, could give us a definition of "hypnotic state" that did not depend on any reference to the act of hypnotizing. If he defines "hypnotic state" (or its synonym "hypnosis") as "state resembling sleep, induced by hypnotizing," then we do have circularity. But it is a circularity not of a single definition, but of a set of (two) definitions. A **circular definition-set** is a set of definitions in which at least one term is ultimately defined in terms of itself.

Consider this pair, from an unabridged dictionary (dictionaries, by the way, do not worry about circularity, because their job is partly to exhibit the main relationships among words: to report, for example, that "hypnotist" and "hypnosis" are correlative):

> "Tenterhook" : "sharp hooked nail used for fastening cloth on a tenter."
>
> "Tenter" : "machine or frame for stretching cloth by tenterhooks so that it may dry even and square."

The circularity of this set is brought out by substitution. If we accept the definitions, we can replace the defined term by its defining term wherever it occurs, including other definitions. So we can write:

> "Tenter" : "a machine or frame for stretching cloth by *sharp hooked nails used for fastening cloth on a tenter.*"

—omitting the information about the purpose of tenters, since this is not strictly part of the definition. Now we have a circular definition.

This substitution method is the way to determine whether a set of definitions is circular. It can also help us see how the circularity might be avoided. To define "tenter," we do have to mention the nails:

> "Tenter" : "machine or frame for stretching cloth by sharp hooked nails."

That will do nicely; we can then add:

> "Tenterhook" : "sharp hooked nail used for fastening cloth on a tenter."

No circularity now, and the basic terms are clearly separated from the terms we are defining.

A less common sort of self-defeating definition is the *inconsistent definition*: one in which the defining term contains logically incompatible predicates. One could define:

> "Hexapede" : "four-legged biped"

—but the definition would be logically unusable, since to call anything a hexapede in this sense would be to imply two incompatible things about it. An **inconsistent definiton-set**, however, might be more apt to get us confused: It is a set of definitions that contains at least one implicitly inconsistent definition. That is, if we substitute according to the definitions we will end up with a definition, or definitions, with incompatible predicates. Consider this small set:

> "Actor" : "male dramatic performer."
> "Actress" : "female actor."

If we use the first definition to expand the defining term of the second one, we get

> "Actress" : "female *male dramatic performer*"

—and that won't do. The inconsistency is of course readily avoidable; we need only stick to "dramatic performer" as our basic term:

> "Actor" : "male dramatic performer."
> "Actress" : "female dramatic performer."

But an even easier way to avoid the problem would be to go along with—and indeed encourage—the current development in our language to get away from terms defined for a single sex which suggest that there are important role-differences when in fact there are not. We have gotten rid of "sculptress," and have de-sexed "sculptor," so that "female sculptor" is no contradiction at all; and similarly for "poetess' and "huntress." Even most practicing witches (according to reports from active covens) no longer use the term "warlock."

The definition-proposer claims the freedom to change meanings for his own purposes, and this freedom, if we grant it, carries with it certain responsibilities. Of these, the most important is the duty to stick by his own rules, once he has laid them down. He may give a new sense to a word, if he wishes; but then he must continue, throughout the discourse, to use the word in the sense he has given it. He may not fall back on the old sense or senses when it suits him, and thus lead us to confuse the new sense with the old one. Nor may he take unfair advantage of the freedom to define, by using his definition proposals to make it seem that he has proved a statement when in fact he has not.

A **question-begging definition** is a definition introduced in order to make a statement appear to be true when in fact it has not been supported by good reasons, either inductive or deductive. There are two ways of committing this fallacy: one that manipulates the subject of the statement; the other, the predicate.

Suppose the conclusion to be proved has the form "*A* is *B*"— never mind for the present whether it is all, or some, or one. And suppose the desperate and disingenuous arguer is finding it difficult to show that *A* is *B*. A simple solution to his problem is to propose a definition of the term "A" that will make it true by definition that *A* is *B*. To prove that pigs have wings, all you need to do is redefine "pig" as "winged animal"; then pigs have wings by definition. Now if you do this out in the open, the trick will be glaringly obvious, and critical readers, at least, will notice two important things about your impromptu definition. First, you haven't really proved that the animals that you *used* to call "pigs," and that people who speak ordinary English call "pigs," have wings; in changing the designation of the word, you have also changed its comprehension, and the familiar barnyard beasts are no longer pigs, by your new definition, so you are no longer even talking about *them.* Second, in *saying* "Pigs have wings," given your new definition, you aren't saying anything very interesting, for your statement is true by definition, that is, it is a *tautology*. That husbands are married, squares have sides, and food is edible, are true but trivial remarks; and your effort to establish "Pigs have wings" has reduced it to their level. Of course, if you discovered a breed of flying pigs in a far corner of the Andes, that would be different.

To make this maneuver at all plausible, then, it is obviously going to be necessary to disguise it—at least from the reader, but maybe even from yourself. This is done by claiming, or suggesting, either that no redefinition has occurred (the proposed definition is really a report of common, or accepted, or the most approved, usage), or that somehow, despite the redefinition, you are really discussing the same question that the discussion started off being about (in this case, perhaps, whether pigs can fly). A writer in a journal of opinion, say, is trying to convince us that we have a lot more social problems then we need to have, or can afford to have; that the things that bother us are not as serious as we thought, and are more readily remedied. He argues:

> A social problem, as I see it, is a gap between society's expectations of social conditions—people's demands and priorities—and the present social realities. Once this definition is grasped, it becomes clear that the existence of a social problem depends not only on the conditions themselves—how much money people have, how much racial discrimination there is, etc.—but on people's perceiving these conditions as defects. Hence political leaders must pay as much attention to the forces that determine expectations as to those that shape social realities. When realities cannot be changed, we can manage public expectations, in order to close the expectation-reality gap and end, or at least diminish, the problem.

Now this is a provocative thesis, and it does indeed raise some challenging questions that are not adequately discussable here. Perhaps the passage doesn't strike you as a convincing example of a question-begging definition. But it comes close, I think, to satisfying the conditions that make a definition proposal question-begging in the way we have been describing. First, it *is* a definition proposal, and the words "as I see it," seem to concede as much, though the writer might claim that he is giving a more fundamental and important definition of "social problem" than those who would say that our social problems are many and serious. Second, if we accept his definition, it follows, as he says, that one way to eliminate social problems is to get people to stop expecting things they don't have. On this view, slavery would be no social problem at all, if you succeeded in brainwashing the slaves into embracing, or at least accepting, their condition. But third, the redefinition then does have the effect, to some extent, of changing the subject; it purports to be an answer to those who think of social problems in more objective terms—who would think slavery unworthy of human beings, even if they didn't object to it. It really doesn't refute that kind of position.

The second way of "proving" that *A* is *B* is to give a question-begging definition of the term "*B*." A scrupulous definition-proposer will note that when *he* now says that *A* is *B*, he of course, means something quite different from what others would mean: having defined "grievance" as concerned only with the application of the labor agreement, he will note that, on this definition, not all complaints (say, about the location of the water cooler or about the language of the office supervisor—assuming that the agreement does not cover these matters) are grievances, technically speaking. It does not follow that they are not important, or that nothing can be done about them; it does follow that they are not handled according to the formal grievance procedures spelled out in the agreement, which provide that if a grievance is not resolved at an earlier stage, it can ultimately be submitted to binding arbitration. So when we say an employee who complains is not a grievant, in this proposed sense, we are not begging any questions.

The trouble comes when the shift of sense is not clearly marked and admitted, when there is a lingering reliance on the old discarded sense, and when there is the suggestion that something new has been proved mainly by a juggling of terms.

> The clearest and most satisfactory definition of "intelligence" is that it is what is measured by intelligence tests. Thus if a person passes the tests, he is intelligent, by this definition; if he fails, he is not. The group I tested turned out to be well below average in their intelligence-level, and certainly they cannot benefit from the kind of educational or employment opportunities that more intelligent people should have. It is a waste of resources to try to help them further.

This is a very sketchy version of what could be an elaborate and important line of argument. So we should be cautious in analyzing it. It does seem that this proposed definition of "intelligent" is really a redefinition; it is far more usual among psychologists to think of intelligence as a general capacity to adapt to one's surroundings, and as being made up of a great variety of skills, some of which may or may not be well indicated by familiar kinds of intelligence tests. Whenever a definition proposal is offered—especially one that diverges widely from ordinary usage—we always have the right to ask for a good reason to accept it. What is the point of defining "intelligent" as "able to pass intelligence tests"? Well, it is certainly simple, and saves a lot of thought—but after all, thought is what we expect from scientists, including psychologists, so that's not a very good reason. In any case, the main fallacy comes at the next stage. If the writer is looking only for a simpler way of saying that *X* can't do well on an intelligence test ("*X* is not intelligent"), all right; but it does not follow that *X* is not intelligent in other, more usual, senses. Yet this author immediately goes on to draw practical conclusions, to recommend an educational policy—and surely this is wholly illegitimate. The only thing that makes it seem at all legitimate is that we may still be clinging to the older sense of "intelligent," in which, indeed, a person who cannot adapt very well to his surroundings, or handle simple problems, cannot go far educationally. (There is another fallacy here, too, in jumping from the premise about the average of a group to a conclusion that no member of the group can benefit from educational opportunity.)

Since "intelligent" is a word with some emotive force, conferring approval on anyone it is taken to denote, this example could also be used to illustrate an important variation on the second kind of question-begging definition. In this variation, the redefined predicate "*B*" has a marked emotive force, positive or negative. In the original, or ordinary sense, of "*B*," *A* is not *B* at all; but "*B*" is now assigned a new sense, and as redefined it means something a good deal less emotion-arousing (less strongly approved or disapproved) than it had before. But after he has proposed his new definition, the writer (or speaker) keeps the old emotive force alive, so that when we accept his "proof" (by definition) that *A* is *B*, we feel nudged toward approval or disapproval of *A* through the emotive force of "*B*." Such a definition is a **persuasive definition.**

Consider, for example, the way the term "national security" is handled in the following paragraph:

> I think all of you gentlemen will agree, realistic observers of the world scene as you are, that nothing is more important for America than to preserve its national security. We must therefore take the most serious possible view of anything that constitutes a threat to national security. I know there are irresponsible people who claim that this term has not been adequately defined, but I will be glad to enlighten them by proposing a definition. By a "threat to national security" I mean any overt act, or attempt or plan or conspiracy to act, in such a way as to make it more difficult for the United States to defend itself in case there should be a war or in such a way as to lower the respect, regard, or esteem for, or the sense of power of, the United States on the part of any other nation with which we might at some future time come into armed conflict. And that is why I insist, and continue to insist, that the protests by Catholic priests, Vietnam war veterans, housewives, college students, and others, against the policies of our government, are indeed threats to national security.

Here the emotive force of "threat to national security" is built up first, then an extremely—not to say absurdly—broad definition proposal is made (its absurdity is evident the moment we think of examples of conduct, involving the clearest exercise of First Amendment freedoms, that would fall under it). We can try to keep in mind that, under the new definition, picketing the White House or writing a letter to the newspaper protesting the expenditure of so much of the budget on military hardware would indeed be a "threat to national security." But the term itself is so emotion-laden, that we cannot escape completely from its narrower and more familiar—and more powerful—sense, in which it designates acts that go beyond free speech. The trick works if it makes us believe that, somehow, the speaker has shown that outspoken objections to the government's military policies are a terrible thing—when in fact he has shown no such thing. The trick does not work (at least on us) if we are on to what is going on, and we see how the redefinition is used persuasively, that is, to arouse our feelings, while concealing the means of doing so.

A check-up quiz

Point out circularities and inconsistencies in the following sets of definitions.

1. (a) "Smog" : "smoke and fog."
   (b) "Smain" : "smoke and rain."
   (c) "Smail" : "smog and hail."
   (d) "Smow" : "smog and snow."
   (e) "Smight" : "night smail."
   (f) "Smightoff" : "smight without fog."

2. (a) "Certified shop" : "shop in which a union has been certified as collective bargaining agent for employees in the shop."
   (b) "Closed shop" : "certified shop in which an employee must be a member of the union at the time of hiring."
   (c) "Union shop" : "certified shop in which the newly hired employee who is not a member of the union at the time of hiring must become a member within a stipulated period."
   (d) "Agency shop" : "certified shop in which all employees must pay union dues whether or not they are members of the union."
   (e) "Union" : "organization serving as bargaining agent in a certified shop."

3. (a) "Lunch" : "light midday meal."
   (b) "Breakfast" : "first meal of day."
   (c) "Brunch" : "meal serving for both lunch and breakfast."
   (d) "Dinner" : "main meal of day."
   (e) "Snack" : "repast that is not a meal."

4. (a) "Organic food" : "food grown in soil treated only with natural (not chemical) fertilizers and not sprayed with chemicals or watered with polluted water."
   (b) "Natural food" : "food not processed or treated with preservatives, artificial coloring or flavoring."
   (c) "Ecological food" : "food that is both organic and natural, and also nutritious."
   (d) "Health food" : "food that is either ecological or good for dieting or of medical value."

(e) "Nutritious food" : "health food that is high in vitamins and minerals."

5. (a) "Bloog" : "astrogynized tork."
   (b) "Mang" : "chiz that is both an ord and a bloog."
   (c) "Ord" : "plisted woop."
   (d) "Stip" : "plisted frud."
   (e) "Tork" : nonplisted frud."

OUTLINE-SUMMARY: chapter six

A *definition* is a rule of synonymy between a term to be defined and a defining term: " 'Scale' to have the same designation as 'balance for measuring weight.' " It may be introduced into a discourse by a *definition report,* which is a statement that this rule is actually observed in a range of contexts by a certain group of people: " 'Scale' (in musicological discourses) has the same designation as 'ordered series of pitches used as the basis for musical compositions.' " A definition report is complete when its defining term specifies all the necessary conditions for applying the term to be defined, and it may be checked by testing to determine whether the defining term is too broad or too narrow for the term to be defined. A definition may be introduced into a discourse by a *definition proposal,* which is an imperative or optative sentence stipulating that this rule shall be observed in a certain context or range of contexts: " 'Fallacy of unequal negation' (in *Thinking Straight)* shall have the same designation as 'violation of the logical rule that in a syllogism the number of negative premises is to be equal to the number of negative conclusions.' "

A set of definitions is a group of definitions in which the defining terms in some are the terms to be defined in others. A *circular definition* is one in which the whole of the term to be defined appears in the defining term; and a circular set is one in which at least one of the definitions can be made circular by substituting according to the others. (Example: If "true" is defined as "not false," then "false" cannot without circularity be defined as "not true.") An *inconsistent definition* is one in which the defining term contains logically incompatible predicates; and an inconsistent set is one in which at least one of the definitions can be made inconsistent by substituting according to the others. (Example: if "fact" is defined as "proposition known to be true," then "misinformation" cannot consistently be defined as "false facts.")

A definition is *question-begging* if it is introduced into an argument as a definition proposal to make a certain statement true (for example, "Do-gooders are neurotic"), by presenting a new definition of either the subject or the predicate (for example, "By a 'do-gooder,' let us understand someone who has an abnormally strong compulsion to manipulate the lives of others for his own satisfaction"). When the predicate has emotive force, and the new definition broadens its designation to make it apply to the subject in the *new* sense, while at the same time the emotive force (positive or negative) of the *old* sense remains active, it is a *persuasive definition* (for example, "traitor" might keep its strong disparaging flavor even if momentarily broadened in meaning so that the charge of treason *in the new sense* is not nearly as serious as in the older and usual sense).

Exercise 26

For each of the following terms, give a full definition, if you can (taking the term in its most familiar sense); if you can't, list some necessary properties and some nonnecessary properties that might be used as criteria.

1. umbrella
2. stoned
3. situation comedy (on television)
4. to putter about
5. final examination
6. to tinker
7. commune (current usage)
8. to zap
9. snow job
10. to goof

Exercise 27

Criticize the following definition reports. Point out where the defining term is too broad or too narrow, and where it is ambiguous or very vague; and point our circularities and inconsistencies.

1. "Cemetery" = "place where human bodies are interred and identified by name."
2. "Environmental impact" = "effect on the ecological balance, aesthetic character, or habitability of the environment."
3. "To lie" = "to tell a lie."
4. "Progeny of *A*" = "those descended from *A*."
5. "Chess champion" = "the person who has defeated the preceding chess champion."
6. "Mud pie" = "pie made of mud."

7. "Funny" = "laughable."
8. "Fresh" = "not stale."
9. "Witness" = "one who gives eye-witness testimony concerning an event."
10. "Traffic light" = "light for regulating the flow of traffic."

Exercise 28

Analyze the use of definition proposals in the following passages. Point out ambiguity, excessive vagueness, and the need for further definitions. Point out question-begging definitions (including persuasive definitions).

1. [A judge's instructions to a jury] Before you retire to consider your verdict in this case, it is my duty to instruct you concerning the applicable law, as I interpret it. We are concerned with the defendant's pamphlet, *Notes on a Mountain Strike,* which describes his efforts to aid the strike of coal miners a few years ago, and contains derogatory statements about the chief of police, the sheriff, and the publisher of the local newspaper. You are to find the defendant guilty if the statements were false and libelous. I define "criminal libel" as "any writing calculated to create disturbance of the peace, corrupt the public morals, or lead to any act which, when done, is indictable."

2. Ever since the Supreme Court declared Bible-reading and prayers in public schools to be unconstitutional, people have been trying to find some way of getting around that decision. Now the great idea is to teach "spiritual values" in the schools, without violating the separation of church and state. But what are "spiritual values"? The best definition of this term that I can think of is that they are values that guide conduct in accordance with one's fundamental faith. Suppose the teacher is trying to make children believe that lying is wrong: she has to give some kind of reason. If she says it's wrong because "God says so," then her spiritual value really is based on a religious value. If she says, it's wrong because "Lying hurts other people," then by the mere fact of *not* referring to God, she shows that her basic faith is anti-religious, which is still a basic faith. It's impossible to teach "spiritual values" without religion, in the broad sense.

3. "Intelligence" is simply evaluated information. If we learn that someone has landed on the coast of Cuba with a guerrilla band, and is attacking the Castro government, we have information. Intelligence tells who he and his associates are, political aims and principles, their chances of success, the results of their success or failure, etc. The CIA, by its basic charter (The National Security Act of 1947), exists to gather information and convert it into intelligence. Its mission is to supply this vital intelligence to all branches of the government—especially the State

Department—that need it. And what could be more reasonable and desirable than that? How could anyone who understands what intelligence is, and why it is needed, object to the CIA?

4. The police and their supporters are always crying out against "political interference," whenever the Mayor or the City Council lays down new regulations about the way the police department should operate. But amid all the outcry, few stop to ask what "political interference" means, or should mean. "Political interference" can best be defined as "guidance by duly elected authorities"—it's really another name, as I see it, for the police being responsible ultimately to civilian authority, rather than a closed corporation with freedom to do anything they want, like the infamous secret police of totalitarian societies. I say more political interference is what we need, and the sooner the better!

5. There are two things we can all agree upon, I think, in regard to this matter of achieving genuine equality of opportunity in employment for groups that have been discriminated against. One is that we must achieve equality of opportunity, as a matter of right and as a matter of social survival. The other is that we must not establish the infamous quota system that would set up absolute percentages, of blacks and women to be hired by each company, etc.—as in the bad old days, the medical and law schools set quotas of 10% or 15% for Jewish students, etc. Now the government has come up with its so-called affirmative action plan, which everyone seems to be praising: requiring the employer to make positive efforts to recruit minority group persons, to make an intensive search for them, to reinterpret traditional criteria of qualification that they found it hard to meet, to reexamine hiring and promotion policies that work against them, etc. It sounds good. But let me tell you, it is not good. What is the quota system, after all? It may be simply defined as a system under which certain groups are singled out for preferential treatment in order to achieve the goal of having some percentage of them in the company—even if the percentage is vaguely stated. That's the essence of it, and that's what affirmative action clearly is, since it aims to increase percentages of minority groups hired and promoted.

REVIEW

As technology advances, as the store of human knowledge about nature and about man continues to grow, as our horizons of awareness widen to include the problems and preoccupations of people of other nations, cultures, races, and social classes, the individual who is trying to cope rationally with his environment finds his task becoming harder and harder. And he needs a larger and more constant supply of reliable information about what is going on, and why.

The great media of mass communication arise to supply this information—newspapers, radio and television, magazines of every character and inclination. For most of us they are the main source of knowledge about the deep issues of politics and government, the predicted consequences of basic policies, the trends of official thinking and world opinions. Yet, despite their power, these media are subject to the control of such a bewildering variety of special interests, and the largest of them are so deeply affected by particular economic and political groups that have a large stake in forming public opinion in certain directions, that even at best they pose formidable problems from a logical point of view—problems of linguistic interpretation and of logical evaluation.

And communication in the other direction takes on new difficulties—when it is up to us to make our views known and to defend a conviction or a proposal, to try to exert influence on the local school board or on those who are working with us in a business or civic organization. For to make a good case, and an effective one, we not only have to compete with stronger opinion-molding forces that may be arrayed on the other side, but we have to be master of more facts, able to marshal and connect them and draw cogent and convincing conclusions.

These are the tasks that this book is designed to help with. It is not, of course, a complete compendium of principles of interpreting and reasoning; it is more like a little home manual, covering the common diseases of discourse, giving clues for diagnosis, methods of treatment, and some precautions against further infection. In the course of the discussion, we have touched on a number of things to keep in mind when you find yourself in the role of reader (or listener) or of writer (or speaker). By way of conclusion, it may be well to run over them once more.

As a reader, approaching any discourse from a logical point of view, you are looking for true statements. You may have some definite problem on the back burner, or you may simply be reading for general knowledge about long-standing problems that are always on your mind. The task is a double one: to find out, as well as you can, what the discourse *says*, and to find out whether what it says is *acceptable*—that is, whether it is worthy of belief.

In answering the first of these main questions, you are interpreting the discourse. You begin by getting a good grip on the over-all structure of the discourse. Is it or is it not an argument? And if it is an argument, what are its main points and lines of reasoning? If the discourse is confusing, or its structure complicated, you may have to outline it or summarize it, so as to be able to keep the lay of the land in view while proceeding to examine the details.

Next you turn to the details of the language. Are there words or phrases that are ambiguous, highly vague, or indefinite? Do any of them appear to shift their meaning in the course of the discussion? It may be that the discourse will turn out to be so unsatisfactory at this stage that there is no point in pursuing it further. If you can't resolve the ambiguity, you can't even take the discourse as saying one thing or the other, and so the question of acceptance doesn't arise. If there is total obscurity in some part of the discourse, then you have to set it aside. But usually, even if certain words are behaving rather strangely, when they are cleared up there still remains something to be considered further.

Are there words or sentences that have more in them than first meets the eye—connotations or suggestions that are important to make explicit to yourself? Metaphors may call for special analysis. And if there is heavy reliance on emotive language or emotive devices, you may have to try to neutralize the discourse to do a careful job of analyzing it. If the argument hinges on technical terms that are defined in the discourse, you will have to look over those terms and their definitions with particular care to be sure you understand them clearly.

In answering the second main question, you are making a logical evaluation of the discourse: that is, you are estimating its success as an argument. And you begin by asking: what kind of argument is it?

If the argument is deductive, you want to know two things: (1) Is it valid? To answer this question, you have to examine its logical structure: is it a syllogism, a conditional argument, or what? Then you have to apply the rules of validity for that kind of argument. (2) Are the premises true? If they are themselves supported in the discourse, then you have another argument to consider, and the same procedure must be used. If they are not defended there, you must decide, on the basis of your own experience and knowledge, whether you think it safe to assume them.

If the argument is inductive, you must again classify it further before you can say how convincing it is—that is, how much probability it gives the conclusion. If it shapes up as an argument for a generalization, you ask whether the sample chosen as evidence is perhaps too small or too biased. If the argument supports a hypothesis, you make sure you understand exactly what the hypothesis is, and then ask whether the facts at hand can be explained by an alternative hypothesis that has greater simplicity or frequency. Finally, if you are confronted with an argument from analogy, you know that in itself it does not give a proof, but it may suggest a generalization or a hypothesis for which some evidence can be supplied.

There is, of course, no guarantee that a discourse that passes even these tests will never let you down. But it will be a good deal more reliable than one that is not critically examined at all.

Let us turn now to the problem of the writer. As an argument-maker, rather than an argument-receiver, you usually begin with a question, too: perhaps a question raised by someone else, or perhaps one you have posed to yourself.

The first phase of your thinking is the imaginative search. Perhaps an answer to your question can be deduced or induced from facts already known to you; perhaps it can be established with the aid of further facts you must then proceed to acquire; or perhaps it will come only through free and adventurous creative thinking. As soon as you think of an answer, and regard it as supported in some way, then your task immediately shifts from discovery to critical examination. At this stage, you step back and examine your own argument just as if it were someone else's, applying the same tests we have just been reviewing.

When you write out an argument for others' eyes, you are working out its details. If it is complex, you should probably outline it before you write, so that the main points can be kept before you. And as you work out the sentences, you must as far as possible look at them objectively—reading them over with an eye for semantical and syntactical ambiguities, obscurities, excessive vagueness or indefiniteness—matters you can still correct, before it is too late, by changing the grammar here, shifting paragraphs there, adding, refining, making more precise—perhaps with the help of carefully constructed definition proposals.

Throughout the process, you must be careful always to maintain authority over your words—to watch the connotations and make sure they are the relevant and desirable ones in the context, to watch the suggestions and make sure that they do not go beyond what you want to say, to guard metaphorical expressions against extravagance and looseness, and to keep the emotive force of the language within due bounds. There are many temptations along the way for the writer to let himself go—but perhaps it will help you to avoid them, when you recall some of the examples of wild and woolly thinking and writing that we have examined in this book. Here is where writing and thinking are intimately connected: As you correct your writing, you are forced to sharpen your thinking. And the more clearly you can say what you believe, and why, the better you—as well as others—can see whether what you say is worth believing.

The best way of finding out how well you have mastered the principles set forth in this book, and indeed of increasing that mastery at the same time, is to apply them to some fairly substantial and complicated arguments you have come across in your reading: a magazine article, a newspaper editorial, the account of a recent political speech. But as a transition from the comparatively circumscribed examples I have discussed or offered as exercises so far, it may be helpful to include a few more general ones, in which fallacies of various sorts are mixed and you may have to consider various possibilities before you decide exactly what is wrong—or right.

Exercise 29

Analyze the mistakes in reasoning that are made in the following dialogue.

TERM PAPERS FOR SALE?

TEACHER: I see they finally closed down that sleazy little business—run no doubt by a bunch of drop-outs from the University—that wrote term papers on order for students.

STUDENT: Yeah. Too bad. That was one organization that cared about students and was rendering a public service.

TEACHER: Public service! Surely you don't defend the practice of students' handing in papers they paid to have written for them? That's cheating!

STUDENT: Cool the emotive language. Sure I defend it. It's the only way some students can get a college degree, without which you're lost in this degree-mad society; that's what it adds up to.

TEACHER: But isn't it unfair to the other students who work hard and write their own papers? How can unfairness be justified?

STUDENT: Those other students already have the advantages: they happened to be born with brains and they were brought up to work hard, so it's actually easy for them to write papers, and even fun for some of them. You aren't claiming that people ought to be rewarded for having fun, I hope?—otherwise, why not reward people who get fun out of having somebody else write their papers? My idea of fairness is to even things up. So if one person has brains, it's fair for somebody who is less bright to have his term papers written for him.

TEACHER: But is it fair to students who don't have the money to pay for term papers? Those papers cost five or ten dollars a page, I gather, and not everyone can afford that. Anything that aids the disadvantaged student is good; I'll grant that; but buying term papers does not aid the disadvantaged student, and so it must be bad.

STUDENT: Students who don't have the bread should be given charity. The way it is now, a student looks for a friend who took the course last year, and asks him if he can copy one of his papers. I had three Freshmen copying papers of mine last year, which is a fair number. The practice is evidently widespread.

TEACHER: But if you're the type that lets people copy your papers—that is being an accessory before the fact in a gross academic deception—I'm afraid your evidence is not very acceptable. We can hardly credit what you say, if you're that dishonest.

STUDENT: Dishonest! I'm the only honest one here, since I'm telling it like it is, instead of pretending that everything is on the up and up. As far as fairness goes, the point is this: a student who belongs to a high-class fraternity can always get papers to copy for his courses—fraternities keep a big file of them over the years, and he can copy any one he likes, for free. The term-paper business evens things up: a kid who doesn't belong to a fraternity can get a paper done for him, too.

TEACHER: But what about the student himself? O.K., so he gets the good grade, and even his degree; but in the back of his mind, he knows didn't really earn it, and that he cheated. He will never know if he was good enough to do it on his own. Is he being fair to himself? Buying a term paper must be a bad thing to do, because it can lead to pangs of conscience, since the person who does the buying knows in his heart that it is a bad thing to do. I feel sorry for him.

STUDENT: Maybe there are a few soft-headed students who feel that way. But most students only resort to buying term papers because they realize that the system is rotten; the term paper itself has become a farce in the eyes of the students, since they are required to go through the mechanical motions, month after month, of putting things down tediously on paper, writing correct sentences, organizing their paragraphs and ideas, thinking up arguments to use, and all those rituals—surely you aren't going to claim that that is education? Real education is ecstacy, the peak experience, as Andy Warhol has said somewhere.

TEACHER: Andy Warhol! The term paper is supposed to be, at its best, an exercise in logical reasoning. When the agency writes the papers, they get the exercise, and the education; the student who buys it gets only the grade. Any student who can write a good term paper deserves to graduate; but students who buy their papers evidently cannot write a good one, and so they do not deserve to graduate.

STUDENT: In my opinion, the ability to write a term paper should not be a necessary condition for graduating. After all, plenty of students have written term papers and then flunked out, and deserved to.

TEACHER: Your line of argument leads nowhere. Suppose we say it's O.K., to buy term papers. Next thing you know, students will pay an agency to come in and take exams for them; next they'll sit in on the whole course for him, and the student won't even have to go to class. Inevitably, we would have to admit that a student might be justified in never going to college at all, while somebody else went as his substitute and got a degree for him.

STUDENT: I'm fed up with all this talk about degrees—as though nobody could do anything useful in the world unless he has a B.A. or M.A. or Ph.D., etc. What good is a degree? It's really a waste of time to go through the agony of getting one; the best things in life are not in books or laboratories or office buildings, after all. The important thing is to be *free*.

TEACHER: But don't forget that the faculty has rules against handing in work that is not your own—and the penalty is severe. You'd better change your ideas if you don't want to be out on your ear.

Exercise 30

Analyze the following essay carefully from the logical point of view.

PROPERTY RIGHTS AND HUMAN RIGHTS

by PAUL L. POIROT

Tricky phrases with favorable meanings and emotional appeal are being used today to imply a distinction between *property* rights and *human* rights.

By implication, there are two sets of rights—one belonging to human beings and the other to property. Since human beings are more important, it is natural for the unwary to react in favor of *human* rights.

Actually, there is no such distinction between property rights and human rights. The term *property* has no significance except as it applies to something owned by someone. Property itself has neither rights nor value, save only as human interests are involved. There are no rights but human rights, and what are spoken of as property rights are only the human rights of individuals to property.

Expressed more accurately, the issue is not one of property rights versus human rights, but of the human rights of one person in the community versus the human rights of another.

Those who talk about two sets of rights apparently want to discriminate between property income and labor income—with the implication that the rights to rental and investment income are inferior, as a class, to the rights to income from wages and salaries. Actually, this is an unwarranted assumption. It must be evident that all persons have rights which are entitled to respect. Safeguarding such rights is essential to the well-being of all. This is the only just principle. Thus, the problem is not to establish priorities on human rights in the community, but rather to determine what the respective rights are in the particular cases under dispute. This is the real problem in human relations, and it is one that calls for the exercise of wisdom, restraint, and true administration of justice under law.

WHAT ARE "PROPERTY RIGHTS"?

What are the property rights thus disparaged by being set apart from human rights? They are among the most ancient and basic of human rights, and among the most essential to freedom and progress. They are the privileges of private ownership, which give meaning to the right to the product of one's labor—privileges which men have always regarded instinctively as belonging to them almost as intimately and inseparably as their own bodies.

The ownership of property is the right for which, above all others, the common man has struggled in his slow ascent from serfdom. It is the right for which he struggles today in countries emerging from feudalism. The sense of this right is so deep-rooted in human nature, so essential as a stimulant of productive effort, that even totalitarian regimes have been unable to abolish it entirely.

It is a mistake to belittle the importance of property rights. Respect for these rights is basic to organized society, and the instinct of individuals to acquire property is at the root of all economic progress. Unless people can feel secure in their ability to retain the fruits of their labor, there is little incentive to save and to expand the fund of capital—the tools and equipment for production and for better living. The industrial development of this country, which has given us the highest standard of living in the world and has made possible a miracle of production in war and peace, is dependent upon the observance of property rights. Who is going to work and save if these rights are not recognized and protected?

The right to own property means the right to use it, to save it, to invest it for gain, and to transmit it to others. It means freedom from unreasonable search and seizure and from deprivation without due process of law or without just compensation. It might also be fairly taken to imply a limitation upon taxation because "the power to tax involves the power to destroy." For a like reason, it should imply assurance against governmental dilution of the money whereby the government takes property which otherwise could be claimed by wage and salary checks and other credit instruments. Further, it should insure against other measures so burdensome or restrictive as to prevent the employment of savings in legitimate productive enterprise with a reasonable prospect of gain. Violation of any of these rights can nullify, in whole or in part, the right to property.

The Bill of Rights in the United States Constitution recognizes no distinction between property rights and other human rights. The ban against unreasonable search and seizure covers "persons, houses, papers, and effects," without discrimination. No person may, without due process of law, be deprived of "life, liberty, or property"; all are equally inviolable. The right of trial by jury is assured in criminal and civil cases alike. Excessive bail, excessive fines, and cruel and unusual punishments are grouped in a single prohibition. The founding fathers realized what some present-day politicians seem to have forgotten: A man without property rights—without the right to the product of his own labor—is not a free man. He can exist only through the generosity or forbearance of others.

These constitutional rights all have two characteristics in common. First, they apply equally to all persons. Second, they are, without exception, guarantees of freedom or immunity from governmental interference. They are not assertions of claims against others, individually or collectively. They merely say, in effect, that there are certain human liberties, including some pertaining to property, which are essential to free men and upon which the state shall not infringe.

THE CLASS STRUGGLE

To many people, the expression "putting property rights first and human rights second" brings to mind the oft-drawn political picture of a struggle between a few "rich plutocrats" and "soulless corporate monopolies" on the one hand and the great body of humble citizens on the other. Much of what the public reads and hears about the recurring steel wage controversy conveys the same impression, with emphasis almost entirely on "the workers" versus the "big companies." John L. Lewis' blast against what he called the "rapacious and predatory" steel industry illustrates the point. In a message to Philip Murray, President of the United Steelworkers, offering a loan of $10,000,000 of coal miners' dues from the union treasury to back up the 1952 steel strike, Mr. Lewis said:

> We are conscious of the strength of the vast array of adversaries which confront you. Rarely has a union membership faced such a formidable grouping of financial and corporate interests as now oppose the steel workers of the nation in their long-standing struggle to achieve their rightful aims and objectives in the industry.

In all such talk about the "big companies" and "formidable groupings of financial and corporate interests," hardly anything is said about the shareholders, little and big, who are the real owners of the business and whose money, plowed into plant and equipment, has made possible the large employment and the record output.

WHO ARE THE "PROPERTIED CLASSES"?

Actually, ownership of property cuts across those imaginary lines between economic classes in the United States; and in no other country is the stake in property rights so great and so widely distributed. While we hear much about large corporations with thousands of employees and millions of dollars in assets, it is probably not generally realized that there are over 4,000,000 non-farm business enterprises in this country. Of these, over nine-tenths are classified by the Department of Commerce as "small business" on the basis of their number of employees or dollar volume of sales. The importance of "small business" in the economy of the country is further shown by the fact that it accounts for 45 per cent of the total employment of all business enterprises.

One of the largest of our "propertied classes"—the farmers—includes nearly 4,000,000 farm owners whose lands and buildings are valued at $55,000,000,000.

Even among large corporations, the ownership of stock is widely distributed; there are now 75 American companies each having over 50,000 registered shareholders. The Bell Telephone System, in its 1951 annual report, showed 1,092,000 shareholders, with no individual owner holding as much as 1/20 of 1 per cent of the total stock. Only five cities in this nation have as large a total population. General Motors, with greater sales volume than any other industrial corporation, has 479,000 shareholders.

A study entitled *Share Ownership in the United States,* just completed by the Brookings Institution of Washington, reaches the conclusion that there are about 6,500,000 individual shareholders of investor-owned corporations. It was found by the survey—contrary to the opinions often heard—that 32 per cent of the shareholders were from families having incomes under $5,000 annually, 44 per cent had incomes of $5,000-$10,000, and only 24 per cent had incomes over $10,000.

WHAT ARE "HUMAN RIGHTS"?

Now what about the so-called human rights that are represented as superior to property rights? What about the "right" to a job, the "right" to a standard of living, the "right" to a minimum wage or a maximum work-week, the "right" to a "fair" price, the "right" to bargain collectively, the "right" to security against the adversities and hazards of life, such as old age and disability?

The framers of the Constitution would have been astonished to hear these things spoken of as rights. They are not immunities from governmental compulsion; on the contrary, they are demands for new forms of governmental compulsion. They are not claims to the product of one's own labor; they are, in some if not in most cases, claims to the products of other people's labor.

These "human rights" are indeed different from property rights, for they rest on a denial of the basic concept of property rights. They are not freedoms or immunities assured to all persons alike. They are special privileges conferred upon some persons at the expense of others. The real distinction is not between property rights and human rights, but between equality of protection from governmental compulsion on the one hand and demands for the exercise of such compulsion for the benefit of favored groups on the other.

THE "RIGHT" TO A JOB

To point out these characteristics of the so-called human rights is not to deny the reality nor belittle the importance of the social problems they represent. Some of these problems are real and important. They are also complex, and in this further respect they are different from the rights guaranteed by the Constitution.

There is no great difficulty nor danger in declaring that certain individual rights shall not be tampered with by the government—and in adhering to that principle. It is quite another matter to say that the government shall seize the property or curtail the freedom of some of its citizens for the benefit, or the supposed benefit, of others. To adopt this view is to cast both the government and the citizen in radically new roles, with far-reaching effects on economic behavior, political practices, and individual character.

Consider, for example, the so-called *right to a job*. This is a fine-sounding phrase that evokes an emotional response. It creates a mental image of an unemployed worker and his family suffering hardship through no fault of their own. No one would deny the reality nor the seriousness of that, especially when the unemployed worker is multiplied by millions. To find the best remedy, however, is a difficult matter, and it is not made easier by the use of such misleading catchwords as the "right" to a job. One man's "right" to a job implies an obligation on the part of someone else to give him a job. Who has any such obligation?

An economy of private enterprise functions by means of voluntary contracts entered into for the sake of mutual advantage. Jobs arise from such contracts. The obligation to fulfill his contract is the only right any person can have to a job. Both sides of the contract have to be fulfilled. The employer's job—his side of the contract—is to anticipate what the consumers will want in the market place. His capacity to offer jobs to employees depends upon how well he understands the market pattern of consumer preferences. He has no right of control over the market. There is a limit to his capacity to provide jobs. And in the final analysis, an employee's so-called *right to a job* is determined by what consumers think the product or service is worth to them.

As with the "right" to a job, so with the other so-called human rights. These are not rights in the constitutional sense of respect for privacy; they are, instead, social programs which the government has undertaken or has been asked to promote. These programs, unlike true rights, are selective, coercive, complex, and experimental. Hence, they need to be carefully considered each on its own merits with due regard to the serious threats they may involve to the real and basic human rights that have enabled free men to build a society with the highest level of material well-being ever achieved anywhere.

TRIPLE THREATS

On the economic side, the gravest threat is that productive enterprise will be so burdened and impeded by high taxes, prohibitions, red tape, and controls that industry will stagnate. Without the products of industry, social programs of any kind become empty promises. New political powers and functions increase the cost of government and drain manpower from farms and factories into administrative bureaus. The great bulk of the money for benefit payments to favored groups must be taken from those who produce by putting forth their own efforts or by investing their savings. Minimum-wage rates wipe out the entire lower range of job opportunities in the business world. Only the government, with the power to tax, can pay more for labor than it is worth. Maximum-hour laws further limit the opportunity to be productive. Artificially pegged prices and wage rates interfere with the normal market process of gearing production to the maximum satisfaction of consumer wants.

On the political side, the increase of power multiplies the opportunities for the abuse of power and the harm that can be done by such abuse. High tax rates expose taxpayers and collectors to strong temptations. The disbursement of billions of dollars in public funds opens new avenues for favoritism and corruption. This system of political distribution of the wealth of a nation encourages government by pressure groups, with the favors flowing toward the groups with the most votes. Demands for more liberal benefits on the one hand and for tax relief on the other converge upon the public treasury. Deficit financing and currency depreciation tend to become national habits which feed upon the savings of individuals and wipe out the means of production and progress.

On the human side, the individual citizen discovers that it is increasingly difficult to get ahead by enterprise and thrift—increasingly profitable to join in the scramble for governmental favors and handouts. The sense of relationship between services rendered and payment received grows weaker. Personal initiative and self-reliance give way to an attitude of: let the government do it. Free citizens tend to degenerate into wards of the state.

These are not imaginary effects, but real ones. They are visible here and now. They are the consequences of placing social programs, mislabeled "human rights," above the *real* human rights, disparagingly called "property rights," which underlie the productive strength of free men.

Essay published November 1952 by the Foundation for Economic Education.

Exercise 31

Explain the fallacies and logical confusions in the following remarks.

CRIME IN THE STREETS (AND ELSEWHERE)

1. They took the Bible out of the public schools; is it any wonder that the crime rate has been rising ever since?

2. It is completely illogical to follow the infamous permissive Warren court and worry about the "rights" (that is, privileges) of the criminal, rather than the needs of the victim. If you make a big fuss about so-called due process, and give every hoodlum and punk the right to a lawyer, the next thing is, to be consistent you'll have to make sure that the police treat him with kid gloves, and warn him not to incriminate himself. It follows that you'll have to give the defense every advantage in court, and hamstring the prosecution to the point where every damning piece of evidence is excluded. You might as well say the criminal has a constitutional right not to be arrested or brought to trial at all.

3. Freedom of speech is all right, but law and order is what we need most, especially these days, when order is constantly being breached. That is why I think the police were perfectly justified in arresting the demonstrators after they refused to put down their signs calling the President a "war-monger," and other such insulting things. After all, the police chief gave them the order to disperse, and to disobey it was a breach of the order.

4. There is no question but that arrested persons who have not yet been indicted should, except under exceptional circumstances, be allowed

to go free on bail. But these alleged numbers writers had been indicted, and therefore they necessarily must be held without bail until they are tried.

5. The three policemen are accused of stealing marijuana and selling it; now they have refused to testify before a departmental hearing to determine whether they should be dismissed, on the ground that their testimony may incriminate them in the criminal suit also being brought against them by the District Attorney. Pleading the Fifth Amendment! I know that the big-name lawyers can twist this around with fancy language. But that's just another name for hiding the truth and refusing cooperate. It's a disgrace to the police force.

6. It is conceivable that the state legislatures will pull themselves together and pass stiff laws restoring capital punishment for vicious crimes. On the other hand, it is conceivable that the vicious crimes will continue to be committed right and left, to the constant terror of the citizenry. A recent survey has shown that more and more state legislatures are reinstituting the death penalty since the Supreme Court's unfortunate decision declaring the California and New York statues unconstitutional. It follows that vicious crimes are bound to diminish.

7. When there are few or no crimes, that means the law is being enforced. Right? O.K., so that's the answer. To stop crime, we can forget about all these liberal panaceas, like drug-addiction centers, etc., and concentrate on one thing: a superbly armed and capable police force equipped with all modern weapons, that is actually out there enforcing the law.

8. The crime-rate curve is horrifying when you see it on a chart; year after year it rises, and most years the *rate* of rise also rises. How is this to be explained?—for, after all, there's no use rushing about trying to cure it, unless we understand why it happens. Question: what else has also been rising, year by year? You guessed it: the number of hours during which people are watching violence on television. More sets, more viewers, more time spent viewing. That is the explanation.

9. I live in the city, and my neighbors are always yammering about crimes and how dangerous it is; but I notice they still live here, like me, and even enjoy city life very much when they forget their morbid fears. Sure, the statistics say there are a lot of crimes, but what is a crime? The list includes offenses like truancy, smoking, running away from home, which constitute a big portion of the half-million crimes committed every year by the young—and it includes offenses like drunkenness, which make up one-third of *all* crimes. So who is hurt when some poor kid can't stand his ghastly parents and runs away from home, or some wino goes to sleep on the sidewalk? I don't see any problem here.

10. Three-fourths of those convicted of felonies had previously been

convicted of misdemeanors, and at least half of the felons now in prison will commit other felonies after release. What conclusion can we draw from these statistics? Only one: that imprisonment does not actually deter crime, but in fact increases it.

11. What I worry about is the danger that's coming more and more from the efforts to "crack down" on crime. When the police start shooting up and down streets from the machine guns and cannon in their special armed cars and tanks, who's going to get hit? Do you know that more than 500 people are killed every year in this country from accidents caused by police cars careening around in pursuit of a criminal, or alleged criminal (more likely a kid who is joyriding in a car he borrowed because the owner left the key in it)?

12. The intelligent person's definition of "crime" is "a deliberate action that violates the rights of someone else," and that is the way I use the term. I do not want to minimize the harm done by those convicted of armed robbery, aggravated assault, homicide, etc.—but I still believe that the real crimes, the most serious crimes, in America are those committed by a society that, with all its affluence and waste, forces so many of its citizens to live under those conditions of poverty and deprivation that drive so many to steal, merely to survive.

13. Ask any criminologist, and he will admit, if he is honest, that crime statistics are meaningless. When you consider all those crimes that go unreported to the police (probably half the crimes committed), or are not reported by the police, or are exaggerated by the police when they want more money, etc., etc., what good are the statistics? (According to the FBI, for example, Philadelphia reported a 70% increase in serious offenses between 1951 and 1952, because in 1951 one police district failed to report 5,000 complaints.) We have to get behind the statistics to the facts, to the human situations in order to understand crime. Take homicide, for example; according to the FBI, 80% of U.S. murders are committed indoors by friends or relatives of the victim; surely we can begin here to ask why we are so violence-prone as a nation, what we are doing to ourselves to make murder so common.

14. Actions that injure other people should always be of concern to society and are justifiably prohibited by law; but so-called "crimes without victims" (such as gambling, prostitution, drug-addiction) are not of this sort. Consequently, "crimes without victims" should never be prohibited by law.

15. There's plenty of evidence that this administration is soft on crime. For one thing, they have spent millions of dollars in long, elaborate trials of persons accused of threatening the Republican Convention with sling-shots, and trying to kidnap Henry Kissinger, putting blood on draft records, and other such violent crimes, but they haven't

convicted any of them. Why not? Surely because they really haven't tried hard, or worked hard, to make these accusations stick. This weakness of will is another item of evidence. How do we know that the Administration lacks firmness of will? That is clear both from the way they have allowed so many draft-resisters to stay in other countries with impunity and, more generally, from their basic softness on crime.

EIGHTEEN FALLACIES

Below is a checklist of common errors in reasoning analyzed in this book, with definitions and examples.

1. **Ad Hominem Argument** (§15). Attacking the arguer, rather than his argument or its conclusion ("Jones's objections to capital punishment carry no weight, since, after all, he is himself a convicted felon").

2. **Affirming a Disjunct** (§4). An invalid form of the disjunctive argument, in which the second premise ("He will work hard") affirms one of the disjuncts in the first premise ("He will either work hard or be fired"), and the conclusion denies the other disjunct ("Therefore, necessarily, he will not be fired").

3. **Affirming the Consequent** (§4). An invalid form of the conditional argument, in which the second premise ("He will work hard") affirms the consequent of the first premise ("If he wants to keep the job, he will work hard"), and the conclusion affirms the antecedent ("Therefore, necessarily, he wants to keep the job").

4. **Argument from Analogy** (§9). An unsound form of inductive argument, in which two things of different sorts are asserted to have a number of properties in common ("My love is like a red, red rose, being lovely, sweet, fair, healthy, and so forth"), one of the two things is then asserted to have a further property ("The rose will soon fade and die"), and it is concluded that the other thing has the same property ("Therefore, probably, my love will soon die").

5. **Begging the Question** (§6). A form of deductive argument in which the conclusion is already assumed (not necessarily in the same words) as a premise ("We can believe what it says in the college cata-

logue, because the catalogue itself says that it is the official publication of the college"). Such an argument is also said to be **circular.** A special kind of circular argument is that in which a **question-begging definition** (§18) is proposed in order to make the conclusion true by definition ("By my definition, 'unbreakable' means 'requiring an unusual degree of force to break'; therefore, these dishes are unbreakable").

6. **Black-or-White Fallacy** (§12). An unsound form of argument, in which it is held that there is no difference, or no notable difference, between two things (for example, between waking and sleeping), because the difference is one of continuous degree, and therefore the difference is the sum of many small and trivial differences (for example, between being "half-asleep" and being very sleepy).

7. **Cross-Ranking** (§9). A fallacy of classification, which consists in using more than one basis of division in dividing a class into subclasses (as when a restaurant menu lists its offerings under the categories of dinners, sandwiches, salads, beverages, and desserts).

8. **Denying the Antecedent** (§4). An invalid form of the conditional argument, in which the second premise ("He does not want to keep the job") denies the antecedent of the first premise ("If he wants to keep the job, then he will work hard"), and the conclusion denies the consequent ("Therefore, necessarily, he will not work hard").

9. **Distraction** (§15). Turning the course of an argument or a dispute away from the point at issue, e.g., by means of an emotive device, and bringing in irrelevant considerations ("You say that you are against raising the sales tax; far be it from me to cast aspersions, but I certainly would like to know what is your personal stake in seeing that retail businessmen do not suffer any diminuation of their profits"—this particular device being an *ad hominem* argument).

10. **Equivocation** (§11). Changing the sense of a word or phrase in the course of an argument in such a way as to make the reason offered appear more convincing (or more relevant) than it really is ("That is an artificial lake; what is artificial is spurious; therefore, that lake is spurious").

11. **Far-Fetched Hypothesis** (§8). A hypothesis accepted on the support of a particular body of evidence when that evidence can be explained by an alternative hypothesis that is simpler or more frequent ("The little Negro church was set afire after the civil rights meeting was over; therefore, it must have been done by the leaders and the minister in order to cast suspicion upon local segregationists").

12. **Hasty Generalization** (§7). A generalization accepted on the support of a sample that is too small or biased to warrant it ("I had a bad time with my ex-husband; from that experience I learned that men are

no good"). ***Post hoc, ergo propter hoc*** (§7) is a form of hasty generalization, in which it is inferred that because one event followed another, it must be the effect of the other ("You notice how the sales went up after we instituted our new advertising campaign; our success is obvious").

13. **Inconsistency** (§5). A discourse is inconsistent, or self-contradictory, if it contains, explicitly or implicitly, two assertions that are logically incompatible with each other (Advertisement of Florida motel: "Indoor cook-outs every Saturday night"). A special case of inconsistency is **special pleading,** which consists in appealing to a general statement in refuting another person's assertion, and then ignoring that statement in defending one's own.

14. **Maldistributed Middle** (§6). An invalid form of the syllogism, which violates the rule that the middle term must be distributed exactly once ("All schoolhouses are fireproof; some brick buildings are fireproof; therefore, necessarily, some brick buildings are schoolhouses").

15. **Oversimplification** (§15). Excluding relevant considerations from an argument or a dispute, e.g., by means of an emotive device that makes it appear that the point at issue can be settled more easily than is really the case ("The D. A.'s campaign for mayor raises again the ugly specter of boss control, as the clubhouses once again renew their efforts to get a stranglehold on the voters; to me, this is the only issue of the campaign: Are you for or against bossism?").

16. **Slanting** (§14). A form of misrepresentation, in which a true statement is made, but in such a way as to suggest something that is not true ("Oh, I admit that our space program will cost a certain amount of money," which suggests that the amount is not great), or to give a false description through the connotations of the terms ("Money is being poured into the space program," in which "pour" connotes heedless and unnecessary spending).

17. **Unequal Distribution** (§6). An invalid form of the syllogism, which violates the rule that an end term be distributed in the conclusion if and only if it is distributed in the premise ("All schoolhouses are fireproof; this building is not a schoolhouse; therefore, necessarily, this building is not fireproof").

18. **Unequal Negation** (§6). An invalid form of the syllogism, which violates the rule that the number of negative statements in the conclusion must equal the number in the premises ("No churches are fireproof; no schoolhouses are churches; therfore, necessarily, all schoolhouses are fireproof").

INDEX

A

B

C

D

E

F

G

H

I

P

Q

R

S

T

U

V